NAPOLEON'S
CONQUEST OF EUROPE

NAPOLEON'S CONQUEST OF EUROPE

THE WAR OF THE THIRD COALITION

Frederick C. Schneid

Studies in Military History and International Affairs
Jeremy Black, Series Editor

Westport, Connecticut
London

Library of Congress Cataloging-in-Publication Data

Schneid, Frederick C.
   Napoleon's conquest of Europe : the war of the Third Coalition / Frederick C.
Schneid.
      p. cm. — (Studies in military history and international affairs, ISSN 1537–
4432)
   Includes bibliographical references and index.
   ISBN 0–275–98096–0 (alk. paper)
   1. Napoleonic Wars, 1800–1815. 2. Napoleon I, Emperor of the French,
1769–1821—Military leadership. 3. France—History, Military—1789–1815.
4. Europe—History—1789–1815. 5. Europe—Politics and government—
1789–1815. I. Title. II. Series.
   DC226.3.S36   2005
   940.2′7—dc22   2004028444

British Library Cataloguing in Publication Data is available.

Library of Congress Catalog Card Number: 2004028444
ISBN: 0–275–98096–0
ISSN: 1537–4432

First published in 2005

Praeger Publishers, 88 Post Road West, Westport, CT 06881
An imprint of Greenwood Publishing Group, Inc.
www.praeger.com

Printed in the United States of America

The paper used in this book complies with the
Permanent Paper Standard issued by the National
Information Standards Organization (Z39.48–1984).

10 9 8 7 6 5 4 3 2 1

In memory of Gunther Erich Rothenberg
(1923–2004)
Scholar, Mentor, Friend

CONTENTS

FOREWORD

Much of the fascination offered by Napoleon is that his career was simultaneously a study in failure and an account of success. If this was true of his political career, it was even more the case with his military one. Frederick Schneid's scholarly and accessible study focuses on military and international success, but it also throws light on some of the causes of failure. It is particularly valuable because Schneid seeks to revitalize the study of grand strategy, presenting it as at once military and political. In doing so, he offers an account that reflects current interest in strategic cultures, because Schneid seeks to locate the short-term with reference to the long-term interests and commitments. As a consequence, the book places the strategic, operational, and tactical dimensions of the campaign in their appropriate long-term context. This wide-ranging character of Schneid's study offers not only a broader historical framework, but also a pertinent geographical one.

Napoleon's successful opportunism emerges from an extensive examination of the motives and conduct of the European states in relation to France and to each other. This gives a dynamic character to his assessment of the Third Coalition. The states given particular attention include not only France and Austria, but also Britain, Prussia, Russia, Spain, and Sweden. Furthermore, far from treating these powers simply as players in a system driven by systemic factors, Schneid shows how European events and internal politics affected their response to tensions. In doing so, Schneid devotes appropriate attention to the French alliances formed prior to the campaign of 1805, particularly exploring Franco-Spanish and Franco-German relations.

The campaign itself indicated the superiority of the French corps and divisional structure over the less coherent and less coordinated opposing forces. French staff work at army and corps level was superior to that of both Austria and Russia, and this helped to vitiate the numbers France's opponents put into the field. The quality of French staff work enabled Napoleon to translate his wide-ranging strategic vision into practice, to force what might have been a segmented war into essentially a struggle in one major theater of operations where he could use the Grande Armée effectively. Although this was true on land, Napoleon lacked comparable facility at sea, and Schneid's book is unusual in that it integrates naval strategy with the land campaign. This brings Great Britain fully into the account, and it also ensures that Franco-Spanish relations receive the attention they deserve because Spain was still a key imperial and naval power. The welcome Atlanticist dimension of this book also ensures that the economic issues that shaped state policy and war receive due attention.

Attention, though, must revert to Napoleon. Able to adapt rapidly to changing circumstances and fresh intelligence, he had a remarkable ability to impose his will upon war. The quest for glory was valued in the culture of the period, and Napoleon's search for fame had a significant military consequence in that it contributed to the morale of his troops and thus to his battlefield effectiveness. War involves imposing one's will on opponents such that they accept defeat. Napoleon did so against Austria in 1805, and far more rapidly than Austria had yielded hitherto. This, however, was to prove only a limited guide to the future.

Jeremy Black
University of Exeter

ACKNOWLEDGMENTS

I was officially introduced to the Archduke Charles in 1988 upon entering graduate school. I had met the Habsburg prince earlier, but only in passing. My interest in the Napoleonic era led me to Purdue, where under the Prussian direction of Professor Gunther E. Rothenberg I studied the history of war. Rothenberg stressed that good military history considered the operations of all armies involved. The problem with studying the Napoleonic era, he argued, was the decided focus on Napoleon's campaigns, with little consideration for the strategic and operational planning of his opponents. Curiously enough, I asked him once why the Austrians failed to produce an official military history of the War of the Third Coalition. "Some things are better left alone," he said wryly. While writing this book I consulted with him often on matters pertaining to the Habsburg war effort. I was deeply saddened by his unexpected death, and it is to his memory that this book is dedicated.

There were many people involved in the development of this book, from its conceptualization to its final publication. Jeremy Black was instrumental in encouraging my work and enticing me to produce it for his series with Praeger Publishers. Peter H. Wilson and Philip Dwyer were kind enough to read chapters and provide valuable comments toward the final draft. Similarly, my friends and colleagues Larry Simpson and James Stitt were invaluable for their editorial advice. Pat Sager at Smith Library, Interlibrary Loan, rose to my many challenges and was able to secure books that should have been well beyond reasonable reach. Her efforts and achievements made this work richer. I am also indebted to Charles White for providing me with a copy of the German General Staff study of Prussian military operations in 1805. I must also thank LeAnn O'Malley, my research assistant in Paris, for her extraordinary efforts.

My friends and colleagues Michael Leggiere, Michael Pavkovic, and Lee Eysturlid were vital in offering comments and acting as a sounding board for questions and problems related to the research and writing of this book. In particular, I want to thank Jack Gill, scholar and master cartographer. Jack's knowledge of the Napoleonic era is matched by his ability to produce beautiful maps. He was kind enough to dedicate time to create the campaign and battle maps for this book, and he gave critical advice concerning the Bavarian, Baden, and Württemberg contingents. I must also acknowledge the work of Heather Staines, editor and friend, who was incredibly supportive and understanding throughout. Peter Kracht, publisher at Greenwood/Praeger, has been a long-time supporter of my work, and I am grateful and pleased to publish with him again.

I am truly appreciative of my family's patience and understanding during the process of writing the book. It was a difficult task, considering my wife Stacy was pregnant and in her last trimester. My children, Craig, Sarah, and Benjamin did their utmost to leave their father alone during his marathon writing sessions. Finally, I thank Abigail, my youngest, who had the patience to wait until her due date to arrive.

Frederick C. Schneid
October 4, 2004

CAMPAIGN AND BATTLE MAPS

Map Symbols

Unit Size

xxxx	·····Army
xxx	·····Corps
xx	·····Division
x	·····Brigade

Examples

xx Bav	·····a Bavarian division
xxxx	**Kutusov 40,000** ·····a Russian army
III	·····French corps are indicated by Roman numerals (here: III Corps)

·····French and allies

·····Coalition and Prussians

·····Engagements

·····Cavalry

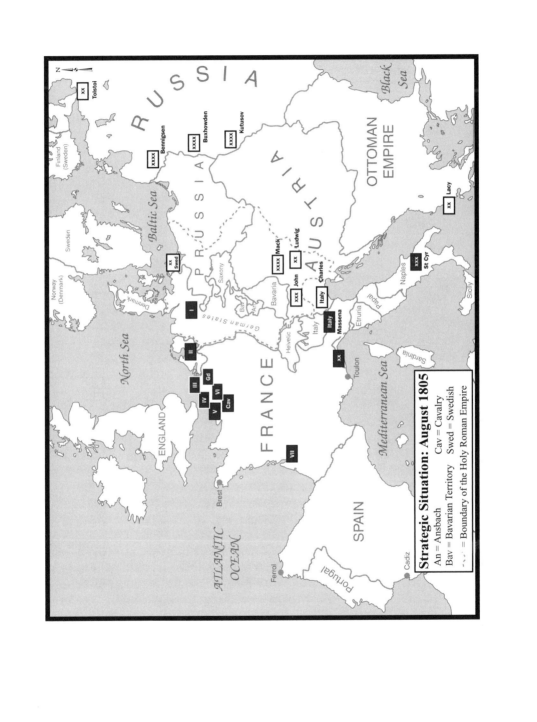

Strategic Situation: August 1805

An = Ansbach   Cav = Cavalry
Bav = Bavarian Territory   Swed = Swedish
ᛌᛌᛌ = Boundary of the Holy Roman Empire

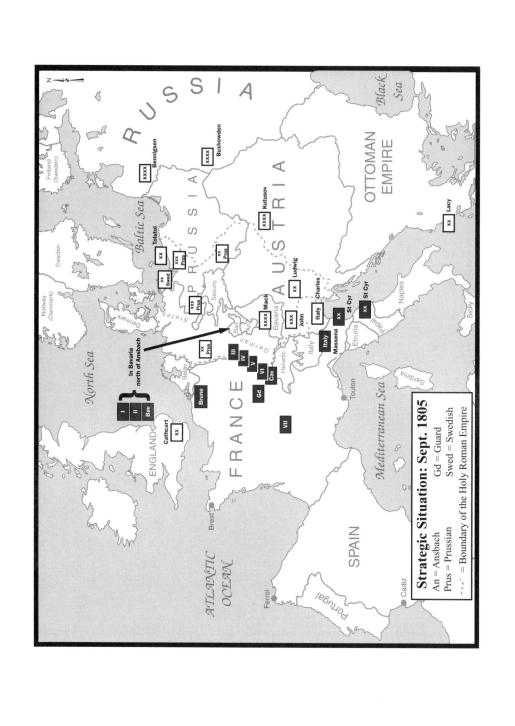

Strategic Situation: Sept. 1805

An = Ansbach   Gd = Guard
Prus = Prussian   Swed = Swedish
˙‑‑˙ = Boundary of the Holy Roman Empire

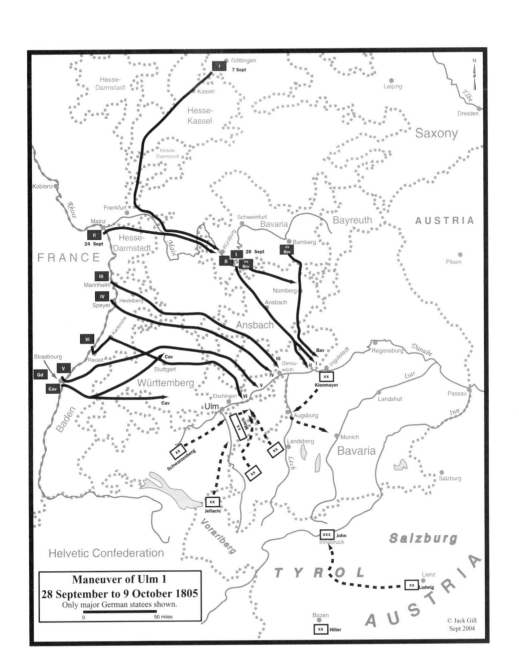

**Maneuver of Ulm 1
28 September to 9 October 1805**
Only major German statees shown.

0   50 miles

© Jack Gill
Sept 2004

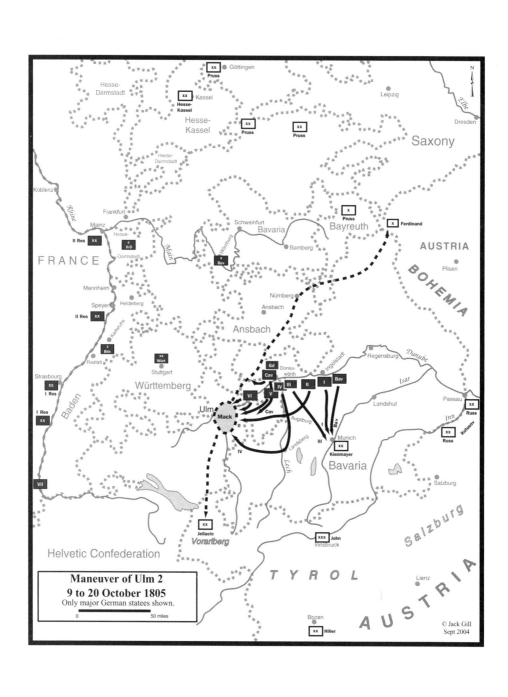

**Maneuver of Ulm 2
9 to 20 October 1805**
Only major German statees shown.

0   50 miles

© Jack Gill
Sept 2004

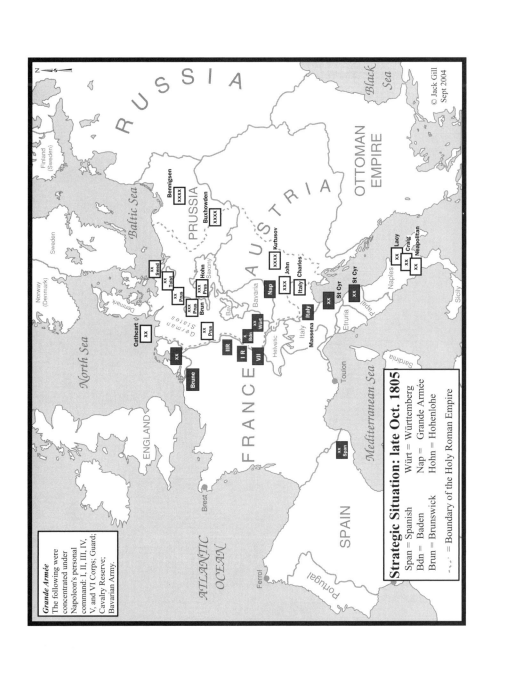

Strategic Situation: late Oct. 1805

Grande Armée
The following were concentrated under Napoleon's personal command: I, II, III, IV, V, and VI Corps; Guard; Cavalry Reserve; Bavarian Army.

Span = Spanish   Würt = Württemberg
Bdn = Baden   Nap = Grande Armée
Brun = Brunswick   Hohn = Hohenlohe

∙∙∙∙ = Boundary of the Holy Roman Empire

© Jack Gill
Sept 2004

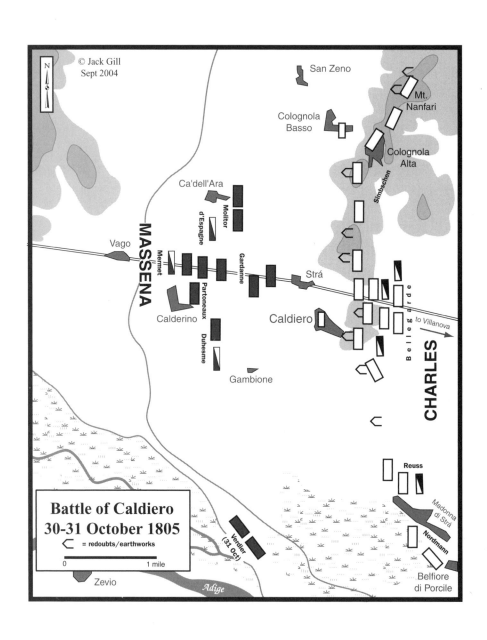

© Jack Gill
Sept 2004

N

San Zeno

Mt. Nanfari

Colognola Basso

Colognola Alta

Simbschen

Ca'dell'Ara

Molitor

d'Espagne

MASSENA

Vago

Mermet

Gardanne

Strá

Belleg arde

to Villanova

Partoneaux

Calderino

Caldiero

CHARLES

Duhesme

Gambione

Reuss

Madonna di Strá

Nordmann

Verdier (31 Oct)

**Battle of Caldiero
30-31 October 1805**

⊏ = redoubts/earthworks

0   1 mile

Zevio

Adige

Belfiore di Porcile

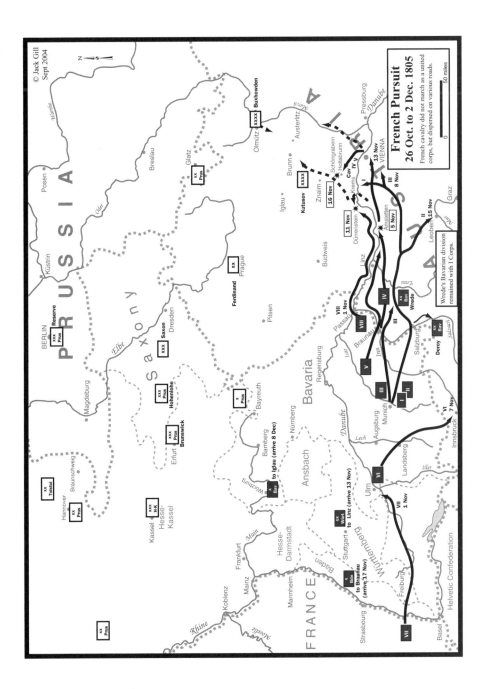

French Pursuit
26 Oct. to 2 Dec. 1805

French cavalry did not march as a united corps, but dispersed on various roads.

© Jack Gill
Sept 2004

0   50 miles

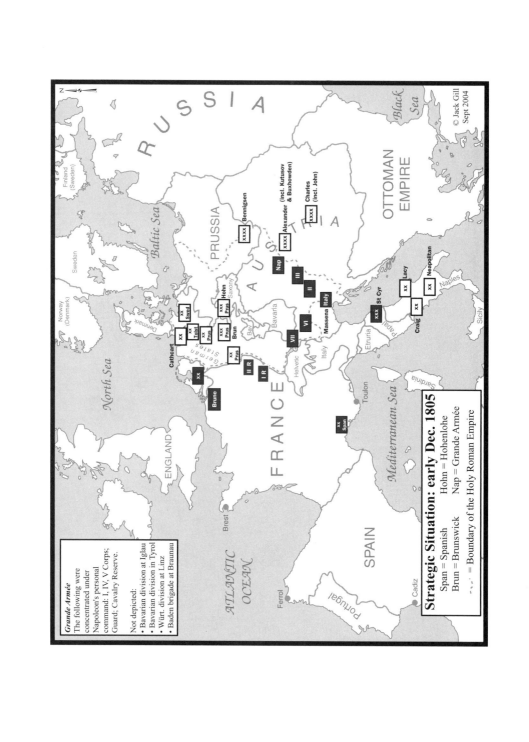

Strategic Situation: early Dec. 1805

Span = Spanish   Hohn = Hohenlohe
Brun = Brunswick Nap = Grande Armée
‑‑‑ = Boundary of the Holy Roman Empire

Grande Armée
The following were concentrated under Napoleon's personal command: I, IV, V Corps; Guard; Cavalry Reserve.

Not depicted:
• Bavarian division at Iglau
• Bavarian division in Tyrol
• Würt. division at Linz
• Baden brigade at Braunau

© Jack Gill
Sept 2004

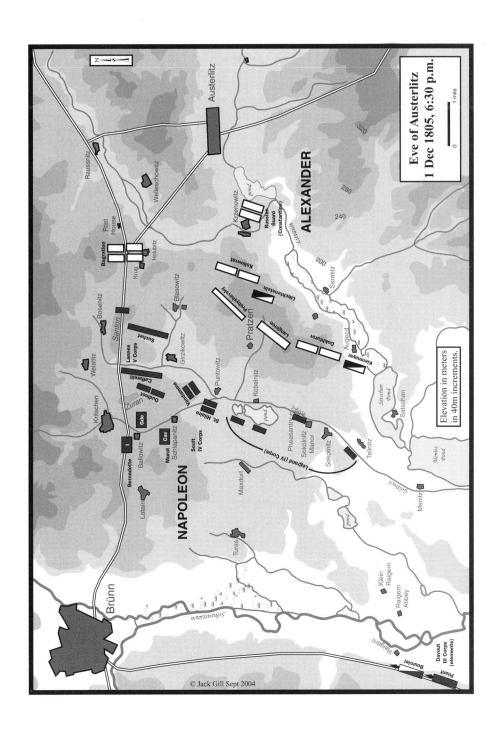

Eve of Austerlitz
1 Dec 1805, 6:30 p.m.

Elevation in meters in 40m increments.

© Jack Gill Sept 2004

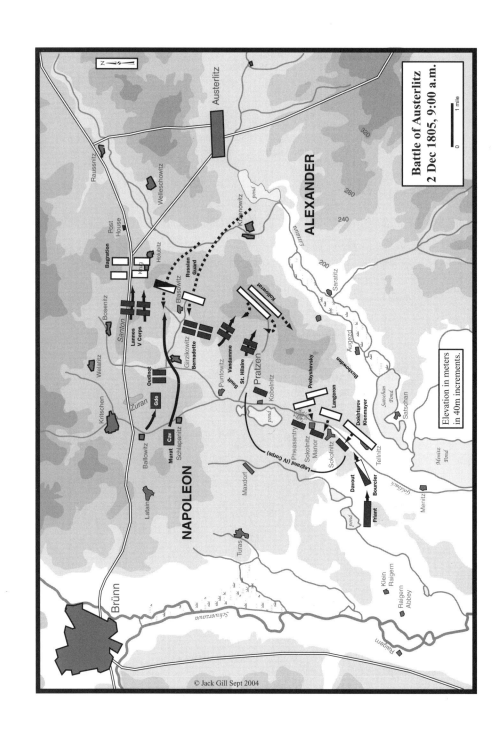

N

Austerlitz

Raussnitz

Welleschowitz

Post
House

Holubitz

ALEXANDER

320

280

240

Bagration

Bosenitz

Santon

Lannes
V Corps

Girzikowitz

Blasowitz

Russian
Guard

Krenowitz

pond

Saratitz

200

Kobelnitz

Welatitz

Kritschen

Zuran

Oudinot

Gde

Murat Cav

Schlapanitz

Bernadotte

Puntowitz

Vandamme

South

St. Hilaire

Pratzen

Kobelnitz

Pheasantry

pond

Prebyshevsky

Langeron

Kollowrat

Buxhowden

Augezd

Satschan
Pond

Dokhturov
Kienmayer

Satschan

Ballowitz

Latein

NAPOLEON

Maxdorf

Legrand (IV Corps)

Sokolnitz
Manor

Sokolnitz

Davout

Friant

Bourcier

Telnitz

Menitz
Pond

Goldbach

Menitz

Turas

Brünn

Schwarzawa

Klein
Raigern

Raigern
Abbey

Raigern

© Jack Gill Sept 2004

Battle of Austerlitz
2 Dec 1805, 9:00 a.m.

0   1 mile

Elevation in meters
in 40m increments.

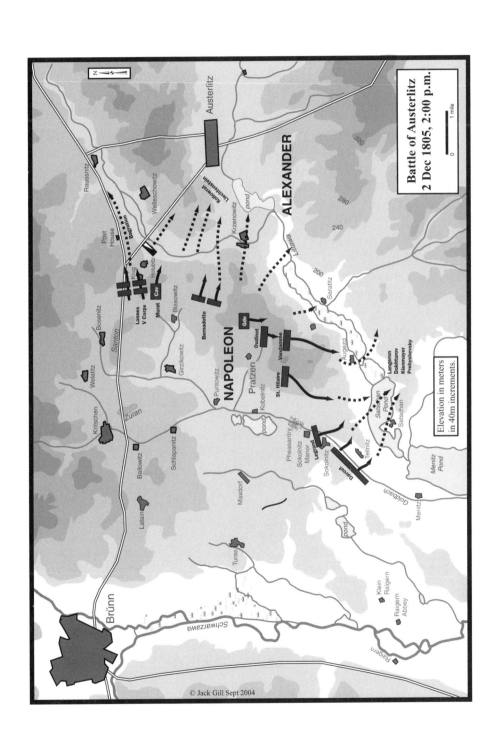

Battle of Austerlitz
2 Dec 1805, 2:00 p.m.

0   1 mile

ALEXANDER

NAPOLEON

Elevation in meters
in 40m increments.

Austerlitz

Rausnitz

Welleschowitz

Kollowrat
Liechtenstein

Krzenowitz

pond

Post
House

Bagration

Kug
Holubitz

Lannes
V Corps

Murat

Cav

Bosenitz

Santon

Blasowitz

Bernadotte

Gde

Pratzen

Oudinot

Vandamme

St. Hilaire

Punlowitz

Kobelnitz

pond

Girzikowitz

Welatitz

Welatitz

Krischen

Zuran

Schlapanitz

Ballowitz

Latain

Maxdorf

Pheasantry

Sokolnitz
Manor

Legrand

Sokolnitz

Davout

Telnitz

320

280

240

Littawa

200

Sarattiz

Augezd

Langeron
Dokhturov
Kienmayer
Prebyshevsky

Satschan
Pond

Satschan

Menitz
Pond

Goldbach

Menitz

pond

Turas

Klein
Raigern

Raigern
Abbey

Brünn

Schwarzawa

Raigern

© Jack Gill Sept 2004

NAPOLEON

NAPOLEON WAS MARS. He was Alexander, Caesar, and Charlemagne. He was the eternal conqueror whom history resurrects periodically. Yet, despite extensive historical accounts of his exploits, Napoleon remains an enigma. His motivations, ambitions, and desires are hotly contested by historians. Through his actions and those of his inner circle, he is presented as an individual who sought nothing more than war for its own sake. But Napoleon was more complex than this. He lived, breathed, and embodied the contradictions of his age. To present him otherwise is to provide an incomplete and, indeed, improper picture. Napoleon was larger than life, but that was only in part his own construct. His epoch provided him with a platform to achieve his goals, the likes of which emperors and kings have only dreamed. He shaped his world, as he was shaped by it.

Napoleon was a soldier and a statesman, a child of the Enlightenment, and a son of the French Revolution. Methodical throughout his career, he was also ever the consummate opportunist. His life spanned one of the greatest periods of transformation in European history, which spawned many of the movements that shaped the later course of Western Civilization. As a general of the Revolution, as first consul, and as emperor of the French, Napoleon ruled first a country and subsequently a continent that required his constant attention not only to high politics, but also to a myriad of mundane issues and ideas. Circumstance both forced and enabled Napoleon to manipulate the circumstances of the day to his own long-term advantage.

Opportunity was provided by events in Europe. Through 1804 Napoleon had no control over the evolving politics of the European monarchies. While the guillotine operated in France, the European states pursued their interests elsewhere. Prussia, Austria, and Russia finally absorbed the kingdom of Poland. At the same time, the Holy Roman Empire was in the process of secularization, which would lead to its eventual dissolution.[1] These events became critical to Napoleon later as consul and emperor. They allowed him to take advantage of the new geopolitics of Europe, to play upon them, and to permit him to devise an appropriate grand strategy for himself and France.

Generally confused with strategy, *grand strategy* is a term rarely used today. It refers to a state's aims in waging war and the resources and means necessary to achieve the objectives. Grand strategy and strategy itself are intertwined. Carl von Clausewitz, the Prussian military theorist and contemporary of Napoleon, best defined strategy as, "the use of engagement for the purpose of the war."

> The strategist must therefore define an aim for the entire operational side of the war that will be in accordance with its purpose. In other words, he will draft a plan of the war, and the aim will determine the series of actions intended to achieve it: he will, in fact, shape the individual campaigns and, within these, decide on the individual engagements.[2]

Political objectives establish the aim of the war. The strategy developed will either be limited to the resources available, or the resources will be expanded to accommodate the strategy. The variable is based upon the nature of the government and its relationship to its military institutions. In a democracy, where the civil and military institutions are separate, the civilian government establishes the political objective and the military leadership must tailor their strategy based upon the resources allocated by the government, and within the confines of the political aim. If, however, there is no clear delineation between the political and military leadership, as in the case of Napoleon, the commitment of resources toward achieving the political objective can be changed at the will of the political-military leader. Therefore, the boundaries between grand strategy and strategy correspondingly tend to be blurred in such cases.

Napoleon singularly held power in all its manifestations. When he assumed control of France he assumed responsibility for the shaping of French foreign and domestic policies. During his reign there were no effective institutional checks and balances to limit him. Nor was there initially any public desire to do so. To compartmentalize the Napoleonic era into the fields of war, society, and politics is to do a disservice to history. One cannot differentiate between the conqueror and the man who produced the Code Napoleon. Napoleon defined the geopolitical reality not only for France but eventually most of the continent. His grand strategy was wedded to the resources of his state and directed by his personal ambitions. Overall, they were formed and fostered by his unique character.

Upon assuming power Napoleon inherited the wars of the Revolution; the condition of the state and the war were not of his making. The Peace of

Campo Formio, which he negotiated with the Austrians in 1797, had already been superseded by events as a second European coalition formed against France. While Napoleon was in Egypt during 1798 and 1799, his conquests in Italy were lost. The military campaigns undertaken by the new first consul were an effort to regain the territory forfeited by the previous French administration and also to solidify his political power. Although his victories tended to legitimize his reign, Napoleon's success at Marengo in 1800 did not end the war. Only with the victory of General Moreau at Hohenlinden did the war come to a conclusion. Napoleon could not hope to pursue his own interests and objectives until hostilities ceased, and the domestic politics of France stabilized. Between 1789 and 1799 there were no less than five different governments—essentially ended by violence or force.[3] The weakness of the Revolutionary regimes was not lost on Napoleon. In 1795, he helped save the National Convention from an attempted Royalist Coup. In 1797, he sent General Pierre Augereau to support the coup of 18 Fructidor.[4] Coming to power in 1799 was the easy part for Napoleon; establishing a stable, well-ordered regime, however, was another matter. He had to reconcile a host of factions and entities within France, and only then, with domestic political stability, could he chart his own course.

War fed war during the Revolution, often without an ultimate goal. It is a mistake, however, to define Napoleon in similar terms. Although the vast majority of his life was spent under military influence, one must be cautious in applying this to his raison d'être. There were clear aims during the years preceding the creation of the Empire, and indeed through 1807. Afterward, Napoleon's objectives grew opaque. There is little doubt that by 1812 his policies and ambitions became increasingly irrational. He did not, however, conceive a master plan for world domination, nor even a desire to reestablish a Carolingian Empire, as some historians have argued.[5] Napoleon's geo-strategic ambitions evolved as he did. They changed with circumstance, through both his initiatives and in reaction to those of others. Napoleon, the rational statesman, eventually gave way to Napoleon the conqueror and romantic, who overcame the former. To understand this development, it is necessary to strip away lore and explore the relationship between Napoleon's grand strategy and the evolution of his character. Both are inexorably intertwined. To better understand this it is crucial that one examine the development of Napoleon's character from his youth through his rise to power.

Napoleon was born in Ajaccio, Corsica, in 1769. He was one of eight children. At the age of nine he was enrolled in the French military academy at Brienne. Napoleon remained there until 1784, when he was admitted to the royal military academy, the École Militaire, in Paris. After only a year of instruction, he successfully placed out of further study by passing his exit exams. Commissioned as a second lieutenant in the artillery, he was assigned to the royal artillery regiment, La Fère, at Valence. In 1788

Napoleon was sent with his regiment to the artillery school at Auxonne, where he remained through 1789. After the Revolution of June, Napoleon went on leave to Corsica, where he remained through January 1791. He rejoined his regiment, now back at Valence, but again returned to Corsica in the fall. There he became embroiled in island politics. He was ordered back to France, but only appeared there briefly, ultimately taking leave once more to rejoin his family in Ajaccio. In 1793, the Bonapartes were chased from Corsica, and Napoleon finally returned to military service, where his star would soon rise.

A number of excellent studies have sought to explore the influences and events of Napoleon's early life. Certainly, in the past twenty-five years works that use psycho-historical methodology have placed considerably greater emphasis on Napoleon's youth and how it impacted on his later actions.[6] Psychohistory is considered by some the cutting edge of historical interpretations, but others have argued that it is impossible to provide a cogent psychoanalysis of a person who died 200 years ago. Nonetheless, it is imperative that when providing a biographical sketch the historian must make certain assessments regarding personality.[7] Although psychohistory often highlights the negative influences in a person's life, one can certainly apply the methodology to Napoleon in a more positive manner to determine what issues, events, and individuals were instrumental in the development of his character, thought, and actions.[8]

Paramount to Napoleon's character were the contradictions between reason and romanticism as revealed by his actions and words. Napoleon exhibited a capacity for reasoned statecraft, quite reminiscent of eighteenth century rulers.[9] At the same time, he directed the military energy of France and his Empire to fulfill wholly romantic ambitions. This was a manifestation of his earlier life experiences—particularly the years from childhood to early adulthood. Much of what he saw and experienced growing up in Corsica or attending school in France is consistent with the contradictions of the age. The late Enlightenment was a period of intellectual and political change that ultimately became a social and political revolution where reason and romanticism overlapped. Napoleon was himself a product of the same influences as those who attended the Estates General and National Assembly in 1789.

The contradictions in Napoleon's life extended beyond his intellectual experience. Perhaps one of the greatest crises in Napoleon's early life involves his search for identity. Was he Corsican or French? Born in Corsica, Napoleon lived his first nine years there with his family, but he subsequently spent thirty-six years calling France his home. Although Corsica had been in prolonged rebellion against its former Genoese rulers, resistance to the French, who acquired the island in 1768, was short lived. Napoleon's father and mother participated in both rebellions, but by the time of his birth they had accepted French rule and settled in the capital, Ajaccio. Thus, he grew up in a relatively peaceful atmosphere. Although in some of his biographies there is a tendency to discuss the "brutal nature" of Corsican society, with particular emphasis on the role of the vendetta, it was not part of the Bonaparte's cultural heritage. The closest they came to waging vendettas was in the courts. Litigation against members of the extended family, as well as neighbors, seemed to occupy much of his family's time. This was not unusual, as Carlo, Napoleon's father, put down the gun in 1768 and picked up the pen as an attorney. If there was a violent side to Corsican society it was not pervasive in the capital city. There was a prominent distinction between the cosmopolitan Corsica of the coast and that of the agricultural interior.[10] This difference would be key in the lives of Napoleon and his brother during the early years of the French Revolution.

The cultural violence of Corsican society was not an influence in Napoleon's youth, yet conflict with his eldest brother Joseph was certainly common- place. The second son of eight children, Napoleon was only a year apart from Joseph and often fought with his brother. This has been discussed as perhaps an illustration of Napoleon's will to dominate. Yet, one could certainly ask whether this was merely a matter of everyday sibling rivalry, where two brothers close in age fight for a variety of reasons, or for no reason at all.[11] His relationships with fellow students at the provincial military academy of Brienne have also been examined. Napoleon was steadfastly tied to his Corsican identity, and this often led to fights with the other cadets. There is also some debate surrounding the origin of Napoleon's assertion of his "Corsicaness" at Brienne. It has been suggested that initially it was thrust upon him by his classmates.[12] Whatever the impetus, Napoleon's acceptance and proclama- tion of his Corsican birth can clearly be viewed as an attempt to set himself apart from the others. Napoleon's conduct, however, may not be unusual for a child of the eighteenth century—or the twenty-first—attending school a great distance from home and family. How does one establish individuality in such an atmosphere? His constant scrapes with students were not an indi- cation of a proclivity toward violence. There is little similar analysis of the other cadets involved in these altercations. Few have argued that Napoleon was the class bully. In many ways fighting among teenage boys at a military academy could be nothing more than a rite of passage, or the product of hor- monal activity.

Little, however, could have prepared Napoleon for his role as leader of the family. Shortly after he graduated from the École Militaire in 1785, his father, Carlo, died. Although Joseph was the eldest, Napoleon became the de facto head of the household. Unusual as it was, Napoleon was the only son who had a career and was able to take responsibility for the leadership of the family. Joseph at that time was torn between entering the army as an artil- lerist or continuing with his religious studies. In either case, he was in no position to provide financial support for his family. Since second lieutenants of the artillery did not receive a substantial salary, Napoleon borrowed from fellow officers in his regiment.[13]

The weighty responsibility of family provider had much to do with his extended leaves in Corsica from 1788 through 1793, when he continued his education. Napoleon was an avid reader and his taste in literature was symptomatic of the age. His early education in Ajaccio consisted of traditional reading, writing, mathematics, and religion. The latter, however, came from family instruction. Enlightenment culture was prominent in Corsica as the count de Marbeuf, the French military governor, sought to rationalize the French administration, enabling a more efficient assimilation of the island into the kingdom of France. The Corsicans themselves, or more properly, those of the nobility and the more affluent bourgeoisie—of which the Bonapartes were a part—were taken by the ideas of the Enlightenment. There was a difference, however, between Marbeuf's Enlightenment and that of the Corsicans. To Marbeuf, the model was enlightened monarchy, whereas the Corsican champion was Jean-Jacques Rousseau.[14] Napoleon read Rousseau. He also read Montesquieu, Voltaire, Mably, and Mirabeau.[15] There is correspondingly no doubt that the Enlightenment had a profound influence upon Napoleon.

The military academies he attended from 1778 to 1786 were instrumental in introducing him to the Enlightenment. Brienne was one of several military schools established as part of extensive military-education reforms in the wake of the debacle of the Seven Years' War. Napoleon attended that school from the age of nine through fifteen. Curiously, in the latter half of the eighteenth century the Royal Army was one of the few institutions in France that greatly benefited from enlightened and rational reforms.[16] Although one might be inclined to perceive the army as a bastion of conservatism in its desire to preserve the existing order, its primary role was to defend the monarchy. The abysmal performance of the French army during the Seven Years' War compelled it to reform.

The purpose of the Enlightenment, as an intellectual movement or a function of monarchical reform, was to establish reasoned order.[17] These aspects of the Enlightenment seem in many ways contradictory, but the French Royal Army was able to draw from both. At the heart of the matter was the French nobility, whose desire to assert their social privilege within the army corroded the fundamental law of subordination to military leadership.[18] The French aristocracy sought to restore their privilege within those institutions they believed were exclusive to their caste. The officer corps was such an institution.[19] To address this dilemma, the reforms established a respect for military hierarchy and opened the army gradually to men of talent.[20]

Far from being a progressive institution, the Royal Army was nevertheless the most successful of all the bureaucratic institutions of *ancien regime*

France to reform. This was illustrated by the army's performance in America during the American Revolution. It was a marked difference compared to its actions two decades earlier. Napoleon was a beneficiary and a product of this institution and its reforms. But, the French aristocracy's attempt to reassert itself posed a threat to Napoleon's career. It is also a reason why Napoleon and many of his contemporaries in the artillery later supported the Revolution.[21]

Cadets at Brienne were carefully guided through aspects of enlightened thought, but both the military traditions and the nature of the French system sought to limit their exposure. Virtue—not in the republican sense but as defined by the counter-enlightenment, pre-modern romanticism—was institutionalized. Although the soldiers marched in cadence to geometrically precise maneuvers, it was the Roman martial virtue of *honneur et gloire* that motivated them.[22] The curriculum at Brienne and its sister schools mirrored those of the private academies that future revolutionary leaders attended in their youth. In particular the schools emphasized classical studies, notably Livy, Tacitus, Sallust, Plutarch, and Virgil. At Brienne there were additional readings in ancient military history, such as *Caesar's Commentaries* (the conquest of Gaul and the civil war).[23] It was here that the educated youth of France were introduced to the concepts of "a society of self-made men, . . . by virtue of their eloquence rise to hold the highest positions in the state."[24] Napoleon was not the only student who took to heart the concept that glory and virtue brought opportunity and advancement to men of talent, but Robespierre and Marat advocated these points from a different perspective years later.[25] Opportunity for men of talent was one of several classical ideas that permeated both the advocates of Enlightenment and those of the established order who rejected reform.

These contradictions emerged at the moment Napoleon was introduced to logic and reason. "The army," said historian David Bien, "was locked in a cold war with the court, wealth, cities, the whole French 'constitution.' It was a struggle to realize a professional ideal that was at once bureaucratic and moral, modeled on exaggerated pictures of public virtue in Sparta, the Roman republic, and Prussia."[26] Under these circumstances could a child of nine, ten, eleven, or twelve truly understand the complexities of his age? Yet Brienne was one of several institutions purposefully established to address the excesses of eighteenth century luxury and privilege. Napoleon lived and learned in a school that was created as a purposeful contradiction to the existing system.[27]

One of the greatest difficulties was wedding military values with current intellectual trends. "Glory," wrote Voltaire, "is reputation joined with esteem, and is complete when admiration is superceded." He continued, "It always supposes that which is brilliant in action, in virtue or in talent and the surmounting of great difficulties."[28] In this definition, enlightened concepts of virtue, merit, and talent are merged with romantic notions of glory and action. Glory could be applied to the nation and the individual. This melding of Enlightenment with counter-Enlightenment romanticism formed the core of Napoleon's thought. He accepted reason, but was consistently motivated by romantic calls to action.

Certainly Napoleon had been exposed to concepts of revolt in Corsica long before 1789, although he never personally experienced such until the French Revolution. Difficulty arises, however, in the application of the concepts of honor and virtue. Montesquieu defined honor as associated with monarchy, and virtue with democracy; however, Voltaire rejected those definitions.[29] Lacking his own clear definition of honor, Voltaire believed virtue was "that which does good for society."[30] These definitions are insufficient in explaining how Napoleon saw them. French revolutionaries favored Montesquieu and Rousseau initially, but Napoleon was a product of the military institutions of royal France and therefore accepted "virtue, honor, and glory" as defined by the military caste prior to 1789. As a contemporary of Napoleon, Clausewitz referred to these concepts as "military virtue," which incorporated this trinity. He referred to bravery, courage, nationalism, honor, and spirit.[31] This held true for the French Royal Army as well.[32] Their ideas were a critical part of Napoleon's military education. Brienne and other similar institutions established during the 1770s stressed these ideas and indoctrinated their students, stressing the association of these concepts with service to the state.

The philosophes raised the history of antiquity and particularly Rome to a level that often exceeded historical reality. The virtue of Cicero and Caesar were paramount. To the philosophes, Cicero was a better representative of Roman ideals. But they also found Julius Casear and Augustus acceptable.[33] This was the root of virtue in the military definition. Napoleon's concept of virtue was associated with martial responsibilities.

> Virtue had been awarded ultimate prestige and, detached from both theology and ethics, was now equated with military masculinity, dominance, simplicity, frugality, ignorance and a preference for the archaic; in short, the antithesis of every value prevailing among the influential classes of French society in the eighteenth century.[34]

At both Brienne and the École Militaire these concepts of virtue, honor, and glory were emphasized increasingly as a reaction to the admission of "outsiders" into the once monopolized domain of the noble-officer corps. It was necessary to teach these future leaders of the French army what it was believed they did not inherently possess. The innate concept of honor, which was possessed by the *noblesse d'epee*, or so they believed, had to be taught to the new and socially questionable attendees of the military academies.[35] Leadership by example, loyalty to the king and regiment, and the manner by which one motivates men requires the evocation of emotion. This was codified as *esprit du corps*. It was a military necessity during the transformation of French military institutions from professional to national armies. No more than one-third of the French Royal Army was composed of foreign regiments in 1789. The remainder was drawn from national recruitment.[36]

Napoleon was a product of the eighteenth century armies and education, and he could not avoid being influenced by these concepts and seeming contradictions. He was after all under the care of the French military system from the age of nine to seventeen. Upon his commission and subsequent leave from the army, he returned home to Corsica where he brought along a considerable number of books, including those by Montaigne, Montesquieu, Plato, Tacitus, Cicero, Livy, and Plutarch.[37] His interests broadened to both subjects of nature, but he also retained a keen interest in history, particularly in the ancient world and specifically Rome.[38] His fascination with history was therefore a consequence of the Enlightenment as much as it was tied to his search for his identity.

There is little doubt that he was struggling with his identity during the time he attended Brienne. He outwardly proclaimed himself a Corsican, but in that statement there was contradiction as well.[39] What did being a Corsican mean? His parents had accepted French rule and his mother was the favorite of the French military governor. Certainly, his family's perceptions of being Corsican were filled with contradictions. In the end, years of education and life in France led to his ultimate rejection of a Corsican identity as Corsica rejected him: "I am not Corsican. I was brought up in France, therefore I am French."[40] If upon departing Brienne and graduating from the École Militaire Napoleon left his island, what of his youth did he take with him to the artillery school at Auxonne and thereafter? How did he see himself? If he could not reconcile the contradictions by which others sought to define him, then perhaps he could define himself.[41]

His father, Carlo, defined his family's social identity. He spent years and a great deal of money the family did not possess to acquire patents recognizing the Bonaparte's nobility. This only became a priority after Carlo and Napoleon's mother, Leitzia, accepted French rule. Prior, it was a matter of Corsican patriotism verses Genoese overlordship. Napoleon could not have gained entrance to Brienne were it not for Carlo's pursuit of familial legitimacy and the support of the French governor of Corsica.

Curiously, within the examination of Napoleon's quest for an identity as a Corsican, a Frenchman, or both, he has been isolated and studied in a vacuum as if the experiences of his brothers in their youth were irrelevant. The entire Bonaparte family after 1768 seems to have tied their futures to France. Carlo understood all too well the opportunities opened to his family. His efforts to establish the family's social legitimacy clearly indicate that the patriarch was not a revolutionary in the republican sense, but a man of the eighteenth century. Patronage was as critical as social standing. The

Bonapartes' affiliation with the Count de Marbeuf extended to the count's brother, the Bishop of Autun.[42] Both Joseph, the eldest son, and Lucien, the third, were enrolled at the College d'Autun in preparation for the church while Napoleon entered Brienne.[43] Of all the institutions of the *ancien regime*, the church and the Royal Army were two of its most ardent supporters. Napoleon's family saw French rule as an opportunity for advancement.

Napoleon championed Corsican independence as an adolescent, but during the Revolution he rejected Pasquale Paoli, the leader of the Corsican independence movement since his father's day. The great break between the Bonapartes and Paoli was dramatic, but a long time coming before 1793. Just as Napoleon had ardently called for Paoli's resurrection as a student at Brienne, his family found themselves at odds with the Corsica leader. The confrontation was founded on Paoli's British sympathies.[44] Paoli returned from exile in England in July 1790. Napoleon and the Corsican Jacobins, such as Chrisophe Saliceti, believed Corsica's fate stood better with France and the Revolution. In short, by 1793 there were those in Corsica who believed that the island should remain a part of Revolutionary France, those who were counterrevolutionaries, and those such as Paoli who believed Corsica was better off under British protection. The Bonapartes were of the former faction, and denounced Paoli. Napoleon's hero in youth became his enemy in adulthood.[45]

By the time of the French Revolution what Napoleon had learned was that the world was filled with contradictions. Ability determined one's fate. This, above all else, seemed to form the core of Napoleon's character. He possessed a great deal of confidence in himself and pride in his achievements. He saw in the history he read, particularly the ancient histories, that men of ability and virtue (the pre-republican definition) were limited only by their own ambitions.[46] Opportunity was the key to achieving ambition, and Napoleon reached maturity in an age when opportunity abounded. The French Revolution enabled a young second lieutenant in the artillery in 1789 to become commander in chief of the French army of Italy by 1796. The Revolution provided Napoleon the opportunity to utilize his ambitious nature and understanding of reason and revolution. The child of the Enlightenment became a revolutionary, and the contradictions of his youth afforded him the tools to succeed as an officer in the army, as first consul, and as emperor of the French.

CHAPTER TWO

FRANCE AND SPAIN

NAPOLEON NEEDED SPAIN. He needed its navy, and, most importantly, he needed its silver. In the first instance, the union of the Spanish and French fleets was a critical precursor for a successful invasion of England. Twice before, the combined Franco-Spanish fleets had challenged the Royal Navy for control of the channel, once in 1781, the other in 1797. The former was a success, the latter a miserable failure, but the possibility of wresting control of the channel was paramount to Napoleon's plan to invade England after 1803. In many ways, this was putting the cart before the horse.

Spanish silver was desperately needed to assure France's financial stability. It was sought after more than the Spanish navy. Napoleon did not understand high finance but clearly appreciated the value of gold and silver. The collapse of the French economy prior to 1789 was due to the state's inability to pay its extensive and overwhelming loans. Financing war was a difficult affair. The economic crisis was not resolved when the Revolutionary government declared war on Austria in April 1792. The creation of paper money, the *assignat*, in 1789 led to the eventual elimination of the short-term national debt; however, by 1792 the demands of war led to the printing of more *assignats* and, subsequently, inflation running at 20 percent.[1] Confidence in the French government and its ability to pay the debt was severely lacking. This created an atmosphere that was not conducive to a successful issuance of government bonds, as was done by the monarchy in the 1770s and 1780s. High inflation continued through 1795, and it was only the introduction of monies "confiscated" by General Napoleon Bonaparte from the Italian states in 1796 and 1797 that brought some stability to the French economy. To the Revolutionaries, war fed war, and "contributions" from "liberated peoples" and the defeated powers was the only means to finance the war effort. When Napoleon seized power in 1799, he was faced with the legacy of the Revolution's failed fiscal policies. Under the Consulate and Empire, he financed his wars by returning France to a bimetallic standard beginning in 1803.[2]

Unable and unwilling to finance the state and the wars by floating bonds, Napoleon relied almost exclusively on taxation and foreign "contributions." This enabled him to pay down the existing debt, which was done in specie, and carry France through fifteen years of war without accruing a substantial deficit. Although the state was solvent, the French people were taxed to the hilt. The Revolutionary regime had eliminated indirect taxes on goods, but Napoleon restored the policy so that in 1805 the tax receipt on commodities was 17.5 percent, dropping to 13 percent in 1806, and rising to 20 percent by 1813.[3]

The military budget for Napoleonic France included the cost of war, the military administration responsible for the army and the navy. On average this represented 60 to 65 percent of the total national expenditure.[4] The ability of the Napoleonic government to cover the cost with hard currency restored some confidence in the economy and interest on government bonds, called *rentes* and *consols*, declined steadily.[5] The secret to Napoleonic finance, however, was not only a strict adherence to a tax-based system, but his ability to shift a large part of the cost of supplying and maintaining the French army upon his allies, the defeated, and the "liberated." Between 1805 and 1808, the kingdom of Italy contributed more than 22 million francs each year for the maintenance of the French army stationed there. Other satellite states did the same.[6]

Napoleon took the opportunity to stabilize the French economy when in 1802 the Peace of Amiens ended war between England and France. State revenue during the last year of the conflict amounted to 500 million francs. Military expenditure for 1802 was 314 million. There were sufficient funds to cover public expenses, but not a great deal more. During 1803, 624.5 million francs were collected in revenue, and by the end of the second quarter only 100 million was dispersed to the Ministry of War and Marine.[7] Napoleon balanced the budget for the next three years on the assumption that peace would hold. He anticipated naval expenditure at 210 million francs between 1803 and 1805, and 630 million for the War administration.[8]

The Bank of France was responsible for the accumulation of specie in state coffers and the issuance of bank notes. In 1803, the bank dispersed 30 million francs in bills.[9] The outbreak of war in May 1803 completely undermined Napoleon's budget and threw France into an economic crisis that reached its zenith in the autumn of 1805. The French deficit increased dramatically as war demanded greater military expenditure. Pressed to find means to pay the bills, Napoleon exacted contributions from the Italian states and Holland.[10] These were wholly inadequate to address the growing problem.

Napoleon saw Spain as a cash cow. Its extensive overseas empire possessed a ready source of silver. Although Spain continued its economic decline in the eighteenth century, it experienced a renaissance in silver mining by the 1790s. The irony of Spain's economic condition was plainly stated by historian John Lynch: "[T]he climax of the silver age and the peak of the transatlantic trade coincided with the destruction of Spain's maritime power and the closure of her imperial routes."[11] Napoleon was not solely responsible for these events, but the wars of the French Revolution, and Spain's role throughout, illustrated—all too clearly—the conundrum of Spanish foreign policy.

The first consul did not simply conclude that Spain's silver should find its way to France. His interests were tied to both the recent and long-term relationship between the two countries. Since the succession of the Bourbon family to Spain in 1700, both monarchies had maintained strong economic and political ties. They made common cause against England regularly in the eighteenth century, and fought against Habsburg interests in Italy during the War of Austrian Succession. The special relationship was codified on three separate occasions. The Bourbon Family Compact was last renewed in 1761 during the Seven Years' War, and common cause was made again in 1779 with a Spanish declaration of war against England, which came two months after a secret Franco-Spanish convention and almost two years after French intervention in America.[12]

The French Revolution drastically shook Spanish policy. Carlos III's reign was one of economic recovery and reconstruction of Spain's fleets and overseas trade. Alliance with France was beneficial. Unfortunately, Carlos IV, the new king, had to cope with the Revolution and its implications on Spanish policy. War and the overthrow of the French monarchy strained relations. The Girondin government in France initially sought a Spanish alliance, but that was while Louis XVI, cousin to Carlos IV, remained tentatively on the throne. After January 1793, when Louis lost his head Spanish reaction turned hostile. For the first time in a century Spain and England found themselves reluctant allies.

Joint naval operations were conducted during the years of the Terror (1793–1794), largely providing support to counterrevolutionaries in the French Mediterranean ports of Toulon and Marseilles. The alliance, however, felt unnatural to both Spanish and English sea captains. Distrust and dislike did not lend itself to effective military cooperation. More than this, Spain was separated from France only by the Pyrenees. A Spanish army crossed into France in late 1793 and met with initial success. By 1794 the French recaptured Marseilles and Toulon, reinforced their armies in Perpignan, and then crossed into Catalonia, bringing war to the Spanish kingdom.[13]

Carlos IV and his ministers desperately sought an exit strategy. Seeing opportunity when Prussia signed a treaty with France in April 1795 Spain followed suit. Carlos found the new French government, the Directory, more receptive than their *Terroriste* predecessors. At the end of July Spain and France were no longer at war.

Beyond the pleasantries of the treaty's preamble and the usual articles related to the withdrawal of forces from conquered territories, the Treaty of Basel required Spain to mediate between France and the Italian states. It also sought particular Spanish intercession with the papacy, seeking to mend relations that were defined by the papal interdict imposed upon France in 1792.[14] The conclusion of war also introduced possibilities and opportunities for both states.

The Directory benefited from Spanish neutrality, but perceived greater reward if Spain restored the Family Compact (*sans bourbons française*), agreed to wage economic war against England, and unite their fleets in the Mediterranean to the exclusion of England.[15] What the French wanted, however, was not clearly what Carlos IV desired. Alliance with England over the past three years had allowed for the continued flow of revenue from the Americas to Spain, but the cost of the continental war was substantial. Similarly, there is a general misunderstanding when considering Spanish finances. The availability of silver is often seen as a ready source of Spanish revenue. Yet, Spain suffered from having to service enormous debts, and in order to generate revenue as quickly as possible for the war with France, the Spanish government preferred to take loans based upon the estimated value of the annual silver shipments. Thus, most of the silver was already spent before it made the long journey across the Atlantic.[16]

The lessons of Spain's participation in the war of the First Coalition were hard. The English alliance was a marriage of convenience. Carlos IV's hand was forced with his cousin's execution. Even English foreign minister Lord Grenville commented upon the signing of the agreement in 1793, "[It] cannot be considered a very solid foundation of friendship."[17] Nor was it. Almost immediately following the Peace of Basel, there was great concern in England that Spanish neutrality was temporary, and the natural order of things—a Franco-Spanish alliance—would soon follow. Spain's possessions in the Caribbean and the Americas were substantial. When the English learned the Treaty of Basel included the transfer of Santo Domingo to France, giving them the entire island of Hispaniola (Haiti being the other half), they were truly distressed.[18]

The potential threat to Britain's Caribbean empire was real enough. It had happened before during the American Revolution. The united fleets bullied their way into the channel, and naval operations in the Caribbean and South America placed Jamaica in significant peril.[19] During the reign of Carlos III, the Spanish navy experienced a recovery. Its performance during the American Revolution and its size during the French war was a reflection of a renewed financial commitment to the fleet and an understanding that

Spain's economic health was tied to its colonies in the Indies and New Spain. Although the Spanish had been able to extract goods and silver from the Americas, this was useless unless they could ship them to Spain. A massive naval building program was undertaken and continued through the 1790s. By 1794, Spain possessed 79 ships of the line, compared to France's 76 and England's 115. Furthermore, 25 percent of Spain's fleet was composed of first-rate ships of the line, which exceeded eighty guns. Six monsters, 112 guns each, were built in the Havana shipyard in the preceding decade.[20]

All of this meant that although the Spanish monarchy had to address the financial impact of the war it had just fought, it was by no means a weak and insignificant factor in international affairs. The English took them seriously enough, as did France. Enter Manuel de Godoy y Alvarez de Faria. A colorful figure in an age filled with color, Godoy has not benefited from the judgment of history. Carlos Secco Serrano, biographer of Godoy, wrote, "[A]t the moment when Europe found itself in the midst of reorganization, Godoy under-bid, a victim of fear and personal vanity, shipwrecked without a pilot in the storm."[21] His rapid rise at the court of Carlos IV was tied initially to his relationship with the Queen, Maria Luisa. In 1787 at the age of 20 he was a cadet in the Spanish Guards. Within four years he was promoted to lieutenant general, then captain general, given title as duke de la Alcudia, and appointed secretary of state.[22] Despite the queen's attentions, his appointment marked a turning point in court politics. Godoy was nobody made somebody by the monarchy. His liaison with the queen had ceased by 1796, when he married a cousin of the monarch (although he had already taken a lover).[23] Godoy was largely responsible for directing the Spanish ship of state through the Revolution and into the Napoleonic era. Although he was responsible for taking Spain to war in 1793, he was also credited with extricating it from the conflict in 1795.

In 1796 Spain was pressured by England to maintain it's neutrality, and pressured by France to convert it to an offensive military alliance. Initially, Godoy maintained Spain's neutrality. Peace meant full restoration of trade with France, and neutrality meant that England would not want to push Spain into French arms by trying to retard or prevent Spain from trading with its neighbor. As Godoy perceived, France could now emerge from economic isolation by importing goods from overseas via neutral Spain, and vice versa.[24] Indeed, peace was translated rapidly into currency. The Spanish navy was now tasked with shipping silver directly from the Americas. Between the autumn of 1795 and that of 1796, there were eight such shipments made, totaling 636 million *reales*, half going to the royal coffers.[25] It is no surprise then that under these circumstances Godoy wanted to protect Spanish neutrality and its overseas trade. He entered into conversations with the Swedish minister baron d'Ehrensmert regarding a league of armed neutrality to preserve and protect what Spain had. Both Sweden and Denmark, although competing for Baltic trade, were none too pleased with Britain's heavy-handedness related to French trade. Godoy thought an armed league, similar to one formed in 1780, would have greater success.[26]

Despite his apparent interest in keeping Spain on course for gradual economic recovery, Godoy eventually saw opportunity. Perhaps in one of the most irrational moves of his career, Manuel de Godoy recommended to Carlos IV that Spain accept French overtures for war with England. Godoy's *Memorias* do not shed any light on this decision.[27] This is not surprising because the result of Spain's alliance in 1796 was the beginning of the end of Bourbon Spain. Godoy was conscious of this when he wrote after the fact. Therefore we can only speculate and examine the events of 1796 as they appeared.

Napoleon's conquest of northern Italy in 1796 marked a dramatic shift in the strategic situation in Europe. By the summer, French troops occupied Piedmont, Habsburg Lombardy, and Modena. According to the Treaty of Basel, Carlos IV was required to mediate between France and the Italian princes. When the treaty was signed, however, the French had a foothold in Genoa, but had yet to break across the Alps and into the Po valley. Spain's role in Italy was minimal through 1795. The Bourbon dynasty extended to the Duchy of Parma and the Kingdom of the two Sicilies. The special relationship between Spain and the Catholic Church made it a fundamental player in papal affairs too. The result was that Spain was now required to play its role and intercede on behalf of France and their dynastic cousins in Italy. More significant was the request that Spain mediate an agreement between Pope Pius VI and General Bonaparte in order to prevent French occupation of the Papal States.[28]

The Spanish ambassador to Rome, José Nicholas Azara, directed negotiations between the Papacy and Bonaparte. Azara was later rewarded for his successful service with his appointment as ambassador to France. He would remain at that post through 1808. The Spanish were able to secure the sovereignty and neutrality of their Italian cousins and assuage French anti-clericalism by securing papal funds as an illustration of friendship. The elimination of Habsburg forces in Italy combined with Neapolitan neutrality gave Godoy the notion that Spain could regain Minorca and Gibraltar, perhaps even seize Tobago. The possibility of victory in the Mediterranean and the reduction of British interests in the Caribbean enticed Godoy. Furthermore, the Directory encouraged Godoy to consider extending Spanish influence to Portugal. The Iberian kingdom was an ally of England, and the historic animosity, competition, and relationship with Spain was certainly played upon. French support at sea and against Portugal gave Godoy illusions of grandeur. One must not forget that he was able to convince Carlos IV to follow his advice. Thus in October 1796, Spain and France entered into an offensive alliance affirmed in the Treaty of San Ildefonso.[29] The treaty formed the basis of Franco-Spanish cooperation through 1805 and tied Spain both willingly and unwillingly to French foreign policy, from the Directory to the Consulate and Empire.

The articles of the treaty are usual enough, but what is striking is that neither France nor Spain defined the objectives of the conflict. It was an offensive-defensive alliance against England, in which both countries pledged to protect the integrity of their respective states, territories, and overseas possessions. For the war both were required to commit and maintain no fewer than fifteen ships of the line, and no fewer than 18,000 men for service in Europe or in their colonies. Their naval contingents would act in concert for the duration of the conflict, although union of the fleets was not strictly required. Among the secret articles France pledged to convince the Dutch to accede to the agreement, putting their navy and colonies at the allies' disposal. This was merely a formality, as Holland was already a French satellite and at war with England. Nonetheless, the only requirement firmly stated in the treaty was that the king of Spain would use either influence or force to compel Portugal to close its ports to English goods.[30]

The war Spain embarked upon in 1796 was an unmitigated disaster, and it put the Spanish Bourbons on the road to ruin. Certainly one cannot blame Godoy in 1796 for not being able to predict the future. The last time Spain and France allied against England in 1779, the outcome was positive. Indeed in the months following the new treaty, England's strategic situation was grim. The Admiralty was forced to withdraw its fleet from the Mediterranean in the face of superior numbers. The island of Corsica was abandoned by the British, having to contend with the French fleet at Toulon and the Spanish squadron at Cartagena, which joined with a Spanish fleet from the Atlantic and entered Toulon toward the end of October. Adding to this problem, the Italian states were now either under French occupation or neutral, resulting in·the withdrawal of the Neapolitan squadron from the English Mediterranean fleet.[31] This was only the beginning. Fortified with confidence, the Directory planned for an invasion of Ireland. A combined Franco-Spanish fleet, reinforced by the Dutch, would provide ample numbers to challenge the channel fleet and enable an expeditionary force to land safely. The plan was set in motion in the first months of 1797.[32]

William Pitt the Younger was twenty-four when he became prime minister of Great Britain in 1784, the year following the loss of the American colonies. Pitt remained at this post through the French Revolution and resigned in 1801, having failed to achieve Catholic emancipation in Ireland. An ardent enemy of Revolutionary France, he witnessed the progressive erosion of the First Coalition. First Prussia, then Spain, signed separate agreements with France. Russia remained a constant source of frustration. Catherine II refused to embroil her empire in the European conflict. Finally, in the summer of 1796, she agreed to send an army, but her price was extraordinary. Catherine was neither easy nor cheap. At the moment when Spain declared war on England it appeared that Catherine might agree to less, but 1796 was not a good year for Pitt and England. Catherine died in November. Paul I, her son and heir, was not interested in entertaining any foreign military commitments at this time.[33]

Matters worsened in the first months of 1797. Britain was on the verge of financial disaster due to its generous foreign subsidies and domestic military expenditure. Furthermore, the French and Spanish fleets left the Mediterranean for Atlantic waters. The Dutch were also assembling their flotilla at Texel, complete with Irish rebels and Franco-Dutch troops. The French fleet headed north to Brest, but the Spanish lagged behind for some days. Regardless, both fleets separated still outnumbered the English fleets at Gibraltar and Spithead, respectively. On 14 February 1797, Admiral Jervis with fifteen English ships of the line gambled and intercepted the Spanish fleet of almost twice its number. The battle of Cape St. Vincent, as it became known, was a resounding victory for England. The Spanish fleet limped back to Cadiz. Jervis was given the title Earl St. Vincent, and one Captain Horatio Nelson was promoted to Rear Admiral for capturing two ships of the line while his own was dismasted.[34] The immediate threat to Great Britain abated.

Pitt would not soon forget the danger posed by the Franco-Spanish alliance, and Godoy was about to realize his gamble did not pay off. The English fleet placed Spain under blockade and began to prey upon her seaborne empire. The dramatic impact of the Royal Navy upon Spain and its colonies cannot be overstated. The statistics are shocking when looking at the nine major Spanish ports that imported and exported goods. During the years of peace, 1795 and 1796, Spain received 264 and 299 million *reales,* respectively, in exports and 233 and 307 million *reales* in imports. At the end of 1797, after war resumed, only 19 million *reales* were collected in exports and 34 million *reales* in imports.[35] In short, Indies revenue composed 20 percent of funds in the state treasury in 1796 was reduced to 1 percent in 1797. They would only be restored to their pre-war levels in 1802 after England and France concluded the Peace of Amiens. What further frustrated the Spanish economy was that any economic recovery that began in 1795 was quickly eroded by substantial deficit spending. Silver piled up in Mexico and remained there. The Spanish government returned to securing loans with American silver as collateral. By 1804, however, Spanish credit was so poor they had difficulty convincing bankers and financiers to raise new loans.[36]

The French were not terribly pleased with their allies' performance. Truthfully, Spain exceeded its obligations to France. From the moment San Ildefenso was negotiated, and before it was officially enacted, the Spanish had put to sea their entire fleet, far more than the fifteen ships of the line required. One could also argue that Napoleon's ability to embark on his Egyptian endeavor in 1798 was the result of the Royal Navy having to dispatch ships to blockade Spanish ports, thereby reducing the ability of the fleet to maintain a squadron of a respectable level to keep an eye on Toulon. On the other hand, Spain had failed to exert promised pressure on Portugal. For all Spain's contributions to the war at sea, there was none on land. Godoy made it clear in negotiations with France that the Spanish alliance was only applicable to the war with England. The treaty specifically stated that Spain was not at war with any of France's continental enemies; this meant Austria.[37] This was not a factor after late 1797, when Austria acceded to the Peace of Campo Formio ending its participation in the coalition. Events changed more significantly in November 1799, when the Directory was overthrown in a coup d'état. Napoleon, recently returned from Egypt, became the first consul and head of France. It was hoped that the change in government would give Spain "wiggle room."

Spain was poorly served by the French alliance. Their fleet was manhandled at Cape St. Vincent and their dynastic interests in Italy were compromised by the complete collapse of French power resulting from the Austro-Russian offensive in northern Italy and the successful San Fedesti Revolt in Naples in 1799. Furthermore, the Spanish economy was on the verge of collapse due to the English blockade and the inability to import and export goods and specie from America. The Directory, too, came to see Spain as an ineffectual ally. The Spanish were unable to keep the English fleet occupied in the western Mediterranean, resulting in the battle of Aboukir Bay in 1799, which destroyed the French fleet at anchor in Egypt. Discussions regarding the transfer of Louisiana from Spanish to French suzerainty had fallen flat, and Spanish promises to invade Portugal, as required by the treaty of San Ildefonso, failed to manifest.[38]

Godoy lost credibility with the monarchy. The Prince of Peace, a title awarded him for extricating Spain from the coalition in 1795, was blamed for the disastrous effect of the French alliance. In 1798 he was temporarily relieved of his duties as secretary of state by F. Saavedra, who resigned the following year due to illness. At the time of the coup d'état of 18 Brumaire, Mariano Luis de Urquijo was charged with directing Spanish foreign policy. His tenure was brief but marked by a cautious approach to Napoleon's new government.[39]

Certainly, the first question considered was whether Spain was still obligated by treaty to the new French government. The answer was tied to Spanish perceptions of Napoleon. Ignacio Múzquiz, the Spanish ambassador in Paris, wrote Urquijo in glowing terms that this government looked much more promising in its policies and direction than the previous ones.[40] Jose Nicolàs de Azara, the Spanish ambassador to Paris and the former mediator between General Bonaparte and Pius VI in 1796, also "talked-up" the promise of this new government. Well-disposed toward the French general since the days in Italy, Azara was close to the Abbé Sièyes, a key participant in the coup. In the first weeks of the new regime, before Napoleon pushed out the "politicians," Sièyes worked assiduously to solidify and give credibility to the post-Directorial administration.[41] Perhaps more important was the opinion of French émigrés in Spain who reinforced these notions, claiming Napoleon's administration was conservative and inclined to reestablish a constitutional monarchy.[42]

One cannot fault Múzquiz, Azara, Godoy, and ultimately Carlos IV for their expectation that Napoleon marked the end of the revolution. In the corridors of the Hofburg in Vienna this too was discussed a year later during the heated negotiations at Lunèville. Hope that a decade of revolution and radicalism was at an end and that a moderate government led by a general might provide order and stability worked to convince the French public as much as many European leaders that Napoleon was acceptable. For Spain, support for Napoleon was based upon a desire to find a solution to their financial predicament.

Urquijo was not convinced that Napoleon's government would benefit Spain. He remained obstinate against ever-increasing pressure from the queen and Godoy's faction at court. Unfortunately, Urquijo could not move cautiously, but only urged caution. Napoleon understood the significance of the Spanish alliance, and he acted swiftly to reinvigorate the relationship. Spain still had a navy and maintained substantial influence in Italy, and Napoleon was aware of the secretary of state's reluctance to advise continued support to France, as much as he was aware of Godoy's perspective. It was in French interest that Godoy return center stage, but Napoleon was careful not to interfere too plainly in Spanish court politics.

Urquijo's most important work related to the war with England was the restoration or, at the very least, maintenance of the Spanish economy. He embarked on an ambitious and controversial policy of purchasing church lands in Spain and using them as collateral to pay off loans. At the same time, he revaluated paper currency, the *Vales Reales*, and transferred increasing amounts of funds from the regional treasuries to the central government. These measures enabled Spain to avoid immediate economic crisis and keep the navy on a war footing. In order to prevent economic collapse in New Spain and the Caribbean, Carlos IV reluctantly permitted limited free trade with the United States in 1798. Mercantilist policy was the order of the day, and there was growing fear in Madrid, as well as Cádiz, that even under the most extreme circumstances a loosening of trade restrictions would have a drastic impact on the peninsular economy. The viceroys of New Spain and the commercial houses in the Americas demanded these concessions and were relieved when they were granted. Yet, they were short-lived, as fear of lost revenue and widespread abuse of limited commercial freedoms resulted in the rescinding of the royal decree in 1799.[43]

All of this factored into Urquijo's considerations of Spain's relationship with Napoleonic France. The French ambassador to Madrid, Charles-Jean-Marie Alquier, believed that Urquijo would be a better ally to France than Godoy once he came around. Talleyrand and Napoleon, however, considered Godoy more reliable and, perhaps, more pliable. Thus, in November 1800, Napoleon dispatched his younger brother Lucein to Spain to reestablish the Franco-Spanish alliance. Similarly, Lucien was instructed to improve relations with Godoy whose star was rising once again.[44]

The diplomatic impasse was resolved as in 1796. Napoleon's victory over the Austrians at Marengo on 14 June 1800 and his subsequent re-conquest of northern Italy provided him with the valuable carrot of Parma, a Bourbon state tied by marriage to Spain. Aggrandizement of dynastic interest was on the negotiating table. Napoleon's "Italy first" strategy bore substantial fruit. Discussions between Urquijo and General Alexandre Berthier, Napoleon's chief of staff, to renew and reinvigorate the treaty of San Ildefenso began in July 1800. The ink was dry and ready for signature by 1 October. The agreement not only reaffirmed the Franco-Spanish alliance, but also included transfer of Louisiana to France and the exchange of Bourbon Parma for an enlarged kingdom in Tuscany. Napoleon also pressed for Spanish action against Portugal, and he pledged troops and money for the adventure. In short, there was little difference between San Ildefenso 1796 and that of 1800 except that it marked a new relationship between the two states for the next eight years.[45]

The alliance was less than three months old when Lucien Bonaparte and Pedro Cevallos, the new Spanish foreign minister, concluded a secret military agreement for war with Portugal. The accession of Cevallos marked the passing of Urquijo and the return of Godoy. Napoleon pledged 15,000 men for the invasion of Portugal, agreeing to allow them to serve under Spanish command. Napoleon wanted guarantees, however, that Spain would not offer Portugal a generous peace as they had done in 1797. He demanded that the war continue until the Portuguese agreed to cease trade with England and that they prohibit commerce of any sort related to English trade.[46] Godoy was given the honor of directing the military campaign, and the Spanish army mobilized for operations.

By May 1801 a Spanish army of 60,000 men with a French contingent of nearly 15,000 en route prepared to invade Portugal. Napoleon dispatched General Gouvion-St. Cyr to "advise" Godoy. It is clear from his letter to Talleyrand on this issue that he had little confidence in his ally.

General St. Cyr, Councilor of State, is going to Madrid. Before leaving, he will receive your instructions:
Make it known that his mission has two objects:

1. That, if the court of Portugal is to enter into negotiations, the French minister must avail himself of his presence at Madrid in order to insure advantageous conditions [for France].
2. That, if the Spanish are truly resolved to make war, he must direct all operations, taking appropriate measures not to offend Castillian pride. He will recommend and check all military plans to be executed, and he will, with the [French] ambassador insure that the Prince of Peace [Godoy] is treated with the proper respect.[47]

Proper respect was a problem St. Cyr had with those who were "supposed" to be his superiors. It caused him trouble in the past and continued to do so in the future. Nonetheless, the war proceeded as planned.

The Spanish army advanced in three columns into Portugal on 20 May. The Portuguese offered minimal resistance, their cities along the frontier falling rapidly to Spanish forces. A major engagement at Aronches resulted in a Spanish victory, and the Portuguese army withdrew to Abrantes in the face of overwhelming numbers. Within three weeks, on 8 June, emissaries of the Portuguese regent arrived in Badajoz to negotiate. In the course of the brief and glorious campaign, Godoy sent the queen-regent of Portugal, who was also Carlos IV's daughter, a gift of oranges. Henceforth, the conflict is referred to as the War of the Oranges.[48]

Napoleon received the news of the Portuguese capitulation with great anger. He was infuriated that the Spanish army halted its advance before it reached Lisbon, and French troops under General Leclerc were sitting in Cuidad Rodrigo, not having crossed the border into Portugal. The object of the war was to strike at England. As far as the first consul was concerned, Portugal's defeat was a forgone conclusion. The occupation of Oporto and Lisbon would compel the Portuguese to accept unconditionally Spanish and, more importantly, French demands. To halt operations and negotiate a moderate settlement flew in the face of Napoleon's plans. He considered the Spanish shortsighted.[49]

The military alliance clearly stated that the two powers were waging war to strike at England, restore Spanish colonies to His-Most-Catholic Majesty, and return several Caribbean islands to France. The war removed one of England's last continental allies. Portugal was compelled to honor the agreement they signed with France in 1797 against English trade, though France and Spain had never enforced it. Portugal was required to prohibit trade with England, close its ports to neutral shipping with English goods, and endure Franco-Spanish military occupation.[50] Portugal would be hostage until England came to terms. Napoleon, therefore, interpreted Godoy's willingness to negotiate while halting operations as either Spanish duplicity or ignorance.

Napoleon wrote Talleyrand, instructing him to inform the Spanish that France would not recognize their arrangements with the Portuguese, that the

English minister Lord Hawkesbury be informed that these agreements between Spain and Portugal were "nul and void," and that the French would continue their attacks in Portugal and occupation of territory. "If it [England] wants, in negotiations, to accept the *status quo ante bellum* for Portugal," Napoleon demanded, "it must equally recognize *the status quo ante bellum* for the Americas."[51] He followed his heated correspondence with instructions to General Berthier, his chief of staff. General St. Cyr should make it clear to the Spanish that he will personally command an army composed of Leclerc's corps and a Spanish contingent of equal number. St. Cyr was directed to occupy northern and central Portugal, including the city of Oporto.[52] He also apprised Godoy that there were 10,000 additional French troops prepared to reinforce his army.

1801 was not 1808. Napoleon was not Emperor of France, he was not the conqueror of Europe, he was merely a French general who had managed to remain in power for a year and a half. True, he had concluded his war with Austria in February, but one must not misinterpret his heated response to Spanish policy as incurring his wrath. Carlos IV and Godoy were quite clear in their respective replies to Napoleon, and in no uncertain terms were they going to entertain a continuation of the conflict when the objectives were already achieved for little cost in men, money, and time. Godoy related in his memoirs that St. Cyr pestered Carlos IV all the way from Madrid to Badajoz. He relayed Napoleon's demands with the greatest of courtesy. Godoy echoed the monarch's perspective. "The reason for the invasion of Portugal has ceased entirely: French troops came as auxiliaries for Spain's war with Portugal."[53] The Portuguese agreed to restrict English shipping and that of neutrals carrying English goods. Their ports were closed to all manner of the Royal Navy or ships carrying English letters of marque. Indeed, Godoy remarked that Lucien Bonaparte, Napoleon's brother and French ambassador to Spain, monitored and reviewed the negotiations and ultimately the text of the treaty. In all he gave his ascent.[54]

The simple fact was Spain met its contractual obligations. There was nothing in the Franco-Spanish alliance that called for the occupation of Portugal until England agreed to negotiate. There was no duplicity and no ignorance. Napoleon continued to press Carlos IV, and regretted that he previously had supported Godoy's return to power. Leclerc's troops remained in Spain through the summer. Napoleon, stubborn and seething, refused to recall them. According to the treaty with Spain the French auxiliary corps was paid by France and victualed by Spain. Neither Carlos IV nor Godoy intended on bending to Napoleon's will. Spanish supplies gradually dried up, and it was clear to Leclerc that they had overstayed their welcome. Infuriated, Napoleon threatened to negate the agreements concerning Spanish dynastic interests in Italy. He demanded that the Spanish continue to feed his troops and treat them as allies.[55]

Neither Carlos IV nor Napoleon budged. When in September negotiations with England moved significantly, Napoleon finally accepted the fait accompli in Portugal. On 29 September 1801, the French and Portuguese representatives signed a treaty terminating hostilities between the two states. Although no French troops operated in Portugal, and despite the Spanish treaty ending their war in June, this treaty compelled Portugal to pay an indemnity to France, cede territory in South America, and pledge to uphold their agreements with Spain.[56]

The War of Oranges and the subsequent arguments between Napoleon and Carlos IV illustrate Spain's resolve to act in their own interests. They did not perceive, nor did they cave in to, threats. Napoleon did not negate his previous agreements regarding Bourbon interests in Parma and Tuscany, he did not move actively to marginalize the Spanish, and he did not eliminate or significantly reduce Spanish claims in the Peace of Amiens with England. He needed Spain. Godoy, for that matter, learned much from this early experience. Although Spain benefited from its victory over Portugal, Napoleon's determination to push and pull Spanish policy was not well received. In a letter to Queen Marie Luise concerning Spain's position in Europe, Godoy wrote, "Russia is important to us for its commerce. . . . Prussia is always important to us, their army is respectable."[57]

CHAPTER THREE

SPAIN, FRANCE, AND WAR WITH ENGLAND

THE TREATY OF AMIENS WAS A GREAT RELIEF FOR SPAIN. It removed the costly burden of war that ravaged their commercial economy and menaced their mercantilist policy. The pressure to maintain strict trade regulations emanated not only from the crown, but also the merchants and regional governments throughout Spain. The Franco-Spanish alliance benefited France more than Spain in hindsight. Yet, this was not due to French duplicity. Spain entered the conflict to improve and secure its colonial position in the Americas. This could only be achieved through a successful naval campaign against England. Failing that, Spain was limited in its ability to press the war beyond the invasion of Portugal.

Perhaps the only sticking point of the treaty was Britain's retention of Trinidad. Carlos IV expressed his frustration to Godoy over Napoleon's willingness to secure French and Dutch interests at the expense of Spain. The archipelago was strategically significant to Spain's American empire. The English understood this well, and they were quite content to add it to their possessions in the West Indies. Napoleon's failure to demand Trinidad for Spain was a shot back at the Iberian kingdom for failing to continue the war with Portugal, and Carlos IV perceived this as a slap in the face. He explained to Godoy that despite the military and economic sacrifices made by Spain in the name of the French alliance, Napoleon saw fit to ignore it for his own interests.[1]

Spain's financial situation remained bleak for some time after the restoration of peace. In order to finance the war Spain issued *libranzas*, bills of exchange equivalent to the value of goods sitting in the Americas but unable to reach Europe due to English naval supremacy. Peace meant that the goods could be shipped and the bills paid. It would take some months before trade could create a positive cash flow.[2] Although peace also provided an opportunity for Spain to reform its economy and move away from mercantilism—something strongly desired in the Americas—it returned to pre-war mercantilist policy under the pressure of the regional governments and merchant houses in Cadíz and elsewhere.[3] In 1801, Spanish exports to the Americas were valued at 80.6 million *reales de vellón*, while imports ran at 33.3 million. The following year, with Amiens signed at the end of March, exports to the Americas jumped to 383 million, with imports at 294.6 million *reales de vellón*. In terms of percentages, by 1803 Indies revenues counted for 23 percent of funds in the General Treasury, compared to less than 1 percent for 1800 and 1801.[4] The short-term debt and deficit spending were reduced substantially. There was no greater illustration of the profits of peace.

England, for that matter, desired to restore relations with Spain as quickly as possible. Sir John Hookham Frere was sent to Madrid in his capacity as British ambassador. Lord Hawkesbury, the British foreign minister explained Frere's mission in quite clear terms. Spain should be drawn away from the French sphere. It must be, "the constant and persevering object of all your attention."[5] The naval threat to England remained so long as Spain was well disposed to France. The other issue of equal if not greater concern was the territorial exchanges between Spain and France in the Americas, threatening Britain's colonial empire in the West Indies. Napoleon's colonial ambitions seemed substantial in the first years of his reign. Egypt remained in French hands through September 1801, and in the Caribbean Portugal ceded Guiana to France that same month. The Treaty of San Ildefenso provided the cession of Louisiana and Santo Domingo to France.[6] Florida was on the negotiating table, although nothing was ultimately decided. In short, prior to Amiens French possessions, while potentially formidable, were no immediate threat to the British West Indies. With peace in Europe, Napoleon could now claim those territories and establish himself comfortably in the Western hemisphere. This was the perception and fear of the British government. Events would soon preclude any concerns regarding a French colonial threat.

At the end of November 1801 General Leclerc, having returned from Spain, was given charge of an expeditionary force to occupy Haiti and Santo Domingo. Both were under the control of Toussaint Louverture, a former slave who led a rebellion against France and ruled the island since 1794. As the war with England prevented an expedition to recover the island and troops were desperately needed elsewhere, this was the first opportunity for Napoleon to reclaim the French colony and occupy Santo Domingo from Spain. Leclerc's force of 23,000 landed in January 1802 and proceeded to conquer the island. By the following year, however, disease claimed much of the French garrison, including Leclerc.

The cession of Louisiana was provided for in the Treaty of San Ildefenso. Its transfer, however, was contingent upon the exchange of Parma for Tuscany. The Habsburg duke of Tuscany was to be compensated with land in Germany. The Holy Roman Emperor, Francis II, agreed to the exchanges, but it was not until February 1803 that the Imperial Diet granted its ascent. The inevitable acquisition of Louisiana concerned England and the United States greatly. There is little doubt that if the expedition to Haiti and Santo Domingo had succeeded, Napoleon would have increased French presence in Louisiana. As it was, the ultimate failure of the expedition and the clear signs that the peace of Amiens was not long to last led Napoleon to consider other options. Thomas Jefferson, president of the United States, was most distressed over French acquisition of Louisiana. He dispatched James Monroe to Paris to negotiate its purchase and Napoleon was quite interested.[7]

It was abundantly clear that maintaining a colonial empire was an expense in men and money France could ill afford. The French franc was shifted to a bi-metallic standard, and for the same reason Napoleon had needed the Spanish alliance three years earlier, he also entertained notions of selling Louisiana. The United States could and would pay. This would keep the territory out of English hands and maintain good relations with the United States. The United States was to pay in specie to banks in London, Amsterdam, and Paris. Monroe and François Barbé-Marbois, the French minister of the treasury, signed the Treaty of Cession on 30 April 1803. The United States purchased Louisiana for 60 million francs. The agreement eliminated France's American debt and immediately improved relations.[8]

The sale of Louisiana, while beneficial to France and the United States, was problematic to Spain. The specifics of the Treaty of San Ildefenso and the subsequent reaffirmation of the territorial exchanges in 1801 as part of the Treaty of Aranjuez stated that the retrocession of Louisiana would not take place until six months after territorial exchanges in Italy. In fact, only two months had past. This was a mere technicality that did not truly disturb the Spanish court. The implication, however, of the transfer of Louisiana to the United States was grave. American merchants benefited greatly from the commercial freedom granted briefly in Spanish America during the 1790s. After the licenses were rescinded American merchants continued illegal trade. The British posed a threat to Spanish America; American merchants posed a commercial threat to Spanish mercantilism.[9] The acquisition of New Orleans would make it far easier for American merchant houses to operate and reap greater rewards in Spanish America—revenues desperately needed in Spain.

It was in Spain's strategic interest to cede Louisiana to France in 1800 as part of a general political and military alliance. It threatened the British in the West Indies and protected it from American expansion in North America. By selling Louisiana to the United States Napoleon weakened Spain's position in the Western Hemisphere and its commercial economy in Europe. This was not Napoleon's intention, but he was not thinking of Spain when he sold it.

The Spanish monarchy did not soon forget too that the island of Trinidad was not returned to Spain as part of the Peace of Amiens, further reducing the security of Spanish America.

The Treaty of Amiens did not insure a general peace between England and France. As Campo Formio in 1797 was considered "temporary" in Vienna until they regained their strength, so too was Amiens perceived in London. There was little way England could accept many of the territorial provisions. The treaty provided for the recognition of the Batavian Republic, formerly the Netherlands, which had been under French occupation since 1795. Furthermore, the island of Ceylon and the Cape of Good Hope would be restored to Dutch control. The British agreed as well to abandon Malta to the Knights of St. John, putting an end to the island's neutrality. As Malta was the strategic jewel of the Mediterranean, this was a difficult pill to swallow. Conversely, Napoleon promised to withdraw French troops from the kingdom of Naples and the Papal States. He also provided that several smaller islands in the Mediterranean, evacuated by the British, could be garrisoned by Neapolitan troops.[10]

In theory, Amiens seemed to balance Napoleon's continental interests in exchange for Britain's overseas concerns. Prime Minister Pitt did not see the negotiations through to their conclusions. He resigned in March 1801 over a disagreement with the English crown concerning Catholic emancipation in England. Henry Addington took his place but fell far short of Pitt's reputation and determination. At the heart of the problem was that neither Napoleon nor Pitt trusted the other, and in the end each was correct in assuming the other would not fully honor his contractual obligations. As early as November 1802, not more than seven months after the signing of Amiens, Pedro Cevallos, the Spanish secretary of state, was informed by Larrea, his *chargé* in London, that it was only a matter of time before the general peace would be shattered.[11] Tensions continued to build, but the peace held until 18 May 1803. This time, the news came from Nicolas Azara, Spain's ambassador in Paris.[12] None of this was pleasing to Godoy's ears. The Spanish economy was improving steadily, and it was clear to even the simplest of minds that the rupture of Amiens would be followed by French demands for support and English pressure to remain neutral. Spain was caught in the same dilemma facing them since 1793. Exacerbating the crisis was Carlos IV's reaction to Napoleon's sale of Louisiana the previous month. He was ill-disposed to the first consul. In a scathing letter to Godoy, Carlos IV wrote, "You know of the duplicity of the French, who have sold Louisiana to America. It reinforces our right to remain neutral; because they have not asked our permission to sell it, and they have done so for a mere pittance."[13] Carlos was strongly inclined to cast off France and remain neutral in the coming conflict. "Peace for my house," the king proclaimed to Godoy, "neither break with France, nor break with England."[14]

Indeed the situation facing Spain was grave. Godoy wrote to Azara in Paris and Anduaga, the new ambassador in London, that they should immediately offer Spanish mediation between the two parties. Talleyrand responded that France was capable of carrying out its own negotiations with England.[15] It is unclear if Godoy thought the offer serious, or if he was merely biding his time. The Spanish minister informed Talleyrand that he was merely abiding by the articles of San Ildefenso calling for Spanish mediation in a conflict between France and Great Britain. Unfortunately, this was not the wisest move, as Napoleon demanded that Spain honor its other obligations under San Ildefenso, particularly those clauses pertaining to a military alliance. There is some confusion here, however, as the Treaty of San Ildefenso was not intended as a permanent alliance between Spain and France, but merely to reaffirm the alliance that was forged by Carlos IV and the Directory in 1796. Certainly, Napoleon perceived it as more than this. He saw it as a reaffirmation of the old Bourbon Family Compact that bound France and Spain throughout the eighteenth century. Carlos IV and Godoy might have seen it in this light if Spain's colonial economy did not suffer as much as it had during the course of the previous conflict.

Anticipating French demands once war became imminent, Godoy instructed his ambassador in St. Petersburg, Count de Noroña, to determine Russia's interest in forming a league of armed neutrality.[16] Relations between the two peripheral states improved with the accession of Alexander I to the throne in 1801. During the War of the Second Coalition, Spain and Russia were technically at war, although the two powers never directly engaged each other. Spain and Russia reaffirmed their friendship in August 1802 with an exchange of ambassadors.[17] Perhaps an alliance of European powers determined to remain outside of the conflict would provide Spain with the influence and power needed to avoid taking sides. The fact that Godoy looked for such an opportunity indicated that he understood Spain's difficult position of facing a British blockade if he sided with France or Napoleon's ill disposition if he failed to choose wisely.

Neither France nor England approached Spain initially, but it was only a matter of weeks after the Spanish ambassador in St. Petersburg proposed a new League of Armed Neutrality that Talleyrand approached José Martinez de Hervas, a Spanish financier in Paris. He proposed that Spain could maintain its neutrality in the new conflict if they agreed to subsidize the French war effort.[18] Talleyrand told Hervas that the agreement would not be an alliance but an understanding. It would supersede Spain's requirements as established in San Ildefenso—though the Spanish continued to interpret the treaty as a matter of history. The price for Spanish neutrality was 6 million francs per month for the duration of the war, payable to the French Public Treasury. The first payment was due immediately and thereafter could be dispersed quarterly.[19]

Godoy took his time to respond to Talleyrand's offer. He waited for a response from Russia. Through June, Godoy and Talleyrand exchanged a series of diplomatic notes. Godoy eventually rebuffed the subsidy proposal. Talleyrand replied to Pedro Cevallos, Spanish foreign minister, that Napoleon was distressed at Spain's desire to distance itself from its friend and ally. Cevallos passed it along to Godoy, who retorted via Azara in Paris that France had done more to distance itself from Spain. He pointed to the sale of Louisiana to the United States, the rejection of Spanish mediation in the autumn 1802, and the fact that France had yet to fulfill its obligations to Spain as specified in San Ildefonso regarding establishing the Bourbons in Tuscany.[20]

Unfortunately, it was not until September that a Russian response was forthcoming. They encouraged the idea of "the courts of the south (Madrid and Lisbon)" forming a league similar to one formed by the northern courts in 1801.[21] Although Godoy interpreted this as a sign of Russian interest, the Russian analogy was problematic from a historical perspective. The league of 1801 was shattered by British naval action in the Baltic, culminating in Nelson's raid on Copenhagen. Elaboration on the Russian note was not forthcoming. According to Noroña, the Russians were not comfortable with Spain. He referred to them as "hispanophobe."[22]

Good news, however, arrived from Valencia, the Spanish ambassador in Berlin. At the end of May, Count Haugwitz, the Prussian foreign minister, communicated Prussia's interest in such a league. He repeated this to Valencia in June.[23] It is unclear, however, whether the proposal was simply to sound out Spain's position or a serious offer. Haugwitz's correspondence with King Frederick William III through June and July 1803 failed to mention Spain. Although there is extensive discussion of the formation of a league in northern Europe, nowhere does Haugwitz discuss a southern league.[24] As fortuitous as it was, timing is everything in matters of diplomacy, and Haugwitz's desire to keep Prussia and north Germany neutral in this new Anglo-French conflict fell flat when Napoleon dispatched French troops to occupy Hanover.[25] Thereafter, there was little discussion and interest in Berlin concerning Spain.

Quite simply, apart from France, Spain was a virtual pariah in Europe. The European monarchies questioned its interests as a consequence of their alliance with Revolutionary and Napoleonic France through 1802. Although Prussia was the first of the European states to make peace with Revolutionary France in 1795 and a number of German princes followed suit, Spain went a step further. Spanish neutrality via the Treaty of Basel would have been acceptable to the European monarchs, but moving beyond neutrality to an offensive-defensive alliance placed Spain within its former eighteenth century context as a consummate French ally. William Pitt saw it as such in 1796, and though it was Addington's ministry who signed Amiens and dispatched Sir John Frere to Madrid to pull the Iberian kingdom from its French orbit, upon Pitt's return to office in 1804 he perceived Spain as a potential and real threat. Godoy was thus in the unenviable situation of desperately wanting to avoid conflict by maintaining strict neutrality, but the failure of past foreign policy and Spain's military inadequacy prevented him from now honestly pursuing this course.

Despite the inability to find ready allies to defend Spanish neutrality, Godoy benefited from Napoleon's greater interest in Spanish silver than its navy. The first consul wholeheartedly supported Talleyrand's initial proposal to supersede Spanish obligations to France as interpreted via San Ildefonso by accepting a subsidy agreement. This is clear from the discussions held between Godoy and General Pierre Riel de Beurnonville, the French ambassador to Spain. Beurnonville replaced St. Cyr in late 1802. Although the latter was well received in Madrid and his council respected, Godoy and Carlos IV despised the new ambassador. He knew nothing of diplomacy and was guided by his own ambitions.[26] In his memoirs, Godoy recounts a lively debate between the French ambassador and himself. Two points, however, are of significant interest. The first is that Godoy argued that Spain met its obligations in the Treaty of San Ildefonso. He continued, "[O]ur treaty of alliance was not the old Family Compact in which common cause was made between the two powers." The current war was for France's benefit, not Spain.[27] The second point served to advance the case for neutrality. "French commerce," Godoy told Beurnonville, "will suffer much from this war; Spanish neutrality can offer a multitude of opportunities."[28]

Godoy argued that Spanish neutrality was more valuable to France, as it offered a means by which French imports and exports could be shipped through Spain, thereby avoiding the British blockade. Furthermore, Spanish neutrality would allow Spain to mediate the conflict if it so desired. Beurnonville remained defiant, countering that Spain's place was at the side of France. Indeed, that was how Beurnonville felt, but Napoleon did not press Spain until August 1803, when he became concerned over Spanish military mobilization. Spain's reluctance to commit itself financially to the French cause, combined with the deployment of Spanish troops in the interior agitated the first consul. At the end of July, Napoleon instructed Talleyrand to get answers from Beurnonville. The first consul received reports of Spanish militia forming at Valladolid, and what incensed him more was that the British warships seized a French merchant ship off the Spanish coast with no Spanish attempt to prevent it.[29]

What is curious about Napoleon's concerns was that he was fully apprised by Beurnonville of Godoy's order to mobilize the Spanish militia and reserves in May. Godoy explained at that time mobilization was to reinforce the Spanish army so as "to conserve our neutrality."[30] If Napoleon was aware of these events in May, why did he decide to complain about it two months later? It appears that although Napoleon used it as a pretext to pressure Spain, mobilization was not accompanied by the fitting out the Spanish navy to preserve its neutrality. In fact, Napoleon told Talleyrand that he must know of Spanish affairs with London. Speculation in Paris said the English offered Godoy £50,000 to join with them.[31]

There is no indication that the English attempted to bribe Godoy. Henry Addington, the British prime minister, worked assiduously, however, to build a coalition against France. In July he proposed a subsidy in excess of £300,000 to Russia and £250,000 to Prussia to enter into a new continental alliance.[32] British monetary enticements were commonplace during the summer of 1803, and the possibility that Godoy would entertain a notion was not without merit. This, perhaps, was the basis of Napoleon's concern. During the first week of August he dispatched reinforcements to the military camp at Bayonne and strengthened the garrisons along the Spanish frontier. The first consul's orders clearly remarked that the regiments bound for Bayonne were to be on a peacetime footing.[33] In military terminology *peacetime footing* meant the regiments would lack their full compliment of officers, rank and file that would otherwise be present in time of war. It was common practice in Europe to minimize military expenditure by allowing officers to take leave and not filling the vacancies in the ranks with conscripts and recruits. Nonetheless, the movement of troops indicated Napoleon's concern for Spain as either a potential ally or enemy.

It was not long before Napoleon became convinced that things were amiss. He received no information from Beurnonville regarding Spanish troop movements, and Napoleon demanded that Beurnonville provide a report on the Spanish army. The first consul turned to his commercial consuls in Cadíz and Madrid for any observations they might have on military dispositions.[34] Godoy's failure to respond in a timely fashion to Napoleon's financial demands (coupled with the rumor of Godoy being in English pay), the fact that Spanish militia were concentrating in north central Spain, and the attack on French shipping by the Royal Navy off Cadíz and Coruña led Napoleon to conclusions. With no news from his ambassador in Madrid, he was left to assume the worst. It was at this point Napoleon presented Spain with an ultimatum.[35] One way or another he would force Godoy's hand.

Spain must declare for France or against it. In the latter case, the first consul threatened that an army 80,000 men forming on the Spanish frontier would invade Spain. If the former, then Spain must demobilize its army to its previous level, and it must allow French ships safe haven in Spanish ports while closing them to English shipping. Spain must also agree to pay a subsidy of 72 million francs for the first year of the conflict. Spain could also opt to declare war on England, in which case it would accede to all of the aforementioned requests and commit two Spanish corps, one to besiege Gibraltar, the other to invade Portugal supported by French troops. The Spanish response must be received by 7 September, or else. . . .[36]

Napoleon's ultimatum was a bluff. He had no intention of invading Spain. His financial and military resources were already stretched, and he was certainly not going to commit himself to invading Spain while concentrating his main army on the Channel coast for an invasion of England. Orders for the construction of military encampments along the coast were first issued in June 1803, and further instructions for the reinforcement and expansion of the camps continued through the summer and into September.[37] The camp at Bayonne, which Napoleon used to threaten Carlos IV, was established at the same time in June for the purpose of guarding the Gascon coast from possible British raids. In fact, Bayonne had the fewest troops of all the military camps; soldiers and artillery were severely lacking in August.[38] A bluff is only effective if the bluffee is unaware of the truth.

French finances were in a critical state in 1804. The Bank of France issued 50 to 60 million francs in notes to address the state's economic demands. Special discounting was offered to members of the bank's board, but the bank possessed an insufficient amount of specie if investors decided to redeem the bills in the short term. The actual expenditures for the French navy were double the anticipated budget of 1803, almost 450 million francs. The War Ministry spent more than 800 million francs by 1805, nearly two-thirds more than planned.[39] Napoleon lacked resources for a war on two fronts.

Sir John Hookham Frere, British ambassador to Spain, worked desperately to keep Spain from joining France. His instructions read, "It is the king's sincere and earnest desire that the Spanish government may be enabled to maintain the strictest neutrality in the war."[40] Godoy's obstinacy toward the French subsidy demands in May was not the product of Frere's diplomatic skill but instead due to economic and political realities in Spain. Godoy conversed freely with Frere concerning Napoleon's threat. The English ambassador was able to provide information regarding the "true" state of French forces at Bayonne. He passed along reports from English spies that Napoleon had no more than 13,000 troops as of mid-August. These estimates were more than double the real strength at that time, but less than a month later there were almost 16,000 troops deployed under General Pierre Augereau.[41] This was a terrible relief for the Spanish minister. Napoleon could neither throw 25,000 troops across the Pyrenees in a week's time, nor concentrate 80,000 troops for the same purpose by month's end.

Carlos IV referred to Napoleon's demands as "the insolent French note."[42] He communicated to the first consul via Godoy that Spain could not commit itself to war. "My financial situation," he wrote, "will not permit the sacrifice demanded and I am determined not to enter into any engagement which I cannot fulfill. . . . The crops have failed again this year all over Spain. If I declare war on England at this moment, I should expose my realm to the horror of war."[43] Godoy hoped Spain could ride out the storm. Napoleon, however, was not to be outdone. He wrote directly to Carlos IV on 18 September, calling for Godoy's dismissal. He told him Godoy was virtually usurping the throne by moving Spain into the English sphere. Napoleon told Carlos he would have to make war on this "new king." Godoy's policies would bring French armies to Spain, and in the end the Prince of Peace would sail to London "with all his treasures."[44]

Godoy was persona non grata to Napoleon. Yet, Carlos IV ignored the first consul's call for his dismissal.[45] This was the second occasion in the history of Franco-Spanish relations since 1800 that Napoleon demanded things of Spain. He threatened, he cajoled, he issued ultimatums, but the king of Spain and his first minister refused to buckle. One should clearly understand that Godoy's objective was to steer a course between England and France, and if the winds were blowing the ship in one direction, it was his responsibility to compensate. To that end, Napoleon would surely not accept a passive Spain, for he already interpreted passivity as a product of English pay. Godoy therefore did the absolute minimum to placate Napoleon while trying desperately not to concern the English. At the beginning of September Godoy permitted 1,500 French troops and supplies to march through Spain to Ferrol, where several French vessels were permitted to seek safe haven from the Royal Navy. Frere reported this to Lord Hawkesbury, the English foreign minister, and it became a cause for concern.[46]

The English perceived Spanish policy as attempting to pursue neutrality by appeasing Napoleon with minor concessions. This, however, weakened Britain's position in Europe and overseas. Carlos IV determined that Spain's best opportunity to remain outside the conflict was to accept Napoleon's demand for a subsidy in lieu of a military alliance. Godoy professed in his memoirs that he had little to do with the agreement. He claimed Cevallos and Azara convinced the king against his counsel.[47] This assessment probably lacks veracity, but nonetheless Azara and Talleyrand signed the Convention of Neutrality and Subsidy in Paris on 19 October 1803. It provided that Spain would remain neutral in exchange for payment of 6 million francs per month to France for the duration of the war, with the first payment dating to the outbreak of the conflict in May 1803. French vessels currently in Spanish ports would be repaired and supplied at Spain's expense. Finally, 2 million francs would be deducted from the dispersements to eliminate the French debt in Spain.[48] Two months to the day of the convention, Portugal signed a secret agreement, an addendum to the one produced by its Iberian neighbor. The price of Portuguese neutrality was 16 million francs and the opening of their markets to French goods.[49]

From the moment England declared war on France, Napoleon sought Spanish specie. He succeeded in the end. Whether his intention was to force Spain to bankroll his military endeavors knowing it would elicit a hostile British response, or whether he simply wanted a subsidy is unclear. The agreement was secret, but Frere was able to glean some information from members of the court. What is abundantly clear is that the English saw the subsidy treaty as a significant threat. Lord Hawkesbury wrote to Frere

> the question, therefore, occurs, how far his majesty would consent that the Spanish government should purchase their neutrality by an advance of pecuniary succours to the French government and would still regard them in the character of neutrals, this must be considered as, in some degree, depending on the amount of the succours so to be advanced, and likewise on the determination of the Spanish government to ensure their neutrality in all other respects; for, at the time when his majesty might be disposed to disregard any small or temporary advance of money, if essential to the attainment of such an object, it would be impossible for him to consider a permanent advance to the extent that stated by you, in any other light than as a subsidy to the French government and as possible most effectual assistance which the Spanish government could afford them for the prosecution of the war.[50]

Frere confirmed the convention several weeks later. The British now were ever watchful and distrustful of Spain. Frere attempted to speak to Godoy and Cevallos in order to ascertain the extent of Spanish support for France. On no occasion was he able to get a straight answer from either. Godoy spoke around the issue, and Cevallos wrote extensively in defense of Spanish neutrality.[51]

At the conclusion of 1803 Britain's strategic situation was grim. Addington's government, at war with France and with no allies on the continent, now faced what they were coming to believe was Spanish duplicity. During the spring of 1804 William Pitt the Younger returned to Parliament. His experience with France and Spain determined his course of action. Throughout the summer of 1804 reports reached Pitt that the Spanish navy was fitting out. French ships, too, were receiving support at Ferrol, and privateers and pirates attacked English shipping in the West Indies from Spanish ports.[52] Pitt, who presided over Commons during the American and French Revolutions, was sure Spain meant war. He refused to pass the initiative and therefore gave permission for the Royal Navy to impose a blockade on Spain and engage in "piracy" against Spanish shipping.[53]

The final act was carried out on 5 October 1804. Four Spanish galleons loaded with £2 million of silver and escorted by four Spanish frigates sailed from Rio del Plata. Sir Graham Moore, commanding a squadron of four English frigates intercepted them en route to Cadíz. One Spanish frigate was sunk and three captured, along with the entire treasure fleet.[54] Despite this clear act of war Carlos IV was reluctant to bring Spain into the conflict. The kingdom remained in debt, an earthquake devastated the province of Malaga, the Basques were on the verge of revolt, and pestilence hit Barcelona and Cadíz.[55] Plagues abounded and war came. There was little choice. Spain could maintain its position in limbo or commit itself. On 12 December 1804 Carlos IV declared war on England, and less than a month later Spain and France entered into an offensive naval alliance.[56]

In Parliament Pitt and his ministers were forced to defend their actions. The opposition used the seizure of the treasure fleet as a means to attack Pitt's government. In both Lords and Commons, Pitt and his supporters laid out the *causus belli* provided by Spain. All argued that the subsidy treaty was a resurrection of San Ildefonso. Lord Mulgrave, the new foreign minister, presented to his colleagues the simple fact that although peaceful intentions were expressed to Frere at every opportunity, the ambassador's queries to Godoy regularly received unclear and vague replies. When Frere requested an explanation over the subsidy agreement, Godoy responded that it was "less advantageous to France than would the furnishing of a contingent." Mulgrave pointed out to his colleagues that this was untrue. The Spanish subsidy could provide for eight times the number of troops required of Spain by the treaty of San Ildefonso. Furthermore, "in 1761, the whole year's treasure was in the ports of Spain: the war is now begun with the treasure of Spain at the disposal of Great Britain."[57]

Pitt advanced the same arguments in Commons. He pointed to 1796, when Spain used the articles of the treaty to declare war on England. Although he understood that in the current situation Spain was forced into the agreement with France, it was England's right to question Spanish intentions. Spain was "a vassalage of France," a term Pitt used frequently.[58] Pitt's recollection of the Franco-Spanish alliance of 1796 is critical to his position in 1804. If not for Jervis's victory at St. Vincent, the combined fleets would have come to control the Channel. This would not happen again.

Godoy did not want war, but Spain lacked the financial and military resources to resist both French and British pressure. Neutrality was only possible if Spain were willing and able to defend it. Armed neutrality, as proposed in May 1803, was an option, but only in theory. Russia's encouragement of a league was never pursued. It was only in 1805 that Adam Czartoryski, advisor to Alexander I, approached Noroña repeatedly. He told the Spanish ambassador that Spain should abandon France. England, he said, would compensate Spain for its losses.[59] By this time, however, Russia, Austria, and Britain had formed the Third Coalition against France. Instead of avoiding war, Godoy found Spain in the middle of a general European conflict.

CHAPTER FOUR

NAPOLEON AND GERMANY, 1792–1803

WHEN THE WAR OF THE THIRD COALITION BEGAN in October 1805, French armies crossed the Rhine and passed through the south German states, not as invaders but as allies. The Austrian forces opposed to them were not perceived as the defenders of the Holy Roman Empire, but as violators of the sovereignty of the south German states. This role reversal was the product of internal crises within the Holy Roman Empire that existed before and during the wars of the French Revolution, and played upon by carefully calculated Napoleonic diplomacy. The failure of the Holy Roman Emperor to defend Germany from French armies during the previous decade created further tensions among the German princes, which were exacerbated as a result of events.

German princes desired to expand their territories at the expense of others. The rise of Prussia during the eighteenth century gave greater voice to the north German princes who in turn sought secularization of the Empire. This movement was also accepted and propagated by the southern German princes. The wars of the Revolution fractured the Empire. This was particularly the case in 1795 when Prussia concluded the Treaty of Basel, ending its participation in the First Coalition against France. Subsequently, the German campaigns of 1796 through 1800 were waged on the lands of the southern princes. Francis II, Holy Roman Emperor, promised these princes to never sell out the Empire in its war with France, but did just that in his settlements at Campo Formio (1797) and Lunéville (1801). By the 1790s the Habsburgs placed dynastic interests over German ones and in doing so they promoted further secularization by seeking territorial exchanges in Italy for archbishoprics in Germany. Their actions alienated the southern princes, who had no common cause with Prussia, but now found Austria's policies hypocritical.

The growing fragmentation of Germany presented Napoleon with significant opportunity. Unlike his predecessors in the Directory, he displayed a more conservative and traditional face to French policy. He supported the notion of *landeshoheit* (territorial sovereignty) over Empire, which appealed to the princes. The Concordat with the Papacy was perceived as a break from the Revolutionary radicalism of the past. Napoleon succeeded in presenting himself as an acceptable alternative to Habsburg power particularly among German Catholics. By 1801 Napoleon was more properly a greater champion of the Catholic Church than Francis II. Napoleon found fertile ground in Germany to develop and ultimately direct its future. He was not solely responsible for the *volte face* in German politics but was merely a catalyst for this change.

Since the Protestant Reformation in the sixteenth century, the Holy Roman Empire was a conglomeration of hundreds of German territories that were undergoing evolutionary change. By the eighteenth century the Empire was, as Voltaire quipped, "neither holy, nor Roman, nor an Empire." Although bound by an Imperial constitution and bureaucracy, the dynamic of the Empire had already been altered. In structure, the emperor was elected for life by several German princes (titled *electors*). By the late eighteenth century there were ten electors. The emperor could only impose policy upon the princes through the approval of the Council of Electors and the Imperial Diet. Before the sixteenth century the Empire was bound by the emperor, the Imperial Constitution, and the Catholic Church, which, through ecclesiastic princes, controlled more than one third of the Empire's territory. The Protestant Reformation and the Thirty Years' War (1618–1648) eroded these pillars of the Empire. The rise of Brandenberg-Prussia in the eighteenth century further weakened the emperor's power. It provided Protestant princes with an alternative German polity to the traditional hegemony of the Catholic Habsburg Austria. Prussian ascendancy during the reign of Frederick II (the Great) accelerated the decline of a centralized German authority, which the Austrians had failed to achieve over the preceding two centuries.

In an age of reason, the Holy Roman Empire was one of the most irrational political institutions in Europe. It was also one of the last bastions of ecclesiastic power and thus a target of secularizing German princes who wanted to absorb ecclesiastic lands into their domains. This process began with the Protestant Reformation and continued through the eighteenth century. It was in effect an evolution of the Empire from a medieval institution to a more "modern" entity. Yet, the nature of the Empire required the emperor to agree to secularization, and as long as the Habsburgs were the dynastic power in the Empire this was not to be.

By the time of the French Revolution there were three distinct entities in Germany: first, the Imperial counts, knights, and ecclesiastic princes whose sovereignty was protected by the emperor; second, the large German states, such as Prussia, Austria (Bohemia), Saxony, and Bavaria, all of which were electorates; and lastly the princes of smaller states who sought greater independence from Imperial influence and Austro-Prussian dominance.[1] The mediatization and absorbtion of feudal states held by Imperial counts and knights provided princes with the potential to expand their holdings within the Empire.[2] It was not until the French Revolutionary Wars that the ability to restructure the Empire through secularization and elimination of feudal estates was possible. This was not apparent when the Empire went to war with France in 1792, but became clear sometime later when the emperor was unable to stem the French invasions.

The War of the First Coalition (1792–1797) was the last Imperial war, or *Reichkrieg*, in the history of the Empire. It began with a French declaration of war against the "king of Bohemia and Hungary." This was an unrealistic attempt to limit the conflict to the House of Austria. Soon the Habsburgs were joined by Prussia. Prussia's participation, combined with the threat to the ecclesiastic electors on the Rhine, precipitated the Imperial Diet's recognition that a state of war existed between France and the Empire. Technically, there was no declaration of *Reichkrieg*, but this is merely a semantic argument.[3]

The *Reichkrieg* was never pressed with as much sagacity as the Empire and its states were capable of. Although troops were raised in three of the Imperial *Kreise* (circles), the core and leadership of the *Reicharmee* was placed in the hands of Austria and Prussia.[4] Despite war with France, Prussia, Austria, and Russia remained occupied with the partitioning of Poland. The German states, including Prussia, failed to meet their military obligations as required by the Imperial constitution. Consequently, the French were able to seize Mainz in the autumn of 1792, and the entire left bank of the Rhine by 1794, including a considerable amount of electoral territory.[5] Austria and Prussia pushed the German princes into a conflict they perceived as not in their interests, but it was the princes who paid the price of the war by losing territory.[6]

In 1795, Prussia abandoned Austria and signed a separate peace with Revolutionary France. The Treaty of Basel was a milestone in the evolution of the Holy Roman Empire. It was abundantly clear to the German princes that in such distressing times it was "every man for himself."[7] By opting for a separate peace, Prussia once again exhibited its independence from the Empire and rejected *Reich* in favor of *raison d'etat*. The clauses of the treaty recognized the French occupation of the left bank of the Rhine and established Prussian neutrality. It further guaranteed the neutrality of northern Germany, as both France and Prussia fixed a line of demarcation that was off limits to French campaigning.[8] This line provided the German princes north of the Main River the opportunity to leave the conflict. Within a year of Basel, Hesse-Cassel, one of the first princely states to support Austrian and Prussian efforts in 1792, withdrew from the war.[9] The princes of Nassau soon followed suit. Several months later in July 1796, the states of the Swabian *Kreis* likewise signed neutrality agreements with France.[10]

The Imperial war ceased after Basel and the strategic focus shifted to southern Germany. The responsibility for protecting the Empire fell upon Austria. Yet, among the German princes there was little confidence in the Habsburg's ability to defend the Rhine. The princes of Baden, Württemberg, Bavaria, and Saxony therefore all negotiated with Revolutionary France, and they all signed armistices, treaties, or both in 1796.[11] The problem, however, was that the Austrian's did not abandon the war so easily. Their holdings in southern Germany enabled them to continue the war on the Rhine, which resulted in a French invasion of those south German states that desperately desired to leave the conflict.

The princes perceived the continuation of the war as purely a Habsburg affair. The campaign of 1796 did more damage to the south German states than four years for war had up to this point. In the end, Austria was still unable to defeat France, as Napoleon's victory in Italy and the subsequent invasion of Austria compelled Francis II to sign his own treaty with France at Campo Formio in 1797. All of this was done with the tacit understanding that the princes would have to work out their own settlements with France.

The Austrian agreements made at Campo Formio demonstrated their willingness to trade Imperial territory to protect their dynastic interests.[12] Greater than Prussia's sins against the Empire in 1795, the Habsburgs broke promises to the German princes and violated their most sacred position within the Empire, that of protector and leader. The clauses of Campo Formio obtained Austrian recognition of French annexation of the left bank of the Rhine, and its secret articles allowed for the accelerated secularization of the Empire. In agreeing to such, Austria abrogated its leadership of the Empire and its protection of the Catholic Church, both of which they had ardently defended during the eighteenth century.[13] Although they had little choice in coming to terms with France, they did have one when it came to the issue of territorial compensation. The Habsburgs promised the German princes they would never agree to a violation of the integrity of the Empire, yet French annexation of the left bank of the Rhine necessitated a reform of the Imperial constitution. The elimination of electoral states and the loss of princely territories to France required a reorganization of the Empire at its most fundamental level. Similarly, at a time when French revolutionaries attacked the Catholic Church, Austria, the defender of the faith in Germany, sold out the church by accepting the archbishopric of Salzburg in exchange for Tuscany.[14] Thus, the largest ecclesiastic state in Germany became a secular possession of the extended Habsburg family.

From the perspective of the south German princes, could the Imperial constitution be defended if the emperor could not and would not guarantee it?[15] Perhaps more galling than this was the hypocrisy of it all. When the princes of Baden and Württemberg signed their respective agreements with France in August of 1796, the treaties provided them with compensation for lost territories. The Austrians initially reacted by disarming those Swabian contingents that remained with the *Reicharmee*. When the Archduke Charles pushed the French armies back across the Rhine in the autumn, he compelled those princes to recommit themselves to war against France.[16] By what right could the Austrians punish the Swabian princes when they made similar agreements with France in the spring of 1797?

Austrian and Prussian attitudes toward of the small and middling territories encouraged the princes to seek protection from larger foreign powers, such as France or Russia, or to form a union to preserve their autonomy. Austria and Prussia's actions during the war merely confirmed what the princes had experienced over the past half-century. No prince saw the Empire as devolving to the point of extinction, but the question remained, what was its future? A myriad of ideas were discussed and debated, from enlightened federalism to a confederation. In the midst of the war preservation of their lands was high priority.

The Directors in France played upon the inconsistencies of Austrian Imperial policy, seeking to separate the princes from Vienna. Whereas the earlier Revolutionary regime tended toward a more radicalized notion of diplomacy, the Directors understood the value of not alienating their potential allies.[17] At the same time they wanted to supplant Habsburg with French military influence in southern Germany. Habsburg possessions, along with a number of Imperial cities and territories (notably the Breisgau), were to be occupied by French troops.[18] This would create a buffer between France and Austria in southern Germany, effectively denying Austria the ability to deploy its armies on the Rhine and forcing them further east to the Vorarlberg. The Swabian states were too small and weak, however, to provide an adequate *cordon sanitaire* for France. It was necessary to enlarge them in order to strengthen them. Therefore, granting territorial compensation in south Germany in return for renunciation of their rights to lands on the left bank of the Rhine made perfect sense from the French perspective. For their part, the princes of south Germany wanted to acquire as much land as possible in their dealings with France.[19] *Mediatization,* the policy of absorbing the independent estates of Imperial counts and knights, was pursued with alacrity. The Holy Roman Emperor ardently defended these Imperial nobles in return for their support of Imperial policy in the Diet. The reduction of their numbers further weakened the power and influence of the emperor in relation to the middling states. The agreement between France and the German princes was a marriage of convenience. The French Revolutionary Wars, however, introduced new opportunities for these princes.

Campo Formio confirmed French and Austrian possessions in Italy, while the Congress of Rastatt in 1798 affirmed those parts of the treaty that applied to the Empire proper. Austrian strategy at the conference was to stall long enough to rebuild its forces. The unknown variable, however, was how long the fragile peace would last. Certainly, the Austrians did not consider the settlement carved in stone.[20] The articles of Campo Formio were simply unacceptable to them, but with the military situation being what it was in 1797 there were few alternatives but to accept it. Time was desperately needed for the Austrian army to recoup its losses and for Baron Francis von Thugut, the Austrian vice-chancellor, to find allies on the continent. When the Second Coalition was finally formed and war renewed in 1799, the Austrian explanation to the German princes was simply that the agreements at Campo Formio were a temporary expedient. It provided a cessation of hostilities, long enough to rebuild and reorganize. Victory in the current war would allow Vienna to abrogate any agreements it had previously made with France. In other words, the clauses of Campo Formio as they were to be applied at Rastatt would be null and void if France was defeated. This was the rationale when Austria compelled the south German princes to participate in the new war.[21]

One question that remains somewhat unclear is why the Bavarian and Swabian princes agreed to contribute troops to the Second Coalition if they saw greater benefit in a French alliance. Perhaps the simplest explanation can be found in the nature of Revolutionary diplomacy and its continued influence in south Germany. Although political overtures were favorable to the princes in 1796, French republican agitation and its growing popular support concerned the princes. Revolutionary diplomacy called for an attack upon the "old" style. The German leaders became wary of further Revolutionary influence that might come with French occupation of their lands.[22] The Austrians' foremost concern, likewise, was the radical assault upon traditional institutions.[23] In the end, however, the geographic position of the south German states compelled them to take sides. When an Austrian army under Archduke Charles forced the French beyond the Rhine in the spring of 1799, neutrality was no longer an option. The princes of Baden and Württemberg also reconsidered their position when Russia joined the Second Coalition. Tsar Paul's wife was the princess of Württemberg, and their son Alexander, the future tsar, married the granddaughter of the duke of Baden in 1799. Furthermore, the British offered these princes 1 million pounds to field their armies.[24]

Although the Second Coalition was able to win impressive victories in Italy and Germany, the coup d'état of 18 Brumaire, which brought Napoleon to power, led to the eventual loss of their short-lived gains. The inability of Austria to defeat France, and the subsequent occupation of Bavaria by a French army, created an irreparable schism between the south German princes and the House of Habsburg.[25] The elector of Bavaria, Maximillian IV Joseph had only come to the throne of the German state in 1799. He was the nephew of the previous Duke Karl Theodor and was from the Duchy of Pfalz-Zweibrücken, which had been under French occupation along with the Lower Palitinate since 1794. A year after his ascension to the Bavarian throne, he now found his new territory under French occupation too. Yet, it was Austria that bore much of the responsibility for this reversal, as they once again failed to defend the Empire adequately. Not surprising then, eight months after the war Bavaria and France signed the Treaty of Paris, promising Max IV Joseph territorial compensation for his loss of Zweibücken on the left bank of the Rhine.[26]

Burgeoning relations between France and the German princes extended to Bavaria's neighbors. The Austrians pressured Frederick II, duke of Württemberg, to join the Second Coalition, only to see a French army march through his lands too. In the midst of the war, Duke Frederick II continued secret negotiations with France that were particularly valuable since Württemberg had signed a neutrality agreement with them in 1796.[27] For the princes of Nassau, the problem before them was one of security. The lands of Nassau were spread between the left and right banks of the Rhine and north of the Main River, which was within the neutrality line established by France and Prussia in the Treaty of Basel. Prussian neutrality and the occupation of the Rhenish states on the left bank placed the princes in a quandry. Freiherr Hans von Gagern, foreign minister of Nassau, initially sought an association of Rhenish princes in order to protect the integrity and sovereignty of their territorial possessions. This was certainly to the deliberate exclusion of Prussia and Austria.[28] In essence, during and after the War of the Second Coalition, Austrian influence gradually faded in favor of a pro-French policy for most of the south German lands.[29]

With Austria and France wrestling over south Germany and the prospects of recovering the left bank of the Rhine looking ever grim, it was the responsibility of the German princes to look out for themselves. General Bonaparte impressed many of the German statesmen during his brief appearance at Rastatt, and they saw him as perhaps someone with whom they could "do business." After the failure of the Second Coalition and the Treaty of Lunéville in February 1801, it was left to the German princes to scramble to secure what they could, since the major powers had already taken what they wanted either by conquest or compensation. Hence, the Treaty of Lunéville (1801) marked a turning point in the history of Germany. The princes of the south came fully into the French sphere and remained there until 1813. If the Treaty of Basel established Prussia as an independent entity from the Holy Roman Empire in 1795, then the princes of south Germany perceived Lunéville as the end to Austrian leadership in the Empire.[30]

Napoleon gained greater force for his German policy by convincing the Russians, who withdrew from the Second Coalition in 1799, that their interest in strengthening the south German princes at the expense of Austria was similar. Russia's role in Germany increased considerably with the Treaty of Teschen in 1779. It granted the Tsar the right to intervene in German affairs. The fact that Tsar Paul I was married to the sister of the elector of Württemberg, who was now the mother of Tsar Alexander I resulted in a significant Russian presence among the German courts. As first consul of France, Napoleon wrote to his brother Joseph, who was in charge of negotiations at Lunéville, that "it [was] difficult to negotiate respecting Germany without the cooperation of Tsar Paul." He believed that Russian support would be decisive in driving home his demands upon Austria. He then instructed Joseph to promise or commit to nothing until the Russians had fully joined with respect to his German policy.[31]

Joseph pressured Habsburg foreign minister Johann von Cobenzl to conclude a treaty under threat of impending Russian intervention, which all believed would be to the detriment of Austria.[32] The tactic was successful as the Austrian position was already untenable. Napoleon's demands were hard enough to concede, and having to factor in Russian interests would have been almost impossible. Having withdrawn from the coalition, Tsar Paul sought indemnification for the south German princes and the right to dictate terms for territorial exchange in Italy too.[33] The question of whether or not Napoleon wanted a Russian diplomat present at the negotiating table is debatable. There is every indication that he desired a formal agreement between Russia and France to use as leverage against Austria. It is unlikely, however, that Napoleon wanted to provide an ambitious Paul with a platform to discuss the future of the Italian peninsula. The latter was certainly part of the Tsar's foreign policy agenda. Paul's interests there stemmed from his desire to extend Russian power into the Mediterranean.[34]

Nonetheless, Russian participation in negotiations was not the ultimate factor that motivated the Austrians to finally accept terms. The decisive element was the defeat of the Austrian army at Hohenlinden at the beginning of December 1800 and the personal report by Francis's brother, Archduke Charles, that the army was incapable of further resistance. On 25 December, the archduke signed an armistice with the French, who were already in upper Austria. Under these circumstances Emperor Francis instructed his vice-chancellor, Baron Thugut, to instruct Cobenzl to secure an end to the conflict. Thugut did so and then tendered his resignation.[35]

The preliminaries were signed at the end of January with the final treaty being completed on 9 February 1801. The articles of the Treaty of Lunéville were nothing more than a reaffirmation of those terms Napoleon had originally demanded at Campo Formio five years earlier. The difference was that Napoleon was no longer a mere general of the Republic, and Austria had run out of allies and options. This was understood both in Paris and Vienna. In fact, Austria's position had deteriorated greatly since 1799. Lunéville provided France with *de jure* recognition of annexation of the left bank of the Rhine. It also gave France possession of a number of cities and territories in Germany that enhanced their strategic and political position at the expense of Austria.[36]

The Habsburgs lost their possessions in Germany that bordered the Rhine. The county of Frickthal was handed over to the Helvetic Confederation (Switzerland), and the Breisgau was given over to the duke of Modena, who then ceded his Italian territories to France.[37] This exchange effectively pushed Habsburg possessions further east. The closest Habsburg territory to the Rhine was now the Vorarlberg, wedged between Bavaria and Switzerland. This provided France with a buffer of states in south Germany, while at the same time reducing the physical Habsburg presence in that region. Perhaps Napoleon's greatest achievement at Lunéville was Austria's acceptance of the now-secularized archbishopric of Salzburg as compensation for the Duchy of Tuscany. This was embodied in article five of the treaty and finalized in an article "*séparé et secret.*" This act essentially discredited the Habsburgs in the eyes of the south German princes and enraged the Catholic Church. By accepting the archbishopric, the Habsburgs completely undermined their position as Holy Roman Emperors. How could Austria justify its resistance to secularization if it were participating in the same? Similarly, it clearly illustrated to the German princes that the Habsburgs were willing to sacrifice German for dynastic interests. As such, Lunéville completely undermined Austrian influence in Germany. It also further legitimized secularization in the princes' eyes.

All articles of the treaty pertaining to the territorial composition of the Holy Roman Empire had to be approved by the Imperial Diet. At the same time the question of indemnification had to be addressed. A committee of German princes was formed to establish the nature of compensation for those princes who lost territory. It was composed of five electors, including the Emperor Francis in his capacity as the King of Bohemia. The king of Prussia, the dukes of Saxony and Bavaria, and the archbishop of Mainz were among the members. In addition, the princes of Württemberg and Hesse-Cassel participated, along with the *Hoch und Deutschmeister* (the grand master of the Teutonic Order).[38] Before the process of indemnification could proceed the Lunéville Treaty was presented before the Imperial Diet at Regensberg and approved. The lack of resistance by the German representatives indicated their support for change in Germany.[39]

The German princes demanded the right to consult with France on the question of indemnities.[40] Francis refused, but they simply ignored him. Napoleon made his initial offers of compensation to the princes in March 1801. By the summer of that year direct negotiations between France and many of the German princes proceeded. In particular, Bavaria, Baden, and Württemberg, along with Prussia and the former archbishop of Mainz, signed separate accords.[41] Bavaria was of utmost importance to Napoleon, as it had a long and amicable relationship with France. Bavarian interests had often led to alliances with France such as had occurred during the War of Spanish Succession (1701–1714) and the War of Austrian Succession (1740–1748). The elector of Bavaria, Maximillian IV Joseph, was far more sympathetic to France than he had ever been to Austria. His first minister, Maximillian von Montgelas, was intensely reformist and also pro-French. Napoleon envisioned a strong bond between the two states as a crucial geo-political and strategic benefit in southern Germany. In its aggrandized form, Bavaria would act as an effective buffer between France and Austria.[42]

During negotiations at Lunéville Napoleon wrote to the Bavarian prince seeking to convince him that Vienna had nothing but duplicity in mind with respect to compensation. Max IV Joseph was greatly concerned with upholding the sanctity of his electoral title. Unfortunately, this derived from his possession of the Bavarian Palatinate, which was situated on the left bank of the Rhine and under French occupation. The fate of his title therefore remained uncertain. Napoleon shrewdly informed the Bavarian elector that he supported the transfer of the title to Munich so that Max Joseph would retain it. Napoleon then contended that Austria sought to transfer the title to one of its hereditary lands, but assured the prince that both he and the Tsar of Russia opposed this.[43] Support and enlargement of Bavaria in the face of Austrian opposition had been the hallmark of French policy for more than a century, and Napoleon pursued it as well.

The acceptance of the German provisions of Lunéville at the Diet of Regensberg cleared the way for a dramatic alteration of the Imperial constitution.[44] Of the ten electoral states that existed in 1792, four were now part of France. The reconfiguration of the most fundamental political institution of the Holy Roman Empire clearly required another meeting of the Imperial Diet to reconstruct the German constitutional system. The princes now scrambled to gain recognition of their territorial desires by the major powers. Under the terms of the Treaties of Westphalia (1648) and the Treaty of Teschen (1779), France and Russia had the right to involve themselves in German affairs on this level. Both states were sympathetic to the south German princes, each for their own reasons, but they also agreed in principle on reducing Austrian influence in the Empire. In effect, France, Russia, Prussia, and Great Britain in George III's capacity as the elector of Hanover supported significant territorial change in Germany. Austria's former enemy, as well as their former allies, compelled them to accept substantial alterations to the Holy Roman Empire.[45]

Between March 1802 and April 1803, there was a flurry of diplomatic activity in Paris as German princes courted French support for compensation.

Napoleon, for his part, determined to guarantee the princes their right to compensation in the face of a reluctant Austria. His interests were far from altruistic, but instead were tied to his own concept of Germany's future. He wrote the duke of Württemberg in June 1802 reaffirming French friendship and assuring him of his state's integrity in the face of imminent change.[46] This was essentially done to mollify the duke, as Bavaria, his neighbor to the east, stood to gain the most in any territorial shifts in southern Germany. Bavaria had the third largest army in Germany, and its close association with France would sandwich Baden and Württemberg between the two. Yet, Baden and Württemberg also stood to gain through secularization of the Empire. Independent ecclesiastic territories and estates held by Imperial counts and knights dotted their lands. All of the latter maintained their independence despite the expansionist interests of the princes because of the protection offered by the Holy Roman Emperor. If the emperor were to abdicate his protection for the ecclesiastic and Imperial states, then they were to be thrown to the larger princes.

All was set for the conclusion of negotiations by the beginning of the summer of 1802. Franco-Russian mediation, which leaned heavily in France's favor, resulted in agreements and conventions signed by Prussia, Bavaria, and Württemberg in Paris.[47] Austrian Vice-Chancellor Cobenzl, who had replaced Baron Thugut, wrote to his counterpart Count Francis von Colloredo that the impact of Lunéville upon Austrian power was critical.

> What a lesson we here receive regarding the slight respect which we enjoy abroad, respect which alone constitutes the security of states. Bonaparte knows us only too well. He has seduced Prussia through the advantages which he secures for her, Russia through the favor shown Baden and Württemberg; he has made his peace with England [Treaty of Amiens]; us he does not need and we have nothing to hope from him. And so it will remain as long as our domestic affairs are in such a state of disorder. All the world knows that we are not in a position to wage war. How then to obtain the execution of treaties from a man like Bonaparte?[48]

Cobenzl refused to accept that Austria was as much to blame as France for its current position in Germany. Yet, Prussia was not "seduced," and although he may have been right concerning Russian motivation, the reality was that Austria lost the war. If the Second Coalition had been victorious on the battlefield, then things would have been dramatically different. To be fair, both Cobenzl and Thugut believed that the Treaty of Campo Formio in 1797, the cornerstone of Napoleon's German policy, was so disadvantageous that it could not be allowed to stand.[49] Thus, the Second Coalition was formed, and though almost victorious, it was ultimately unsuccessful. In the end it should be acknowledged that this was due as much to conflicting war aims of coalition partners as it was to Austria's failure on the battlefield.[50]

Napoleon's role in this was as opportunist. He capitalized upon his military victories and played upon the ebb and flow of European international relations to get what he wanted. He did not orchestrate this from the beginning. He did not bully the German princes into agreeing to his terms. The camps were already set by the time the negotiations commenced. Prussia remained neutral in 1799 not because it was seduced by Napoleon but because King Frederick William III saw no advantage for his state to join the coalition.[51] He desired to increase Prussian influence in north Germany and Vienna was certainly not going to support Prussian demands. The Russians cooperated with Napoleon, albeit reluctantly, because it was to their advantage.

It is true that Napoleon played first upon Tsar Paul's, and then Alexander's, desire to aggrandize the south German princes. This was not contradictory but congruous to French interests. Paul's *rapproachment* with France was symptomatic of the breakdown of the Second Coalition. Russian forces had already withdrawn from central Europe leaving the Austrians in the lurch, and relations with Britain were terribly strained.[52] It should be said, however, that Russia's withdrawal from the coalition began prior to Napoleon's coup in November 1799, but it left the new first consul in an excellent position. Paul's murder in March 1801 came as a shock to Napoleon, but for all his concerns, Alexander I maintained Russian foreign policy in central Europe as it was under his father. Russian support and participation in addressing indemnities and compensation for German princes was so significant that Napoleon instructed his foreign minister, Prince Maurice de Talleyrand, to ascertain Alexander's position through his discussions with Russian ambassador Count Markov and then proceed accordingly. "My intention," Napoleon wrote Talleyrand, "is not to compromise in any manner French affairs in Germany."[53]

Napoleon and Talleyrand were successful in pursuing peace with Russia. On 8 and 10 October 1801, two treaties were signed. The first was a peace agreement, the second a pact to coordinate the process of compensation and indemnification for the German princes, settle affairs in Italy, and accept preliminaries for a peace with the Ottoman Empire.[54] The accord with Russia freed Napoleon to broker the future of south Germany on his own. This is not to say that he ignored Russian interests altogether, or overawed them, but merely that he found common cause with them since they shared similar objectives in the region. France, Russia, and Prussia each desired to reduce Austrian power in central Europe. As issues of Poland and the Balkans were foremost among Russian concerns, the future of northern Germany remained key to Prussian interests.

Prussian neutrality in any conflict with Austria was a significant objective of Napoleonic diplomacy. Such a policy worked well for him within the changing nature of European alliances. Frederick William III inherited the throne in 1797 and continued to guard Prussian influence throughout north Germany. This was to done, however, without committing his state to an entangling and most likely detrimental alliance with Britain, Austria, and Russia in the Second Coalition.[55] Prussia's position was secured by two factors: French promises not to violate north German neutrality as embodied in the Treaty of Basel, and the Prussian army. The former was neither under Frederick William's control nor realistically relied upon, as the French had violated the neutrality zone several times by 1797. The latter was something that the king could control, and Prussian military might remained a tangible threat to all powers.[56] Whether or not Frederick William III would ever agree to commit his army to enforce his policy was another issue.

Unfortunately for the Prussian king, the question was raised relatively early in his reign. As relations between France and Russian cooled in 1800, tensions increased between Britain and Russia. The result was an undeclared naval war between the latter two states. Prussia had been part of the lapsed League of Armed Neutrality (established in 1780), and Paul wanted to resurrect the alliance. Napoleon encouraged Prussian participation, as it added another state to the list of Britain's enemies. Prussian concerns lay not in the Baltic but in the electorate of Hanover. Coveted as it may have been by earlier Prussian kings, it was a possession of King George III of England and beyond Prussia's reach. The dilemma was both in Napoleon's and Tsar Paul's demands that Prussia seize the electorate. Failure to do so would compel the French to do it otherwise.[57]

The Prussian army thus occupied Hanover in April 1801 and remained there until the crisis with Great Britain subsided in November. More than its implication for Prussia, the undeclared war worked well for Napoleon. The Treaty of Lunéville was ratified in Vienna a month earlier, and all things considered, it meant Britain potentially faced a war against France, Russia, and Prussia. Although Napoleon had little to do with the origins of the Anglo-Russian crisis, he profited from it. Paul's growing anger toward Britain provided Napoleon with an opportunity to further French relations with Russia. A cooperative effort over German compensation was now coupled with their hostile stance against Britain. Napoleon also used this diplomatic turnabout to strike at a British possession in Germany through Prussia and with the full support of Russia. The results were quite successful. Negotiations between Britain and France began in earnest. Preliminaries to a treaty were established on 8 October 1801, the same day France and Russia concluded their official peace agreement.[58] For Prussia, the occupation of Hanover was an attempt to reinforce the neutrality zone and prevent French intervention. After Tsar Paul's assassination, Alexander I strongly desired that Prussia withdraw its forces from the electorate.

The period extending from autumn of 1801 through autumn of 1802 was one of significant diplomatic wrangling for France. An official peace agreement between Britain and France was produced at Amiens in March 1802. Relations with the new tsar, Alexander I, remained cordial if not friendly. Napoleon, consequently, was able to focus considerable attention and energy on Germany, where the princes were actively pursuing French and Russian support for territorial compensation. It is fair to say then that Austria was isolated during these negotiations over indemnities and compensations in Paris.

The Austrians learned of the accords between France, Russia, and the German princes when Cobenzl read about them in the French newspaper, *Le Moniteur*.[59] Reaction from Vienna was sharp, but focused exclusively upon the German states. It warned the princes not to act upon their agreements until the Diet met and approved all territorial changes. Prussia simply ignored Austria. Shortly thereafter, a potential crisis emerged over Bavaria's preparations to annex the bishopric of Passau. Austria desired Passau and threatened armed conflict with their German neighbor if Bavaria violated the ecclesiastic state. To preempt any potential humiliation by Bavaria, Austrian troops occupied the bishopric.[60] Napoleon initially sought to mediate the issue, but found it expedient to leave Austria in possession of Passau. It furthered the discord between the Habsburgs and the south German princes and Passau remained a thorn in the side of Austro-Bavarian relations through 1805. Contributing to tensions, the Aulic Council, the body that advised the Holy Roman Emperor, condemned Bavaria's refusal to abide by the emperor's *diktat* not to occupy the territory of Imperial knights until the Imperial Diet approved of such annexations. What irritated the Bavarian elector and his minister Montgelas was that similar condemnations were not forthcoming for their equally guilty neighbor Württemberg.[61] This may have had more to do with the friendly relationship between Württemberg and Russia than with a purposeful move by Austria to isolate Bavaria. Nonetheless, it did not help matters and Austro-Bavarian relations continued to deteriorate.

Austria was presented with a fait accompli by the time the Imperial deputation that was engaged to determine compensation and indemnities submitted its draft to the Diet in February 1803.[62] The committee met for the first time in August 1802 and unilaterally decided the issues. The Imperial Diet accepted the committee's proposals in total. This dramatic alteration of the boundaries and nature of the Holy Roman Empire now necessitated a significant constitutional reorganization of Germany. By accepting the articles of Lunéville, Germany lost three electoral states and part of a fourth.[63] French annexation of the left bank of the Rhine eliminated the Burgundian *Kries*. Annexation and consolidation of territory in south and central Germany altered the nature of the Franconian and Swabian *Kreise*.[64] This was all finalized in the monumental meeting at the end of February 1803, known as the *Reichsdeputations-hauptschluß*, or Imperial Recess.

Francis II accepted most of the provisions, including the alteration to the Imperial constitution, with only a few exceptions.[65] Unfortunately, it did not do much for Austria's position in Germany. The princes achieved greater autonomy from the Empire. This had been the case in northern Germany since the late eighteenth century, but Lunéville and the Imperial Recess did much to reduce Imperial influence in the south German lands. This did not immediately translate into French domination of south Germany, but it certainly extended French influence eastward from the Rhine to the Inn.

Perhaps of more concern to Vienna was the state of international relations in the spring of 1803. Russia was on relatively good terms with France. Great Britain and France were temporarily disengaged, and Prussia remained steadfast in its neutrality. There seemed to be few options for Austria. Assessments of the impact of Lunéville and the Imperial Recess have tended to give Napoleon a great deal of credit for these changes. German historian John Gagliardo writes:

> With these compensations, Bonaparte realized one of the great goals of his German policy: the creation of a group of enlarged German client states one or near the French border, of sufficient size and internal cohesion as to diminish their sense of dependence on Austria, yet not so large as to be able to forget that their recent good fortune as well as their possible further expansion was due to the good will of France.[66]

Eduard Driault, the eminent Napoleonic diplomatic historian, characterized Germany after the Recess as something akin to Poland a decade earlier. He believed that the new Germany was the product of Franco-Russian mediation that was of greater advantage to France, at the expense of Austria and Prussia.[67]

It is certainly true that France benefited the most from the Imperial Recess. The new borders of Germany provided France with greater security and strategic positioning in Central Europe. Moreover, the south German princes became Napoleon's clients. This was, however, a double-edged relationship. Although Bavaria's aggrandizement improved France's position in south Germany at the expense of Austria, it also served to expand the Bavarian state.[68] The Bavarian elector did not consider the territorial exchanges a bad deal. Nor did the dukes of Baden and Württemberg complain of the outcome. As is generally the case, interpretation is relative to the perspective from which one is observing. Hans von Gagern, minister president of Nassau, thus told the Badenese foreign minister in Paris, "the cannon of Mayence [Mainz] and Coblenz dictate to us, as those of Strasbourg dictate to the elector of Baden."[69] When one understands that the duke of Baden received the title of elector as a consequence of the Imperial Recess and with the support of Napoleon, Gagern's wry comment becomes insightful.[70]

One need also consider that throughout the eighteenth century German princes often pursued a schizophrenic policy of seeking greater autonomy from the Empire, but then desiring Imperial protection when their policies found them in difficulties with either foreign powers or other German princes. The middling territories of the Empire, notably Bavaria, Württemberg, and Baden, were able to secure increased influence within the Imperial Diet but at the same time extend their relationships with France and Russia. The Imperial Recess of 1803 provided new opportunities for these princes, but not all would conclude by 1805 that the evolution of the Holy Roman Empire was ultimately beneficial.

CHAPTER FIVE

NAPOLEON, PRUSSIA, AND GERMAN POLITICS, 1803–1805

WHEN NAPOLEON INHERITED THE WAR of the Second Coalition he struck first at Austria and then moved against England. Unable to match them at sea, he was determined to cut them off from their continental allies and commerce. He was fortunate that his ascension to power was concomitant with the formation of the League of Armed Neutrality in northern Europe. Prussian troops occupied Hanover in March 1801, complying with the league's covenant, and, in part, to prevent the French from doing the same. In June, Napoleon convinced Spain to declare war on Portugal. It is clear that these actions were decisive in bringing England to the negotiating table by the autumn of 1801.[1]

When war came in 1803, Napoleon intended to revive his continental strategy. Two month prior to the British declaration of war against France, Napoleon sent General Giraud Duroc to Berlin as a special emissary to the king of Prussia. Duroc informed Frederick William III that England's failure to turn over Malta, a fundamental article of the Treaty of Amiens, would no doubt lead to the collapse of the peace. French troops would then occupy Hanover. The first consul desired to know Prussia's response in such an event.[2] This was a clear threat to the neutrality agreement forged at Basel in 1795, and Napoleon was not looking for Frederick William III to occupy the electorate as he had in 1801.

As Austria's capital faded in Germany, Prussia's strengthened. Two events tested and determined Prussia's role as arbiter of Germany and potentially Europe. The first was Napoleon's invasion of Hanover in 1803, in violation of the north German neutrality zone. The second was in 1805, when continental war seemed imminent and Napoleon prepared to swing his army from northern Europe to south Germany. In both cases Frederick William III, king of Prussia, lost enormous opportunities to present his kingdom as the alternative German power in the face of coming conflict. The princes of Germany sought Prussian guarantees to keep war from the Reich. The Habsburgs were no longer trustworthy, and they had shown in recent years that they were unable to do so. Prussia was preferred to France, and peace to war.

Prussia's political and strategic significance extended beyond its borders to the neighboring *mittelstadt* (middling principalities) of Hesse-Cassel, Hesse-Darmstadt, and Saxony. Both Saxony and Hesse-Cassel were appendages of Prussian military power. During the War of the First Coalition, Saxon and Hessian regiments were not part of the *Reicharmee*, but under direct Prussian command. The duke of Brunswick was a dedicated ally and commander in chief of the Prussian army, while Hesse-Darmstadt was drafted regularly into the Prussian military sphere.[3] Northern Germany increasingly became Prussia's domain in the years following the Treaty of Basel. Frederick William III's accession to the throne in 1797 did not alter this reality but his ministers worked assiduously to enhance it. Whereas many of the south German princes were compelled by Austria to continue their military and economic support of the conflict, central and north Germany territories such as Hesse-Darmstadt and Hesse-Cassel were able to safely emulate Prussia's example. This was done, however, with the knowledge that it placed them squarely in the Prussian camp.

In the decade prior to the War of the Third Coalition, Prussia enjoyed its dominant position in north Germany. When in 1795 Prussia withdrew from the First Coalition against Revolutionary France, military operations ended in Germany north of the River Main. The Peace of Basel was a dramatic and critical event in the history of the Holy Roman Empire, and it contributed to the eventual dissolution of that German institution. By establishing its neutrality and guaranteeing that of northern Germany, Hesse-Cassel was able to make similar terms with France. The electorate of Hanover, a possession of King George III of England, followed the Prussian example and initially participated in the enforcement of the treaty. Francis II, the Holy Roman Emperor, rejected Basel, and Austrian and Imperial forces violated the Main boundary on a few occasions. Similarly, French troops operated north of the Main in 1797. Regardless of these minor infractions, neutrality held, and Prussia, along with the vast majority of north German princes escaped the devastating costs of war that afflicted south Germany.[4]

During the War of the Second Coalition, Prussia refused continued Austrian, British, and Russian pressure to enter the conflict. Prussia's "peace dividend" reduced state expenditure considerably, while allowing the new Prussian monarch, Frederick William III, to settle into his throne and assess Prussia's strategic and diplomatic position in Europe.[5] Frederick William's determination to remain neutral was fortunate, as the Second Coalition failed miserably and Tsar Paul I withdrew from the alliance in 1799, only to establish friendly relations with the first consul of France.

Despite Prussian neutrality, Frederick William III found himself troubled by the conflict's gradual encroachment upon north German neutrality. Britain enforced a strict blockade on continental goods from France and broadly defined its rights to search neutral shipping or occupy Hanseatic towns in search of "contraband." To combat these violations Tsar Paul I, King Gustav IV Adolf of Sweden, King Christian VII of Denmark, and Frederick William III reestablished the League of Armed Neutrality, formed originally in 1781 to protect neutral trade in the Baltic from English strong-arm tactics.[6] Although Prussia entered the league of its own accord, Frederick William III was loath to do more than verbally support it. Yet, pressure from Tsar Paul and Napoleon compelled the Prussian king to occupy Hanover as a hostage against the king of England. British response was Admiral Nelson's surprise attack on the Danish fleet at Copenhagen. Prussian troops, however, remained in Hanover until 1802.[7]

The Peace of Amiens (1802) between England and France ended European conflict for the first time in a decade. Amiens' bearing on the politics of Germany was limited to its impact on German trade in the Baltic and North Sea, but the implications of the Peace of Lunéville, concluded a year earlier, directly affected the constitutional and territorial structure of the Holy Roman Empire. Great opportunities abounded for Prussia. It had lost only minor possessions on the left bank of the Rhine, when annexed by France, and it had a number of significant options for territorial compensation. The question remained where to expand? A decade earlier the Hohenzollerns inherited the territories of Anspach and Bayreuth from their cousins. Prussia, therefore, could seek to increase its possessions in south central Germany, establishing a barrier along Bavaria's northern border. Austria's military failures and the shifting climate of the south German princes reduced the priority of southward expansion.[8]

Growing French power in the west, combined with the earlier threat of French occupation of Hanover in 1801, led Count Christian von Haugwitz, the Prussian foreign minister, to advise expansion in Westphalia. Thus, Frederick William III pressed for the acquisition of large, wealthy bishoprics of Paderborn, Ravensberg , and Munster, in addition to princely territories of Lingen and Minden. The French approved this for a price, essentially quadrupling Prussian territory in the west. Furthermore, Prussia managed to acquire Erfurt from under the nose of the elector of Saxony.[9]

The decision taken to strengthen Prussia's territorial possessions in Westphalia as compensation for French acquisitions on the left bank of the Rhine was confirmed at the Imperial Recess in 1803. Prussia's expansion in Westphalia, however, was not welcomed by some of its allies. Wilhelm I, elector of Hesse-Cassel, perceived Prussia's territorial acquisitions as a violation of previous agreements. The new elector desperately desired a number of small territories bordering his principality. Earlier in 1801 he concluded the Pyrmont Convention with Prussia, and Hesse-Cassel was promised Fulda, Paderborn, and Corvey, almost doubling the size of his lands. Indications that Frederick William III might balk came as early as 1802. Nonetheless, Wilhelm dispatched his minister Weitz to Paris to secure French support for these claims. Unfortunately, Talleyrand's price for considering such things far exceeded the elector's willingness to pay. Prussia, on the other hand, paid, and Frederick William III threw in for good measure a gift for the first consul—the Order of the Black Eagle.[10]

Fulda and Corvey were not meant for the Prussian kingdom, but instead for Frederick William's sister Wilhelmina, princess of Nassau-Orange. Ousted in 1795 by French invasion, Wilhelmina, sought compensation for her husband William V, the former *Staatholder*. Napoleon agreed to transfer Fulda and Corvey to the House of Nassau-Orange on condition they cease anti-French agitation in Holland.[11] The resulting relationship between Prussia, Saxony, and Hesse-Cassel soured somewhat as Hohenzollern interests seemed to outweigh conventions and agreements.[12] Despite this, the Prussians regarded these middling territories as satellites.

When in 1803 Duroc announced Napoleon's intention to dispatch troops to Hanover, Frederick William initially threatened both England and France with a preemptive occupation of the electorate if they did not accept Prussian mediation in the impending crisis.[13] Yet, no matter how definitive this statement seemed, neither Britain nor France were willing to accept this ultimatum. Frederick William III had three choices: he could act unilaterally by occupying the electorate, he could seek Russian diplomatic support for occupation, or he could do nothing.[14] In the first case, the character of the Prussian king was insufficient to meet the storm that would come from unilateral action. It would clearly reinforce the kingdom's dominant position in north Germany, but at the same time disturb Napoleon and evoke grave concern in London. Count Haugwitz, the Prussian foreign minister, instructed his ambassadors in London and St. Petersburg to sound out British and Russian responses to a Prussian occupation while he consulted with their respective representatives in Berlin.

The difficulty discerning Russian opinion derived from the seeming disconnect between Tsar Alexander, his foreign minister, and his ambassadors in Europe. Alexander I and Frederick William III sealed their friendship at Memel in 1802.[15] Since assuming the throne after his father's assassination in 1801, however, Alexander went through three foreign ministers. During the Hanvoverian crisis, the foreign minister du jour Count Alexander Voronstov initially pursued a non-interventionist policy in Europe.[16] Hence, Prussian interest in sounding out Alexander on Hanover met with a tentative response. Confusing matters was the full-court press by Count Maksim

Alopeus in Berlin and Simon Vorontsov, the Russian ambassador to England and brother of the foreign minister, to bring Russia directly into a European coalition against Napoleon.[17]

Lacking a definitive Russian response to potential French occupation of Hanover, Frederick William III said no more. Count von Haugwitz did not share his monarch's optimism. He saw the juxtaposition of a French army on Prussia's borders as a direct threat.[18] He maintained close relations with Count Alopeus, trying to gauge Russia's position if war broke. Alopeus pressed Haugwitz to take a stand against France. The Prussian minister was encouraged, but when Prussian notes to St. Petersburg returned with indications Tsar Alexander I was focused on domestic matters, there was little Haugwitz could do to move things along.[19]

Frederick William III determined to maintain north German neutrality. He opposed French occupation of Hanover, but unless he decided to move first he had little recourse.[20] The decision then, determined after heated debate among the king's ministers, was that Prussia would not act preemptively to prevent a French invasion. Frederick William III did not want to place Prussia between England and France. Prussia's desire to annex Hanover was not secret. A preemptive occupation of Hanover would therefore place Prussia, in the king's mind, in a worse position than it would be if it merely reacted to events.[21]

England declared war on France 18 May 1803. Twelve days later, General Adolphe Mortier invaded Hanover with 13,000 men. Field Marshal von Wallmoden, commanding Hanoverian forces, resisted half-heartedly, although the electoral army significantly outnumbered the French. He withdrew behind the Elbe after concluding the Convention of Suhlingen on 4 June. Mortier entered the city of Hanover the following day. George III, in his capacity as elector of Hanover, refused to ratify the agreement. At the end of July, Wallmoden surrendered his command and 4,000 Hanoverian troops, refusing to lay down their arms, were evacuated to England.[22]

The speed of the French invasion in May through June of 1803 precluded any Prussian military intervention. The king's cabinet was still debating this matter hotly when Mortier moved through the duchies of Aremberg and Oldenberg to arrive in Hanover on schedule.[23] Speed was critical to Napoleon. He was not one to spend months negotiating over his right to attack his enemy's possessions. The swift occupation of Hanover and the subsequent surrender of Hanoverian forces established a clear French presence in north Germany. Indeed, Wilhelm I, elector of Hesse-Cassel, in his capacity as commander of Prussian forces in Westphalia, was inspecting the garrisons in the new Prussian territories when French troops skirted north from Holland into Hanover. Napoleon did not want to disrupt the population of the north German states. Mortier was given express orders not to violate the towns of the two duchies en route to

Hanover, and, further, to avoid disturbing the Hanoverian population as best as possible.[24]

Despite an initially mild military occupation, Napoleon pursued an aggressive campaign against English trade. The first consul ordered the construction and deployment of sixty flatboats armed with cannons to choke off English trade up the Weser and Elbe Rivers. Generally English goods were off-loaded in the Hanseatic cities of Cuxhaven, Hamburg, and Bremen, then shipped down these two rivers to central Germany and Prussia.[25] The economic impact of French occupation went beyond damaging Britain's commercial economy; it essentially cut off Prussia and central Germany from either importing or exporting goods to and from England. Almost immediately upon receiving news of the French invasion, Haugwitz wrote to Frederick William III of the threat to Prussian commerce, and that the French intended on seizing Bremen and Hamburg.[26]

Through the summer of 1803 General Mortier's division was reinforced to more than 30,000 men.[27] Supply trains from Holland moved regularly through Aremberg and Oldenberg, constantly in defiance of north German neutrality. Curiously, Napoleon secured permission from Frederick William to move some supply convoys through Prussian territory.[28] Count von Haugwitz believed French military presence on the borders of the kingdom was a real threat to Prussia's dominating position in north Germany, if not a threat to Prussia.[29] Tsar Alexander I gradually found Napoleon's activities in Germany intolerable. King Gustav IV Adolf of Sweden perceived French occupation of Hanover as a threat to his possession in north Germany, Swedish-Pomerania. Furthermore, Wilhelm I, elector of Hesse-Cassel, found himself cast now into a potential European crisis, with French troops adjacent to his electorate.[30]

In retaliation for closing the Elbe and Weser, Britain imposed a naval blockade on the on the rivers' estuaries. All ships in Hanseatic ports and all goods being shipped out of Germany via these two estuaries would now run the risk of confiscation by the Royal Navy.[31] Actions such as this precipitated the resurrection of the League of Armed Neutrality two years earlier. Although Napoleon's actions placed French troops squarely on Prussia's borders, Frederick William III's overwhelming concern was the security of neutral trade and the independence of the Hanseatic cities of Bremen, Hamburg, and Cuxhaven. Baron Lucchesini, Prussian ambassador to Paris, expressed his king's apprehension to Talleyrand and Napoleon. Their response was an unequivocal guarantee that these cities would retain their independence. As for neutral trade, Napoleon made it clear that France had incurred more than 50 million francs in commercial losses due to England. The occupation of Hanover was retribution—a strike at England's economy.[32]

By the end of June, Napoleon's pledge to respect the neutrality of the Hanseatic cities was conditional. Reports arrived in Paris and Berlin confirmed that French troops entered Cuxhaven and Ritzbüttel, seizing English ships and goods. From Hanover, General Mortier demanded that the governments of Hamburg and Bremen embargo and confiscate English ships and goods in their cities.[33] The Prussian king, strenuously encouraged by Haugwitz, finally wrote Napoleon that despite the friendship between their two states, French violation of neutral states and neutral trade threatened their relationship. The king demanded Napoleon explain his actions.[34] His response was not long in coming. The first consul deflected the criticism of the occupation of Cuxhaven, focusing more on the blockade of the Elbe and Weser. "That the Elbe and Weser are closed to French ships is the right of England," Napoleon remarked, "but that the Prussians, the Danish are not able to reach their own waters because the French occupy Hanover [is an act against neutrals]."[35]

The British blockade was clearly calculated to compel Frederick William III to act against France or face economic repercussions. Actions by both states did nothing to move the Prussian king. Napoleon, however, continued to push the envelope of Prussian goodwill. Mortier raided Cuxhaven and Hamburg to seize English goods despite Napoleon's assurances in June that such actions would not occur.[36] This was as much to enforce the first consul's commercial policies as it was to gather funds for the military occupation of Hanover. The expedition's expenditures did not merely involve the pay and supply of French forces in the electorate, but included the cost of constructing boats to guard the Elbe and Weser, along with the improvement to fortifications in the German principality.

French finances by the summer of 1803 were in poor shape. As the Revolutionary government before him, Napoleon expected the conquered or "liberated" to pay for services rendered. Shortly after Mortier arrived in the city of Hanover, the treasury was seized and requisitions were levied upon the provincial estates. Being unable to provide the £3,000,000 demanded, Mortier was given £500,000 and the Hanoverians took out loans in Hamburg to pay the balance.[37] The funds levied on the electoral government remained insufficient to meet costs, and the towns of Celle and Göttingen were also deprived of their treasuries, with the former required to take loans from Paris. New levies were placed upon Hanover in July.[38] Mortier sought loans from the neighboring German states of Mecklenberg-Schwerin and Hesse-Cassel, lacking sufficient funds to cover the cost of military occupation.[39]

Frederick William's failure to act on any of these matters was read as weakness on all accounts. Though Prussian power was substantial, the Prussian king's reluctance to challenge Napoleon resulted in greater interest in north German affairs on the part of Sweden, Denmark, and Russia. The Danes were terribly concerned about the renewed Franco-British conflict. The raid on Copenhagen in 1801 was enough to commit them to strict neutrality. Yet the Russians pressed them to support anti-French measures. The

Danish conundrum was based upon their need to counterbalance Swedish power in the Baltic via close relations with Russia. By supporting an anti-French policy, Napoleon's forces in Hanover could threaten the provinces of Schleiswig-Holstein. These German duchies were critical to maintaining control of the Norweigian kingdom by supplying grain to the Danish army in Norway.[40] Danish crown prince Frederick mobilized troops in Holstein shortly after French occupation of Hanover, but his father Christian VII maintained a "wait and see" attitude.[41]

Tsar Alexander I remained the most significant variable in north German affairs. His lack of interest in 1803 shortly changed to one of grave concern. Napoleon's actions in Italy and south Germany moved the Tsar along, but a change in the Russian foreign ministry seems to have been a deciding factor. Prince Adam Czartoryski became foreign minister in 1804 and perceived France as the great detractor in European affairs. His personal friendship with Alexander gave him the influence necessary to bring increasing Russian pressure upon Frederick William III.[42] Alexander concluded that Prussia would not ally against France without prodding, and determined that he should approach the Prussian king, seeking to assure him that Russia would support Prussian resolve to defend north German neutrality—in other words, prevent further French violations.

Diplomatic maneuvering continued into the autumn of 1803 with little luck in moving the rock that was the king of Prussia. The March 1804 kidnapping of the duke d'Enghien by French troops in Baden, shook Frederick William and his court. Infuriated at the blatant violation of the integrity of the "Reich," he concluded a military convention with Russia in May 1804. It provided that continued French encroachments in north Germany would create a *causus foederis* between Prussia and Russia. It stipulated that France must suspend troop movements through Bentheim and Aremberg, as it violated their territorial sovereignty. Action against Denmark, Danish provinces, or Mecklenberg would not be tolerated. If Napoleon failed to comply, Prussia and Russia would act to preserve north German neutrality. Denmark, Saxony, and the princes of the north would be invited to join the alliance. Alexander equated this to a coalition against France, whereas Frederick William III interpreted it as a guarantee of the *status quo*. Nonetheless, Alexander I and Czartoryski interpreted the convention as a step forward.[43] Unfortunately, the curious king of Sweden complicated this potential shift in Prussian policy.

Gustav IV Adolf passionately despised Napoleon. He often spoke ill of the French consul, and he was a committed enemy of the Revolution. His personal animosity, however, was tempered by Sweden's more immediate concerns with Britain and Russia. By 1801, after the dissolution of the League of Armed Neutrality, Gustav IV Adolf pursued a *rapprochement* with Britain and Russia. Settling affairs, the Swedish king actively entertained British overtures for an anti-French coalition. He found favor in London on this issue.[44] Henry Addington, prime minister since Pitt's resignation in 1801, was desperate for allies now because the extension of French power into north Germany and the subsequent commercial blockade became a strain on available forces. The months immediately following the Peace of Amiens led to a dramatic demobilization of the Royal Navy. Upon the commencement of hostilities, the Admiralty's resources were insufficient. More than fifty ships blockaded French ports from the Mediterranean to Holland, while an equal number were off to the Caribbean.[45] A Swedish alliance would put Gustav IV Adolf's Baltic fleet at England's disposal. When Pitt returned to office in the spring of 1804, he actively pursued a Swedish alliance with as much energy as he did that of Prussia and Russia.

Gustav Adolf's interests were greatly tempered by Swedish parliament. There was little desire in Stockholm to entangle Sweden in continental affairs. If the king wanted to crusade against France, he would need English subsidies. Subsidy negotiations with Britain lasted almost two years, and did not conclude until French armies were already across the Rhine in 1805.[46] Far from allowing the Swedish constitution to restrict royal policy, Gustav IV Adolf did everything in his power to encourage others to war with France. The invasion of Hanover brought the conflict closer to Swedish territory. Sweden's gateway to Germany was the city of Stralsund in Swedish-Pomerania. He proposed landing Russo-Swedish forces in Stralsund in coordination with an English force in Hanover. To this end Gustav IV Adolf proceeded to dispatch troops to Stralsund beginning in the summer of 1803 through the autumn of 1804. By the spring of 1805, the garrison of the city doubled to more than 6,000 men.[47]

In August 1804 the French representative in Stockholm was ordered out of the country and given a note in which Gustav IV Adolf referred to Napoleon as "Monsieur Buonaparte." As Napoleon announced to Europe his imminent elevation to Emperor of the French, the term *Monsieur* would not do. The news of the note and the expulsion were published subsequently in *Le Moniteur*, Napoleon's official newspaper in Paris. Deep concern registered in Berlin, as Frederick William III believed this would be interpreted by Napoleon as an act of war. In fact, he did, stating, "If his Royal Majesty wants war! He shall have it!"[48] In order to preserve north German neutrality as it was in the autumn of 1804, Frederick William III threatened to invade Swedish-Pomerania to prevent the French from doing the same.[49]

If matters had not yet reached a critical level, in October French troops entered Hamburg and arrested the British consul George Rumbold. The violation of Hamburg's sovereignty was clearly a *causus foederis* as stated in the Russo-Prussian Convention.[50] Karl August von Hardenberg, the new Prussian foreign minister, relayed to Alopeus that after a prolonged debate with the king and the duke of Brunswick, the commander in chief of the Prussian army, no action would be taken. Instead, Frederick William III wrote Napoleon, strenuously protesting the illegal act. Within a month's time Rumbold was released. Frederick William claimed victory and believed activation of the convention was no longer necessary.[51]

The abduction and execution of the duke d'Enghien and Rumbold's arrest did enormous damage to Napoleon's relations with the north German princes. Frederick August, the elector of Saxony, was not greatly disturbed by the occupation of Hanover. He accepted it within the context of Napoleon's war with England. The violations of Baden and Hamburg, however, were perceived as blatant disregard for German territorial sovereignty.[52] Wilhelm I, elector of Hesse-Cassel, and Ludwig X, Landgraf of Hesse-Darmstadt, did not attend a meeting between the German princes and Napoleon during his extended visit to Mainz at the end of September. Both dispatched their sons, claiming illness, but these were convenient excuses to avoid having to confront the soon-to-be French emperor.[53]

Frustration with Napoleon and Frederick William registered in Russia. Alexander dispatched General Baron Winzingerode to Berlin on a special mission to determine Prussia's reaction to a war between Russia and France.[54] In October 1804, the same month Rumbold was accosted, Austria and Russia concluded a preliminary military convention against France.[55] Although Russia and England continued to negotiate terms of a military alliance, it was understood that Alexander meant war if Napoleon's expansionist policies and violation of agreements did not desist. Winzingerode arrived in January 1805 and remained in Berlin through March. Shortly after his arrival he accurately assessed that, "[T]hey [Prussia] will never depart from their neutrality." Only threats, he advised, may stir the Prussian monarch from his intransigence.[56]

CHAPTER SIX

AUSTRIA, ITALY, AND THE MEDITERRANEAN

FROM THE MOMENT ALEXANDER I assumed the throne, Addington worked desperately to forge a new Anglo-Russian coalition. Napoleon's activities in north Germany led the Tsar and his ministers to pursue a policy of containment. After May 1803, however, England was at war with France and needed more than an agreement in principle. A Russian alliance was insufficient to conduct a war with France if Prussia and Austria remained neutral. The two powers could do no more than wage war on the peripheries of Europe. Frederick William's odd interpretation of north German neutrality prevented any significant joint military operations in northern Europe, except Holland. The humiliating Anglo-Russian defeat in the Netherlands in 1799 questioned further logic in attempting this a second time without full Prussian participation. In the Mediterranean, Russia possessed limited military power and could do no more, perhaps, than conduct minor operations in southern Italy. Austria was the key.

Habsburg engagement in an anti-French coalition allowed a sizeable Russian army to move into central Europe during the War of the Second Coalition. A Russian army under General Suvarov advanced through Austria and successfully overran French forces in Italy. A Russian corps in Switzerland further threatened French positions in the Alpine cantons.[1] In 1803 little doubt existed in London and St. Petersburg that, without Prussian support, Vienna was critical to waging a broader war against France. Unfortunately, convincing Emperor Francis II was almost as difficult as Frederick William III, but for different reasons.

The Habsburg monarchy was the great bulwark against Revolutionary expansion, but its decade-long conflict with France drained its economic resources and armed forces. The Peace of Lunéville revised the dynasty's possessions in Germany at the expense of its interests in Italy. Habsburg control of

Lombardy, Modena, and Tuscany was abandoned in exchange for German concessions.[2] Unlike the Peace of Amiens (an expediency in the face of stalemate), the Austrians reluctantly, but willingly accepted French terms concluding their role in the Second Coalition. Since the sixteenth century the kingdom of Piedmont-Sardinia formed a buffer between France and Austria in northern Italy. The Franco-Piedmontese alliance that included the military occupation and integration of the Italian kingdom eliminated the buffer. Austria was granted Venetia and its associated territories along the Dalmatian coast as fair compensation. Venice was the new buffer. French forces could stage out of the Cisalpine Republic, as opposed to southern France. This placed Austria in a precarious position as the dynasty's *Erblande* (inherited lands) in the Tyrol was now juxtaposed to the French satellite republics in Italy.

Even if Austria desired to revise Lunéville by force of arms, the monarchy's army was in poor shape. Archduke Charles, the emperor's brother, headed the *Hofkriegsrat*, the Imperial war council. His appointment in 1801 resulted from his significant victories over French armies in Germany in 1796 and 1799. Although he could not restore order to the shattered Austrian army in Italy in 1797 and failed to dislodge a French army from Zurich in 1799, his military reputation led to his appointment. Charles was younger, more intelligent, and more capable than Francis. A certain amount of sibling rivalry pervaded their relationship. Francis relied on Charles to set things right after the disaster of Austrian arms in 1800.[3] Many older and more experienced generals resented Charles's elevation to the War Ministry and looked upon his plans to overhaul the army with suspicion.

The archduke pursued extensive administrative, organizational, and tactical reforms beginning in January 1801.[4] The totality of Charles's reforms precluded Austria from military commitments for some time. Even if Charles was inclined to advise joining a coalition against France, which he was not, losses incurred necessitated recruitment and training of tens of thousands of soldiers. Indeed, the war had led the monarchy to the brink of bankruptcy. Peace allowed the emperor to reduce military expenditure, but Charles constantly argued that reconstruction of the army did not come cheap. Austrian military outlay for 1801, the last year of the war, was 87,371,000 gulden. In 1802, it was halved to 45,377,000 gulden and reduced to 35,902,000 gulden in 1803.[5] Resistance to recruitment and expenditure came from all quarters. The Hungarians chafed at Charles's requests for recruits and the funds to train them.[6]

Few in Austria were talking of war with France in 1803. Charles's supporters dominated the Viennese court and advocated neutrality as expediency. The archduke's detractors often portrayed his faction as the "peace party," but this label should not mislead one. The army counted 83,000 men in 1803, with an additional 25,000 to be recruited.[7] Considering that soldiers were not properly trained and equipped, funds were unavailable, and the archduke's reforms existed only on paper, the thought of war was abhorrent to Charles. Only two factors kept the ethnically and nationally diverse monarchy together: loyalty to the Emperor, and the army. The former was preferred, but the latter necessary if the other was wanting. The Austrian army could not be sacrificed because it was directly tied to the dynasty's ability to control its numerous and distinct possessions.

The military leadership discouraged war, but Count Ludwig Cobenzl, the Austrian vice-chancellor, and Cabinet Minister Franz Colloredo entertained ideas of engaging Russia in an anti-French alliance. In November 1803 he instructed Count Phillip Stadion, ambassador to Russia, to explore negotiations. Charles distrusted Russia's military leadership. They had abandoned Austria in the field in 1799. He blamed the withdrawal of the Russian army from Switzerland for his failure to take Zurich. He did everything in his power to disabuse his brother of any notions of it. The struggle for control of Austrian foreign policy continued for more than a year.[8]

Cobenzl wanted to examine a new Austro-Russian alliance, but there was hesitation on Russia's part. Prior to the rupture of Amiens, harsh feelings remained. Alexander's negotiations with Napoleon and the German princes in 1802 were seen as an attempt to undermine Austrian influence in the Holy Roman Empire. The Russians, for that matter, were horribly upset that Emperor Francis did not do more to limit Napoleon's territorial acquisitions in Italy, particularly Piedmont-Sardinia.[9] In June 1803 Sir Arthur Paget, the British ambassador in Vienna, noted that although Cobenzl sought improved relations, Russian response to Austrian overtures had been "uniformly received with the most discouraging coldness and indifference."[10] By the autumn of 1803 Cobenzl found Voronstov, his Russian counterpart, more amenable to reviving the military relationship between their empires.

During the course of 1803, Napoleon consolidated his influence in Germany, Switzerland, and Italy while Vienna observed. He introduced French forces into Switzerland to settle the disputes among the cantons. The product was the Act of Mediation, which established a federal constitution for Switzerland with France as its guarantor.[11] On the face of it the agreement can be viewed as an extension of French power into Switzerland. It certainly was that; however, it also insured Switzerland would not become a viable theater of war as it had been in 1799. Nine months later, after the collapse of Amiens, France and Switzerland entered into a defensive military alliance, activated upon the invasion of either state by a foreign power. The Swiss cantons, whose forces were established at 15,000 troops by the Act of Mediation, were required to contribute 8,000 men if requested, and the cantons were committed to preventing their territory from being used by enemies of France as an invasion route.[12]

Of all Napoleon's policies, none agitated, disturbed, and angered Vienna more than his mucking about in Italy. One third of the articles of the Peace of

Lunéville addressed the Italian states. The Habsburgs renounced their familial possessions in Modena, Liguria, and Tuscany, and recognized the Cisalpine Republic, a French satellite state. In return, France recognized Austrian acquisition of the Venetian republic and its Adriatic holdings as compensation. Napoleon also pledged that the Cisalpine and Ligurian republics would be independent of France.[13] Within a year of Lunéville, however, Napoleon restructured the Cisalpine Republic, annexed the Kingdom of Piedmont, and integrated the Ligurian Republic into the French military system. He concluded a peace treaty with the Kingdom of the Two Sicilies (Naples), and signed an agreement with Spain to exchange Parma for Tuscany.[14] Indeed, between 1801 and 1803, Napoleon managed to exclude the Habsburg dynasty from the peninsula. He achieved a centuries-long objective of French monarchical policy.

France and Spain came to terms concerning the future of the Bourbon dynasty in Italy. The Treaty of Aranjuez in March 1801 exchanged the Bourbon Duchy of Parma for the soon-to-be-vacated Habsburg grand-duchy of Tuscany. Under the terms of the agreement, the duke of Parma would renounce his claims to his state and his son would be granted Tuscany as compensation.[15] The duke of Parma was married to one of the Carlos IV's daughters; therefore, Napoleon greatly appreciated the Spanish king's support. Although Carlos IV willingly agreed to the terms, no one consulted the duke of Parma until after the treaty was signed. He was not inclined to accede to the terms, thus, the treaty of Aranjuez was held in abatement. The duke of Parma had the good fortune to die in 1803, and his son accepted his stepfather's provisions. In return for his commitment, the grand-duchy of Tuscany was transformed into the kingdom of Etruria.[16]

In 1803 the French strategic situation in Italy was reminiscent of the decades preceding the Revolution. The Bourbon-Habsburg alliance in the 1750s began almost four decades of unprecedented cooperation between the two continental dynasties. England was cut-off from the peninsula during the Seven Years' War and the American Revolution. The combined influence of Bourbon France, Bourbon Spain, and the Habsburgs removed any notion among their extended families sitting on the myriad of Italian thrones, of siding with England in these conflicts. The French acquisition of Corsica in 1768 further weakened Britain's position in the central Mediterranean. This challenge to British naval supremacy culminated in the siege of Gibraltar in 1782.[17] French Bourbon influence in Italy reached its height in the 1770s with the triple marriage between Louis XVI's sister and two brothers and a son and two daughters of Victor Amadeus III, king of Piedmont-Sardinia.[18]

The events of the Revolution did not alter the Italian princes' perspective on their involvement in a general European conflict. The close association of the Bourbon and Savoyard (Piedmontese) houses made Turin, the capital of Piedmont, a center of counterrevolutionary activity. War came to Italy courtesy of French armies in 1792, but only on a limited scale. French threats in 1791 compelled Piedmont to ask the Bourbon princes in Turin to leave in order to avoid being drawn into the conflict. In an attempt to compensate for humiliating defeats in Belgium at the hands of Habsburg forces, however, the Revolutionary government authorized offensive operations against the kingdom of Piedmont-Sardinia in September 1792, with the intention of grabbing the duchy of Savoy and the county of Nice, whose inhabitants were largely ethnic French.

The opening of the Italian front did not immediately result in the commitment of the Italian princes to the defense of the peninsula. Most believed as long as Piedmont held the Alpine gates Italy was safeguarded against French invasion. Austria lacked sufficient forces to conduct a joint offensive across the Italian Alps. Their primary concern was holding Belgium and the Rhine. Scant forces existed to assist in Piedmontese defense, let alone to conduct offensive operations. Forty years earlier, many of the Italian princes willingly accepted a treaty providing for collective security of the Italian peninsula. This was relatively painless, as it occurred in the midst of the Bourbon-Habsburg alliance. The French invasion in 1792 led Victor Amadeus III to promote the resurrection of the Italian League, but jealousy among the princes prevented them from acceding to the agreement.[19] In 1793, when French troops invaded Genoa despite the republic's neutrality, Victor Amadeus again called upon the Italian princes. The Republic of Venice rejected his plea, as did the Neapolitan court. In the case of the former, its proximity to Austria and its distance from Piedmont provided the Venetian leadership with a false sense of security. Similarly, the Habsburgs played a double game by trying to negotiate separate agreements with the Italian states in order to prevent Piedmont from becoming too influential in the peninsula.[20] Venice held its neutral course and Naples entertained Austrian and British negotiations.

France was unable to break across the Alpine passes, and the Austro-Piedmontese line held through 1794. The following year French occupation of Genoa created greater opportunities and placed the Piedmontese in a strategic dilemma, forcing them to extend their line to cover the Ligurian passes to their south. Always wary of Austrian duplicity, Victor Amadeus III was compelled to accept an expanded Austrian auxiliary corps. At the same time 18,000 Neapolitan troops were committed as Austria concluded an agreement with Ferdinand IV.[21] The Alps held through 1795, although French pressure increased considerably. Diplomatic opportunity presented itself that year when Spain joined the Peace of Basel. Carlos IV offered to mediate between France and the respective Italian states. The French hoped to separate the Italian princes from their Austrian alliance, but were ultimately unsuccessful.[22]

It was not until 1796 that there was any dramatic alteration to the situation in Italy. General Napoleon Bonaparte's lightning offensive in April shattered the Austro-Piedmontese army and forced King Victor Amadeus III to sign the Armistice of Cherasco. Beyond separating Piedmont from the First Coalition, the king turned on his former allies providing troops and supplies to the French.[23] Napoleon's campaign changed the equation in Italy. Italian princes defined the French war in terms of past wars. Limited operations in the north conducted over the course of several years resulted in limited territorial exchanges. Furthermore, the general peace that existed in the peninsula for the previous half-century meant the princes maintained much smaller and leaner armies. In short, the Italian rulers left the defense of the peninsula to the Bourbons and Habsburgs. Napoleon's rapid conquest of Piedmont and then much of the peninsula created a revolution in Italian geo-politics.

Italy's strategic significance lay in its geographic position in the Mediterranean, and the fact that it bordered Austria. The Peace of Basel eliminated Spain and northern Germany as theaters of war and the French War Ministry could redeploy forces accordingly. With Austrian armies in southern Germany and northern Italy, Lazare Carnot, French minister of war, called for joint offensives by several armies in Germany and Italy, which would eventually link up in the Tyrol.[24] Attempts to accomplish this in 1795 failed because resources were lacking. By the time Napoleon took command of the Army of Italy its numbers were quite meager, but it was substantially reinforced during the course of operations. Napoleon invaded Piedmont in April 1796, with fewer than 40,000 men, but had 100,000 men in Italy a year later.

Napoleon established French dominance in the peninsula for the next two decades. Nowhere was his influence greater than in northern Italy. The Genoese and Piedmontese alliances allowed them some sense of autonomy throughout the conflict, but Napoleon and the Revolutionary government were determined to eliminate Habsburg control in Lombardy, Tuscany, and Modena. The French government instructed Napoleon to extend his arm into the Papal States. As Italy was not the primary theater of war, Napoleon's ability to accomplish all while deflecting Austrian counterattacks through the autumn of 1796 was severely hampered by a lack of troops.[25]

Napoleon consolidated French political power in Lombardy with the creation of the Cisalpine Republic in May. At the end of December, Modena, Parma, and the papal territory of the Romagna were organized into the Cispadane Republic. Austro-Russian armies overran both republics during the War of the Second Coalition. Upon Napoleon's return to Italy as first consul in 1800, he defeated an Austrian army at Marengo and restored French control in northern Italy. The two republics were united into an enlarged Cisalpine Republic, and a nascent Italian army was formed to augment French military presence in the peninsula.[26]

In January 1802 Napoleon convened an assembly of the Cisalpine political leadership at Lyon. At the *Consulte* of Lyon, the groundwork was laid for the new Italian republic. "Invaded by enemy armies," Napoleon exclaimed, "your existence appeared no longer possible, when the people of France, for a second time, chased by force of arms, your enemies from your land." He proclaimed, "Composed of six different states, you have been reunited under a single constitution. . . . Your people have only regional laws; they must create general laws."[27] Francesco Melzi d'Eril, a Milanese, presided over the state as vice president, while Napoleon accepted his nomination as the republic's president.[28] This clearly violated the provision in the Lunéville accord that expressly guaranteed the separation of the Italian Republic from France. Piedmont's fate was decided that year, too, when Napoleon annexed it in September.

Austria was in no position to challenge Napoleon's blatant disregard for the treaty as Archduke Charles had only begun his extensive military reforms. Habsburg attention focused on the German states. The primacy of constitutional reorganization of the Holy Roman Empire was foremost on the emperor's mind. Italy was abandoned to the French. Tsar Alexander I demanded fair compensation for Piedmont-Sardinia. Napoleon refused, and Alexander failed to recognize annexation, but nothing more.[29]

Concomitant with the restructuring of the Italian Republic, Napoleon concluded a concordat with Pope Pius VII. The agreement restored the Catholic Church in France, and it gave Napoleon enormous legitimacy among conservative Italians. Napoleon's alliance with Spain and their role as mediator between France and the papacy was critical to presenting Napoleon as something other than a revolutionary. At a time when secularization of church lands in Germany became policy not only for the Protestant princes in the north but the Habsburgs as well, Napoleon appeared willing to accept the church as a significant religious institution in France: not the "official religion," but the religion of the majority.[30]

Napoleon's papal coup did much to move along relations with the Kingdom of the Two Sicilies. The southern Italian kingdom was the most problematic of states in the peninsula. Its possessed tremendous strategic significance as it jutted into the central Mediterranean. Unable to seize the kingdom in 1797, Ferdinand IV's participation in the Second Coalition opened the door to a French invasion. Napoleon experienced firsthand the difficulty of coordinating operations against Austria from northern Italy, while having to contend with a hostile Neapolitan kingdom. The Neapolitan army came to the aid of the small papal army in 1796 when the Austrians decided to abandon Italy in order to defend against Napoleon's army in Venetia. Francis II, however, dispatched Karl Lieberich von Mack to Naples to direct their campaign in central Italy.

At the age of forty-six, Karl von Mack's military career spanned a quarter century in Habsburg service. A commoner by birth, he began his military career as a cavalry trooper, but during the Austro-Turkish war of 1787–1788 he was awarded the Order of Maria Theresa for bravery. Ennobled and an officer, Mack served as an adjutant until the wars of the Revolution. Thereafter he became a staff officer. During the campaigns in Belgium in 1792–1793, Mack served on the duke of Coburg's staff, along with the Archduke Charles, then only 21. In 1797 he was quartermaster general of the Austrian army on the Rhine.[31] Mack possessed a considerable reputation in Austria. His writings on war reflected the preponderance of science and rationalism, a hallmark of the eighteenth century.[32] An accomplished officer well known for his meticulousness, Francis believed he was the person to oversee Neapolitan operations.

By the time Mack arrived in Naples in December 1797, Ferdinand IV had already concluded a peace agreement with France.[33] The king later betrayed the treaty and joined the Second Coalition in 1798, believing Mack's presence and Austrian assurances guaranteed their strategic cooperation in Italy.[34] Plans were made in Vienna for a Neapolitan offensive to coincide with an Austro-Russian attack in the Po valley. Admiral Horatio Nelson met with Mack and the Neapolitan monarch prior to the campaign. His assessment of the Austrian general was not flattering. He referred to Mack as the "general who does not move without five carriages."[35] Unfortunately, timing was not one of Mack's strengths. He initiated his operations at the end of November 1798, while the Austro-Russian armies could not take the field until the spring of 1799. This lack of timing would be characteristic of the Austrian general.

> Regarded as "the most scientific soldier" in Europe, Mack . . . espoused the fashionable system of strategy in which the main objective was not the destruction of the enemy army but control of certain topographical points. He designed intricate offensive movements by divergent columns, though he often underrated his opponent's reaction and was completely lost when his complicated schemes did not work out.[36]

Dividing his forces on both sides of the Apennines and advancing in separate columns, Mack intended on seizing Rome in a *coup de main* and advancing rapidly upon Livourno. The right wing of the Neapolitan army would move on Ancona and then Modena and Parma. Mack's offensive began at the end of November 1798 and did not get further than Rome. The French counteroffensive made quick work of Mack's divided army, and by January 1799 the Neapolitan offensive was reduced piecemeal. In full retreat less than a month after taking the field, Mack found himself besieged in Capua by superior French forces. The city's population, accompanied by disgruntled soldiers and officers, blamed Mack for the disaster and compelled him to flee the city. He surrendered to the French on 16 January and spent two years as a French prisoner.[37]

French conquest of southern Italy in 1799 was short-lived. Popular insurrection, guerrilla war, and British support resulted in the collapse of

French control by late 1799. Napoleon's return to Italy the following year and his need to allocate military resources prudently resulted in negotiations with Ferdinand IV. Fortune favored Napoleon as the conclusion of Lunéville in February 1801 removed any notion of Austrian support for the Bourbons of Naples. Similarly, Napoleon's relationship with the Spanish Bourbons removed any assistance from that quarter. Ferdinand found himself without a continental ally. Although England remained steadfast, its paltry forces in the Mediterranean were focused on eliminating the French army in Egypt and could not aid Naples.

Napoleon did not trust the Neapolitan king or his queen Marie Caroline. They signed a peace accord with France in 1796 only to break it in 1798. Napoleon looked to the intercession of the king of Spain to smooth relations. Ferdinand IV of Naples was brother to Carlos IV of Spain. Queen Marie Caroline was the sister of Marie Antoinette, the former queen of France, and therefore decidedly ill-disposed to France. Prince Ferdinand, son of Carlos IV married Maria Antonia, the daughter of the Neapolitan king. This family affair, however, did not seal the relationship between the two states. The Spanish king had little influence on his brother. The Treaty of Aranjuez (signed on 28 March 1801), which gave Tuscany to the Bourbons of Parma, did, however, influence Neapolitan negotiations. On 23 March, representatives of France and the kingdom of the Two Sicilies concluded the Treaty of Florence.[38]

More than a conventional agreement, the treaty provided Napoleon with concrete guarantees of Neapolitan sincerity. Of course, the only means by which Napoleon could be guaranteed this honest desire to abide by the agreement was through French military presence. Secret articles provided for French troops to embark from Otranto and Brindisi for Egypt. It called for the maintenance of 3,000 French troops in Pescara and required Naples to close its ports to English shipping. General Nicholas Soult, with 15,000 troops, entered the kingdom in May, occupying Apulia and levying 425,000 francs.[39] Napoleon made clear to Soult that "[W]e are currently sincerely reconciled with the King of Naples."[40]

After the Peace of Amiens French forces withdrew from the Neapolitan kingdom. With the outbreak of war in May 1803, however, Napoleon invoked the Treaty of Florence, and General Gouvion St. Cyr entered the kingdom once more at the head of 18,000 men and collected 1 million francs to sustain his forces.[41] Ferdinand and Marie Caroline had no recourse but to accept French occupation of their Adriatic ports. They did discuss, however, their options with the new English ambassador to Naples, Hugh Elliot. Napoleon thought little of the Neapolitan king due to his reliance on Sir John Acton, an English ex-patriot who served as the first minister to Ferdinand IV. There was good reason for Napoleon's concern as Acton believed the kingdom more secure with Britain than France. Yet, under the circumstances only discrete discussions could be held. Preparations were made to evacuate the royal family to Sicily if necessary.[42]

Addington's decision to abrogate Amiens by refusing to abandon Malta was done with Italy specifically in mind. Although French forces were removed from Egypt in 1801 and Soult withdrew his troops from Naples in 1802, England could ill-afford to hand Malta to France. Trust was lacking among the parties and each had legitimate reasons to distrust the other. From Malta the British fleet could watch Toulon. Without it there could be no effective blockade with Gibraltar as the only base of operations. Malta allowed the British to keep close contact with Naples, and, under the worst circumstance, secure Sicily from French invasion.[43]

Admiral Horatio Nelson commanded the Mediterranean station. He won his promotion at the Battle of Cape St. Vincent and affirmed it with a spectacular victory over the French at Aboukir Bay. His daring and insubordinate attack on Copenhagen in 1801 placed him among England's greatest naval commanders. The fact that he was posted to the Mediterranean indicated the admiralty's awareness of England's precarious position there.[44] Far from simply containing the French fleet at Toulon and the substantial French presence in southern Italy, Nelson faced the possibility of a French expedition to Greece. To add to the admiral's difficulties, Tsar Alexander gradually reinforced the Russian squadron at Corfu, ostensibly to counter French threats to Greece.[45]

Anglo-Russian relations were strained despite their common concerns. Napoleon initially proposed to give Malta to Russia in lieu of Britain returning it to France. Napoleon's desire to deny England the naval base was paramount to his plans in the Mediterranean. He knew his offer to the Tsar would not be well received in London and used it as a wedge to separate the two powers. Britain needed Malta to control the central Mediterranean, to counter French power in Italy, and to project itself into the eastern Mediterranean. One could not do that from Gibraltar.[46]

Since his exit from Egypt in 1799, Napoleon had not forgotten the far-flung extremity of the French Republic. When the British expedition under General Abercromby defeated the French under General Menou at Alexandria in 1801, capturing the former Turkish province, the first consul did not give up hope that the French would return some day. On 25 June 1802, three months following the Peace of Amiens, Napoleon and Sultan Selim III came to terms. The treaty ended hostilities and normalized relations between the French Republic and the Ottoman Empire, but more importantly it permitted French merchant ships access to the Black Sea.[47]

Six months after the accord the new French ambassador, General Guillaume Brune, arrived in Constantinople. He was a seasoned Revolutionary veteran and his recent military exploits made him the logical choice for the post. British and Russian influence at the Ottoman court remained substantial even after peace with France. Brune commanded the French army in Holland during the War of the Second Coalition, and soundly defeated the Anglo-Russian expeditionary forces there in 1799. Napoleon hoped Brune would restore French prestige in the Turkish capital. There was a long history of cooperative relations between the two states since the seventeenth century. War between the French Republic and the Ottoman Empire had been an anomaly.[48]

Although Brune's embassy seemed successful during his first months in Constantinople, Napoleon hedged his bets. War with England was on the horizon and the first consul studied his options in the Mediterranean. Napoleon commissioned General Horace Sebastiani to assess the military situation in Egypt and determine to what extent British forces remained. Napoleon further directed Sebastiani to ascertain the strength of Turkish forces at Jaffa and Jerusalem.[49] Similarly, he looked to extending French influence to Corfu and Greece. Admiral Decrès received orders in February to proceed with clandestine armaments for the Greeks in Corfu and the Peloponnese.[50] British agents disclosed the report to Selim III, who then demanded an explanation. Brune did his best to smooth the waters, but this was a severe blow to his initial *raproachment* with the Turks. Relations cooled and did not improve until Napoleon sat in Vienna in December 1805.

The purpose of French activity in Corfu and Greece was not exclusively to undermine Turkish power in the Balkans. Italy, being a peninsula, was vulnerable to a British seaborne attack. Corfu's geographic position across the straits of Otranto made it strategically important for controlling the Adriatic. Napoleon said as much six years earlier in 1797.[51] Russia gained control of the island in 1802, and they maintained there a naval squadron and small garrison. Tsar Alexander was more interested in the island's position vis-à-vis Greece and the Balkans than Italy.

Napoleon used Italy to project his power into the Balkans and the Mediterranean at the expense of Britain and Russia. The Neapolitan ports in Apulia were occupied, and Ancona in the Papal States received a French garrison. The French Army of Italy was augmented by the expansion of the republic's Italian army. At the time of the *Consulte of Lyon* the army consisted of 9,000 men. By the collapse of Amiens, it reached 22,000. French forces in Italy were in equal number, but increased through 1805 to 60,000 men.[52] This was adequate to keep the peninsula safe from British raids out of Malta, but not necessarily enough to defend it from a determined Austrian assault.

Napoleon exuded hubris. In 1804 the duke d'Enghien's kidnapping followed by Napoleon's elevation to Emperor of the French in May caused severe consternation in Vienna. Despite Charles's efforts to temper the war party, Francis was moved by Napoleon's bold disregard for the integrity of the *Reich* and his illegitimate assumption of an Imperial title. Nonetheless, this did not translate into Austrian participation in a coalition against France.

There remained a number of unresolved issues among Russia, Britain, and Austria that precluded any formal agreement.

Francis II, Holy Roman Emperor, took the title Francis I, Emperor of Austria, in the summer of 1804. The rationale lay not in the possession of two Imperial crowns, but to preserve an Imperial title. It was an acknowledgement that the days of the *Reich* were numbered. Francis wanted to retain equal billing with Tsar Alexander, whom he did not entirely trust. Russia played a significant role in territorial redistribution of the Empire after Lunéville and continued this role through 1804. It was of great annoyance and concern to Francis. The Russo-Prussian convention in May appeared from Vienna's view another example of Alexander's encroachment in Germany, and it brought Prussia into Alexander's orbit. It is clear that this was not how it was perceived in Berlin, but certainly there was some element of truth to it in St. Petersburg. This, above all, tempered Austria's decision to rush headlong into a coalition against France, despite Napoleon's violations of the integrity of German states.[53]

Cobenzl and Colloredo did not interpret events similarly. They carried out quiet discussions with Russia. At the end of May Alexander proposed an alliance in which Russia would contribute 150,000 soldiers. Furthermore, Austria would receive territorial compensation in Italy.[54] This was more than the vice-chancellor intended, but Alexander wanted action. Cobenzl gave no indication to the English ambassador at Vienna, Sir Arthur Paget, that negotiations were at that level of involvement. Paget reported to Lord Hawkebury, the foreign minister, "[T]he fact is that the very idea of war so appals [*sic.*] the senses of the Government," that they have no clear direction on policy vis-à-vis France.[55] Archduke Charles retained the emperor's confidence, although it was beginning to wane.

Through the summer of 1804, Cobenzl and Colloredo moved quickly and subtly to undermine Archduke Charles's authority in the War Ministry. They removed his two most trusted advisers, Count Duka and General Fassbender. The latter was convinced to join the vice-chancellor and abandon the archduke. Quartermaster-general Mack replaced the former. Mack was an expedient, but he was also a known quantity. The Archduke Charles met Mack first in 1791, and he was impressed with Mack's observations of the art of war. The general became one of Charles's most important military influences.[56] Since leaving Italy, Mack spent 1801 through 1804 working in military administration. Emperor Francis gradually perceived his brother's resistance to war as a significant failing, since the purpose of entrusting him with wide-ranging powers over the armed forces was to prepare for war.[57] As the war party gained momentum in Vienna and a number of disgruntled generals were unimpressed with Charles's reforms, Mack appeared the likely and logical successor. He favored war with France, he was respected by the archduke, and he wrote extensively of military reforms as well.

In the autumn, a frustrated Tsar Alexander I demanded a definitive response from Francis concerning his spring proposal. Austrian indecision compounded Alexander's failure to move Frederick William III.[58] Cobenzl convinced the Emperor to disregard his brother's arguments. Austria must commit itself to an alliance. Francis acceded to Cobenzl, and on 6 November 1804 an Austro-Russian convention was concluded. The two emperors pledged to contain Napoleon's ambitions and compel him to withdraw troops from territories that were declared off-limits by previous treaties. They promised to protect the Ottoman Empire from French threat and demand an indemnity for the king of Piedmont-Sardinia. Alexander and Francis called upon Napoleon to abandon the Kingdom of Two Sicilies and conform to earlier arrangements regarding Italy. In secret articles Alexander gave assurances that Russia would press England for subsidies to underwrite Habsburg military expenditure. Finally, both agreed that an army of observation should be deployed to insure Prussia's pacific nature.[59] There remained some question in Vienna and St. Petersburg regarding Frederick William's true intentions.

The Austro-Russian convention did not formally establish the Third Coalition against France. England was not party to it, and Alexander had yet to come to his own terms with Great Britain. This agreement did provide Alexander with a partner more willing than Prussia. Its signing came at the time of the Rumbold affair, and by November Alexander's initial enthusiasm related to the Russo-Prussian convention was dashed. News of Vienna's acceptance and participation in many ways reduced the Tsar's need for Prussia.

The Archduke Charles lost the battle for Austrian foreign policy. In December he told Cobenzl that it would take six months to mobilize the army. Mack, who was a "can do" man, told the emperor that he would have the army ready in less time. In January 1805, Francis removed Charles as head of the *Hofkriegsrat*, although the archduke remained war minister. Charles, however, no longer held the prominent position he had held three years earlier. Mack was elevated to quartermaster-general and retained the emperor's ear. Cobenzl and Colloredo had won. Austria prepared for war, and Francis informed Charles he had an important role to play in the coming conflict.[60]

There were few regrets at court, as Napoleon's actions in May 1804 made it clear to most in Vienna that war was the only answer. Napoleon took the Iron Crown of Lombardy in the Duomo of Milan and united it with his Imperial title. For the first time since Charlemagne France and Italy were one. Napoleon knew this was expressly prohibited according to Lunéville, but nonetheless it was done. Charles resigned himself to doing all that he could to influence war plans and prepare for a war he did not believe Austria could win.

CHAPTER SEVEN

THE THIRD COALITION

MONEY WAS THE ORDER OF THE DAY. For all the talk of war with France, the formation of a coalition depended upon English subsidies. Russia was determined to limit Napoleon's ambitions in Europe, but they disagreed with England on two issues: the first was money, the second was Malta. The former was eventually overcome, while the latter became an obstacle. At the end of June 1804, Pitt proposed Russia dangle before Austria a carrot of £2–2.5 million. If Prussia could be convinced, they would receive no more than £1 million, while Saxony and Sweden would have to accept £500,000.[1] Hugh Elliott, the English ambassador to Naples, was authorized to offer £150,000 per annum for their adhesion to an anti-French coalition.[2]

Britain spent enormous sums on subsidies during the wars of the Revolution. Most states had yet to pay their war debts. England was forced to suspend specie payments and institute an income tax during the War of the Second Coalition. The outbreak of war in 1803 did not improve Britain's financial situation. The annual deficit increased from £9.43 million in 1803 to £17.25 million in 1805.[3] Pitt faced enormous resistance in Parliament to increasing available funds. He succeeded in securing permission to offer more, and ultimately paid the asking price of all powers involved. Cost, therefore, ran more than £2 million over what Pitt had set aside for an anti-French coalition.[4] These were, however, desperate times, and Napoleon's army was concentrated along the Channel coast. Though the Royal Navy had effectively blockaded the major Spanish and French ports, the threat that they could unite their fleets and enter the Channel was very real.

Napoleon laid the groundwork for an invasion in the weeks preceding the collapse of Amiens. On 14 June 1803, he issued orders for the establishment of six military camps along the French coast from Bayonne to Holland. Each camp would consist of a French corps composed of approximately 20,000 infantry and 2,000 cavalry, each with a substantial contingent of artillery. The corps at Bayonne was intended to defend the Atlantic coast from potential English raids, while the five other camps, Gand, Saint-Omer, Com-pèigne, Saint-Malo, and one in Holland at Utrecht, were the foundation of a future invasion force. The largest of the camps was in Holland. There 18,000 French troops were joined by 12,000 Dutch.[5] The latter contingent formed part of Dutch military obligations.

Napoleon concluded a convention with the Dutch republic at the begin-ning of June. Although Holland was technically independent, French military occupation since 1795 made it de facto a French satellite. The Batavian Republic—its official name—pledged 16,000 men to their defense, while France promised 18,000 men. This was a generous offer, as that was the pre-cise number Napoleon intended on maintaining in Holland. The republic committed itself to providing five ships of the line, five frigates, and sufficient transport to carry 25,000 men. Furthermore, Holland agreed to construct 100 gunboats and 250 armed flatboats to transport horses and artillery for an invasion of England. All was to be prepared by December 1803.[6]

The Batavian Republic was already financially crippled by paying for the privilege of French military occupation. Dutch tax burdens related to Hol-land's obligations to France in 1803 were staggering. On average, the Dutch paid 64.25 francs per capita as compared to 15.18 francs paid by Frenchmen.[7] Dutch military expenditures returned to their pre-Amiens level, nearly dou-ble that of 1802. The national debt continued to rise through 1803 and there-after.[8] Dutch banking and merchant houses were the least pleased with the new Anglo-French war. Indeed, the fear that the war would have enormous consequences on Dutch trade was well founded. Although commerce with England was expressly prohibited, Dutch merchants were permitted to trade with the United States. As such, American merchants became the intermedi-aries between English and Dutch commerce and their respective commercial houses.[9]

The irony of Napoleon's fiscal and military demands on his allies was that he relied more on the Dutch for their naval contributions, while prefer-ring to seek Spanish financial subsidies. Holland hosted some of the greatest merchant and banking houses in Europe, rivaling those of England. Their wealth, however, had waned since 1788, and the nature of their financial strength was in stocks, bonds, and matters of high finance. Napoleon gener-ally rejected these as monetarily unsound.[10] His limited—relative to other demands—interest in Dutch subsidies was not in recognition of the weaken-ing Dutch economy, but of his general preference for hard currency. Spain had a navy, but, better yet, silver.

In his persistence to acquire specie, Napoleon's financial demands on Spain led to one of the most curious economic adventures. Upon the rupture of Amiens and Carlos IV's accession to the French subsidy treaty, notorious French financier George-Julien Ouvrard was sent on mission to Madrid to coordinate the transfer of Spanish funds to France. There he concocted a scheme to import Spanish silver accumulating in the Americas. He convinced Godoy and the Spanish monarch that through his contacts with banking houses in Amsterdam and England he could move the silver from Mexico to Holland using American ships. Facing enormous economic burdens related to the subsidy treaty, Carlos IV was all the more encouraged by Ouvrard's confidence in the project. The French financier would take a percentage, of course, for his services. Napoleon gave his blessing to the endeavor, as it would benefit France in the end.[11]

Ouvrard's participation in the *negotiants réunis*, a consortium of French financiers who underwrote the Bank of France, provided him with numerous contacts in the financial community. Ouvrard's years of business relations as a military contractor also involved him with a number of banking houses. Ouvrard approached Pierre Labouchère, a friend, financier, and partner at Hope & Company, a Dutch finance house. Labouchère began negotiations in earnest with the British bankers Baring Brothers. Baring secured permission for the silver imports from William Pitt in return for significant concessions from Spain. All of this occurred prior to the fall of 1804 when a state of war existed between the two states. English merchants, therefore, would be allowed to trade in Spanish American ports despite the reinstatement of the mercantilist policy of 1802.[12]

A seeming windfall for all involved, the complex mechanisms of political and financial agreements prohibited the movement of funds until 1806. The first shipments of silver did not arrive until that year. In any case, even if the plan succeeded, the only ones to benefit greatly were Ouvrard, the banking houses, and English merchants. France did receive some silver, but that ended rather quickly as the situation in Europe had changed dramatically and Napoleon no longer needed Spanish silver. He could draw on the coffers of the defeated.

Napoleon did not bank on Ouvrard's scheme. He never limited his ambitions, even in the face of fiscal realities. He prepared for the invasion of England through 1804 and into 1805. The French navy had experienced significant changes over the course of the past decade and a half. It stood at almost seventy ships of the line and sixty-five frigates in 1789, but was reduced dramatically by desertions, and plagued by political unrest and the loss of experienced senior officers due to their noble status. Despite the crises suffered through the first years of the Revolution, the navy experienced a substantial building and revitalization program in 1794–1795. Thereafter, it comprised eighty-eight ships of the line and seventy-four frigates. The reconstitution of French naval power enabled the Directory to pursue ambitious projects, such as the failed invasion of Ireland and Napoleon's expedition to Egypt in 1798.[13]

Admiral Horatio Nelson's stunning victory over the French Mediterranean fleet at Aboukir Bay severely damaged the overall strength of the

French navy. By 1805 Napoleon had no more than fifty ships of the line available. In December 1804, he delayed his invasion plans, deciding to send the Mediterranean fleet at Toulon to the West Indies. He ordered Admiral Villeneuve to sail when able, accompanied by an expeditionary force under General Lauriston. The squadron at Rochefort under Admiral Missiessy would join his squadron, carrying another division under General Lagrange. Together they would recapture Guyana, Surinam, Guadeloupe, Martinique, and Saint-Lucia. They were to reinforce French garrisons in Haiti and Santo Domingo. Once done, the combined fleet would sail for Rochefort to unite with the Brest fleet and sail into the Channel.[14] This was not the first time Napoleon was determined to recapture and reinforce French colonies in the Caribbean. Plans were originally issued in September, but they were forced by circumstances to be delayed.[15] Spain's entry into the conflict provided Napoleon with more ships and greater opportunities.

Tsar Alexander I tried in vain to prevent a rupture between England and Spain. Russia had more in common with Spain than England, particularly in regard to Mediterranean interests. The preservation of the Neapolitan Bourbons in the face of French military occupation was foremost on Alexander's mind. As British tensions rose after the signing of the Spanish subsidy treaty in October 1803, Czartoryski, Alexander's foreign minister, employed the Neapolitan ambassador to Spain as an intermediary. All of this came to naught through 1804. Despite Russian and Neapolitan attempts to prevent Spain from being drawn into the French sphere, Czartoryski concluded that French influence was ultimately greater than the Tsar's, and this ran counter to English interests. Alexander blamed England rather than Napoleon, as he perceived England's seizure of the Spanish treasure fleet as leaving Spain with absolutely no recourse but war.[16] This was frustrating, as Alexander's attempt to keep Spain from war failed at the same moment he had difficulty bringing Austria and Prussia into the coalition.

Tsar Alexander I could do no more than push for war by the autumn of 1804, but he knew all too well that Austrian interest in revising the Peace of Lunéville was tempered by their financial situation. The Archduke Charles used this as one of several excuses to avoid conflict, but with Cobenzl's victory over state policy, fiscal realities had to be addressed. The interested parties conducted separate negotiations. Certainly, Pitt hoped for a general discussion on the issue, but the Austrians and Russians purposely kept him in the dark. Sir Arthur Paget, English ambassador in Vienna, and Sir J.B. Warren, ambassador in St. Petersburg, had little information on negotiations between the two powers.[17] Both Russia and Austria formed a united front seeking to limit Pitt's ability to haggle.

Articles pertaining to English subsidies formed the basis of the separate and secret addenda to the preliminary Austro-Russian military convention of October 1804. The Russians were quite generous with English money, pledging to pursue £2 million in initial subsidies with an allotment of £4 million per annum for the duration of the war. This was amended in Vienna several weeks later when the Emperor Francis agreed to accept a lesser sum of £1.5 million initially, and £3 million per annum if England balked at the initial request, although Austria would accept as little as £4 million for the first year. Pitt originally offered £5 million for both Austria and Russia, although he eventually compromised by the summer of 1805.[18] Alexander asked for £1.2 million for Russia, but Austria needed much more.

Austria contributed approximately 235,000 troops in 1799, although it had originally pledged 300,000 to the Second Coalition.[19] Military expenditure exceeded 89 million gulden for that year, and more than 96 million gulden for 1800. England offered a loan of £3.6 million to offset costs, but subsidies did not exceed £1 million by 1800.[20] The Austrian army was substantially smaller in 1804, with military expenditures at almost one-third the level of 1799 and 1800. Russia desired that Austria put 250,000 men in the field.[21] This was improbable. Even if Austria tried to match their contributions in 1799, they would be fiscally pressed. It would require an increase in military expenditure at least four times the current level. State debt had reached significant proportions and taxes already reached critical levels.[22] British subsidies would aid mobilization and supply, but it would be woefully inadequate to make up the shortfall.

Then there was Sweden. King Gustav IV Adolf, perhaps more committed to a coalition against France than Tsar Alexander I, refused to consign his kingdom to the alliance without sufficient funds. Negotiations with Britain were long and arduous. Since 1772 the Rikstag (Parliament) controlled the Swedish monarchy's fiscal policy. Gustav IV Adolf's interest in involving Sweden in a European war ran counter to many in the estates, as he also quarreled with them over constitutional powers. He thus sought subsidies from England, which would allow him to mobilize the Swedish army, transport it to Swedish Pomerania, and maintain it on campaign in north Germany.[23] Sweden possessed fewer troops than Russia or Austria, yet its base in Stralsund opened up strategic possibilities in north Germany, which were of great interest to Britain.

Immediate discussions with the Swedish king involved the use of Stralsund as a forward operating base. British troops would be permitted use of the Baltic port to recruit and train troops under Swedish protection. Hanoverian troops who left for England in 1803, now titled the King's German Legion, would operate from Swedish Pomerania once Sweden formally declared war on France. Pitt pledged £60,000 for the use of Stralsund. Gustavus demanded £100,000–120,000. The king settled on the lesser amount, signing an agreement with England on 3 December 1804.[24]

The exorbitant price for Stralsund was nothing compared to the asking price for 20,000 to 25,000 Swedish troops. Russia and England conducted separate negotiations with the Swedish monarch. The Russians approached the subject as a strategic proposal, promising an auxiliary force of 15,000 men in addition to 10,000 British troops. The English inquired how much the good Swedish king would need to field his army. The standard English rate was £12 10s per man, but Gustavus demanded double.[25] It was far easier for Sweden and Russia to come to terms. A preliminary agreement signed on 14 January 1805 was followed in March by a formal treaty for cooperation in north Germany. Unfortunately, this arrangement hinged on England's acceptance of Gustavus's monetary demand.[26] All of this remained unsettled until the autumn of 1805 when armies were already on the march.

Pitt's difficulties were compounded by the conclusion of a Franco-Spanish military alliance on 4 January 1805. Although Pitt believed Spanish subsidies were the precursor to a Franco-Spanish coalition against England, he hoped negotiations with the continental powers would have borne fruit. As it stood, less than a year after Pitt returned as prime minister, the threat of an invasion loomed even greater. The Royal Navy was capable of containing France, but the addition of the Spanish fleet significantly stretched their resources. Despite England's great naval victories over both fleets in 1797 and 1798, respectively, combined they could potentially wrest control of the channel if the respective squadrons could slip the British blockades and unite.

That is precisely what happened in January. Missiessy escaped from Rochefort, and Villeneuve escaped a week later from Toulon. They headed for the West Indies in compliance with Napoleon's orders of December 1804. Villeneuve returned to Toulon shortly after his departure due to poor weather. Missiessy, however, reached Martinique on 20 February and proceeded to reinforce the French garrison in Santo Domingo. A British squadron under Admiral Cochrane pursued.[27] Villeneuve's failure to make for the Atlantic altered Napoleon's plans for the Indies, but considering the new alliance with Spain, opportunities abounded.

The Franco-Spanish convention committed Spain to providing twenty to twenty-nine ships of the line and 4,700 men by 20 March 1805. Napoleon announced he had thirty-eight ships of the line ranging from Toulon to Brest, not including the Dutch squadron at Texel. At Boulogne and its surrounding camps, 120,000 men and 25,000 horses were waiting to cross the Channel. Indeed, there was a further 30,000 at Texel and 25,000 at Brest, irrespective of the 13,000 troops dedicated to Villeneuve's and Missiessy's squadrons.[28] All totaled it was an impressive assemblage of men and ships. If the Spanish could put twenty-five ships to sea by March, Villeneuve could sortie successfully from Toulon and Missiessy return from the West Indies, Napoleon could potentially have a combined fleet of forty-two ships of the line to lift the British blockade of Brest. This would enable Admiral Ganteaume, with twenty-one ships at Brest, to sail out. Sixty-three ships then, might very well challenge the English for control of the Channel. These figures are quite ominous, but one has to consider the great number of variables required for it to work. In the meantime, Missiessy was in the Indies, Villeneuve at Toulon watched by Nelson, and the Spanish hardly ready to put to sea.

The fact that Pitt had such trouble bringing the continental powers into a coalition indicated that although Russia and Austria saw Napoleon as a growing problem that needed to be addressed, French military dispositions indicated his next move would be against England, and not in central Europe. Time was growing short for England, but not critical for Russia or Austria. It was more than this. The inability of Pitt's government to come to terms with any of the other powers was a consequence of Pitt's foreign policies during the War of the Second Coalition. The failure of the Anglo-Russian expedition to Holland, differing interests on the state of the Italian peninsula, and arguments with Austria were to blame for the eventual *denouément*, which led to the creation of the League of Armed Neutrality against England in 1801.[29] Although there was a general *rapprochement* with Sweden and Russia by 1803, there remained a distrust of England's ulterior motives. The Russians saw Addington's administration as relatively weak and ineffectual. Pitt's return in May 1804 did much to alter their perspective of England's commitment, but recalled the prime minister's direction of the war effort five years earlier.[30]

On 21 January 1805, Pitt proposed a framework for a treaty of alliance with Russia and Austria based upon the general principles the two continental powers agreed on earlier in November. He demanded the restoration of the Kingdom of Piedmont-Sardinia, the evacuation of French troops from Italy, the abandonment of north Germany, the restoration of an independent Holland and Switzerland, and the abandonment of fortresses on the right bank of the Rhine. Assuming Napoleon would reject this, England would subsidize coalition forces at the standard rate. Tsar Alexander was then expected to bring Austria and Prussia fully into line.[31]

As promising as Pitt's proposal was to Alexander, crucial obstacles stood in the way. Prussia remained steadfastly neutral and Frederick William III was still threatening intervention in Swedish Pomerania. Even in Vienna, Franz Colloredo had reservations about rushing headlong into an open alliance against France. He advised Cobenzl, his friend and colleague, that Austria should consider preparing for war in "as greater secrecy as possible. . . . Bonaparte could not resist the temptation to crush those who are defenseless in order to prevent a new coalition, to which he knows well we pursue, but without us cannot exist."[32]

Even the Emperor Francis, who had already dispensed with his brother as head of the *Hofkriegsrat*, requested Cobenzl address his concerns that an Anglo-Russian alliance might reduce Austria's ability to negotiate beneficial terms if it sought to join the coalition. Cobenzl responded that such an alliance could only benefit Austria. Using Russia as an intermediary was a necessity, as direct negotiations would potentially reveal Austria's hand to France. War with France was "inevitable" and therefore an Anglo-Russian alliance was desired. Austria required English subsidies, and Austrian forces were needed in the coming war. In every case, an agreement between England and Russia could only be advantageous to Austria's interests.[33] Francis was concerned with England's and Russia's ulterior motives. Austria desired to roll back French forces and influence in Italy and Germany. They desired this in order to reestablish Austria's position prior to 1797. England and Russia were not necessarily committed to this notion.

On 11 April 1805, Russia and England came to terms. The provisional Anglo-Russia treaty was far more explicit than the framework provided by Lord Mulgrave, the British foreign secretary, in January. Beyond the basic demands for the withdrawal of French forces from Italy and Germany, the agreement called for the expansion of the Kingdom of Piedmont-Sardinia if "circumstances permitted." More significantly, it called for "the establishment of an order of things in Europe which effectively guaranteed the security and independence of the diverse states and establishes a firm barrier against future usurpations."[34] This was a vague and ambitious objective. It came at a moment when Napoleon arrived in Italy to receive his crown and when Admiral Villeneuve had once again sailed from Toulon headed for Cadíz.

Napoleon announced his intentions in Italy much earlier. The transformation of the Italian Republic to a kingdom was presaged by Napoleon's assumption of the Imperial crown in France in December 1804. In reaction, Francis reinforced Austrian troops in the Tyrol, Venetia, and Carinthia under the guise of a *cordon sanitaire*. These forces began to arrive in early 1805 and elicited great concern from the recently self-anointed French emperor.[35] Napoleon responded by ordering the Italian minister of war, General Domenico Pino, to prepare the kingdom's fortresses and magazines in case of war. He demanded regular reports on the concentration of Austrian troops on the frontiers of his Italian kingdom. Napoleon was not convinced Austria meant war and was fully aware of the political conflict in the Viennese court related to British and Russian machinations.[36] Nonetheless, he would take no chances.

For Napoleon, the situation at sea was improving. Missiessy's squadron was still at sea, although supposedly returning to Europe. Napoleon wrote Villeneuve at the beginning of March, sending him to Martinique. Passing Cadíz, he would be joined by all available Spanish ships. Napoleon hoped Villeneuve would find Missiessy returning from the Indies. Admiral Ganteaume received his orders as well, calling on him to escape from Brest at the earliest moment and sail for Ferrol. There he would chase the English squadron away enabling the French and Spanish squadrons present to join with him. If Missiessy arrived before Ferrol having failed to locate Villeneuve, then the former should combine with Ganteaume's fleet. Achieving this, he was to proceed to Martinique where Villeneuve would take command of the combined French fleets.[37]

Villeneuve left Toulon 30 March while Nelson's fleet was at the southern tip of Sardinia. He passed the Straits of Gibraltar on 8 April and arrived at Cadíz the following day, forcing the smaller British squadron observing the Spanish port to withdraw. To his eleven ships of the line, Villeneuve added one French ship and eight Spanish ships. He immediately set off for Martinique.[38] Nelson discovered Villeneuve's departure two days after the fact; gales had slowed his pursuit terribly, and he did not reach Gibraltar until 6 May. Villeneuve at this time was only eight days out from Martinique. Nelson had fewer ships than Villeneuve, but he was responsible for defending the entire Mediterranean. After the Spanish declaration of war, the admiral had to contend with the Spanish squadron at Cartagena. Regardless, Villeneuve was able to slip the Mediterranean because Nelson was convinced of Napoleon's intention to reestablish a French presence in Egypt.[39]

Admiral Ganteaume did not sail from Brest. Opportunity presented itself on 24 March when the British blockading fleet was reduced to fifteen ships of the line. Ganteaume requested permission to sortie against the weaker British force. Napoleon rejected the admiral's request, not being comfortable with the odds. The Brest fleet thus remained in port while the English reinforced their fleet with an additional six ships by 30 March.[40] This was perhaps Napoleon's best chance to unite his fleets. His failure, however, was not perceived by the British Admiralty as relief. Villeneuve's liberty caused extreme consternation in England. Nelson's squadron remained numerically inferior to that of the French.

The French naval threat abated momentarily in the Mediterranean with Villeneuve's departure, but the Anglo-Russian convention ran into opposition from Pitt when the Russians proposed to garrison Malta.[41] Alexander generously offered to occupy the island in lieu of either Britain or France, if English possession of Malta stood in the way of peace. Under no circumstances would Pitt or Lord Mulgrave countenance such a notion. In a strong letter to Simon Voronstov, the Russian ambassador to England, Lord Mulgrave, the British foreign minister, presented a clear statement on Malta's fate.

> The necessity of a secure port in the Mediterranean not liable to capture or a sudden attack at the commencement of a war; and the assuring thereby a ready opposition to the maritime operations of France from her ports and arsenals in that quarter to whatever object they may be directed, are considerations of such importance to the interests of Great Britain, that if they be duly estimated upon the principles of friendly, cordial, and enlightened system of policy of the

Emperor of Russia, his Imperial Majesty will probably not be disposed to urge or to wish for such a sacrifice; which could not indeed be deemed consistent, either with the just consideration due to his Majesty as a member of the proposed concert, with the general feelings of his people or with the essential interests of his dominions.[42]

As Pitt and Mulgrave despaired at Alexander's ludicrous proposition, a British expeditionary force of 5,000 men sailed from England to reinforce Gibraltar and Malta.[43] England was strengthening its position in the Mediterranean. This was non-negotiable. Furthermore, there were almost 10,000 Russians at Corfu. Their presence concerned not only Napoleon, who believed they were to be landed at Naples, but also the British, who were nowhere closer to an understanding with Russia than they were in January.[44] Alexander rejected the English demand to withdraw the article pertaining to Malta, and negotiations stalled on the issue until the end of July.[45]

In the course of these events Napoleon traveled to Italy to receive his crown. He was coronated as king of Italy in the Duomo of Milan on 26 May. A few weeks later Genoa was formally annexed to France. All of this expressly violated the Treaty of Lunéville. The coronation was preceded by the concentration of 40,000 French and Italian troops in northern Italy. They served a dual purpose: to provide the coronation with proper martial splendor, and to act as a counterweight to the growing number of Austrian troops in Venetia and the Tyrol. Nonetheless, Austrian forces continued to flow into Venetia. After Napoleon's assumption to the Italian crown, Francis now desired to formalize the Russian alliance and insure English subsidies.[46] Until the Russians and English settled their dispute, however, a discussion of subsidies was placed on hold. Thus, Austria, England, and Russia agreed in principle to the coalition. Everything now hinged on Alexander's willingness to abandon his claim to Malta.[47]

Indeed, the Mulgrave letters to Russia on this matter were wrought with frustration. Feeding this was the uncertainty of events at sea. Missiessy returned to Rochefort at the end of May after failing to find Villeneuve, and was promptly blockaded. Villeneuve determined to return to Europe by the first week of June, having reinforced French garrisons and been unable to locate Missiessy. As Nelson arrived at Antigua, he prefigured Villeneuve's return to Europe. Turning his ships he made for Gibraltar. The Franco-Spanish fleet headed for Ferrol, as Napoleon provided in his March orders. Arriving there on 22 July, Villeneuve found a British fleet of fifteen ships under Admiral Calder. After a brief engagement, the French entered Ferrol.[48]

The return of the French Mediterranean fleet posed problems for England, as it combined with the Spanish squadron and now severely outnumbered Calder. If Villeneuve determined to challenge Calder there could be serious consequences. The British admiral lifted the blockade and sought security among Admiral Cornwallis's large fleet at Brest.[49] By the end of July, the events at sea were tenuous. Fortunately, Tsar Alexander finally abandoned his position on Malta. On 9 August 1805, a formal treaty of alliance between England, Russia, and Austria was signed. The Third Coalition was given life.[50]

The war aims were quite clear. It was the intention of the coalition to restore the map of Europe to its 1792 borders. The French were to be forced from Hanover and north Germany and completely eliminated from the Italian peninsula. The Kingdom of Piedmont-Sardinia was to be restored. Holland and Switzerland were to receive their independence, and, in a separate and secret article, Austria was to reclaim Belgium. The extent of these aims necessitated coordination and a substantial military effort on the part of all powers. The coalition wanted to commit 400,000 men to the war. The overwhelming majority of forces were to be composed of 250,000 Austrian troops supported by 115,000 Russians, with the balance to be drawn from Sweden, Naples, and perhaps Prussia.[51]

Tsar Alexander dispatched Baron General Wizingerode to Vienna in May 1805 to discuss strategy. As the Austrians had yet to accede fully to the coalition, and the restructuring of the Habsburg military command was still in process, the actual meeting was delayed until 16 July. At that time Winzingerode met with Archduke Charles, Mack, and Prince Schwarzenberg to discuss the framework of coalition strategy.[52] Although Charles was no longer president of the *Hofkriegsrat*, he remained war minister. Mack, however, had the confidence and ear of the emperor. Charles understood that he no longer held influence with his brother. War it was. Charles, however, wanted to insure that Mack's strategic vision, encouraged and inflated by Russian promises, did not take the form of the impractical and irrational. As it was, Charles's presence at the conference was merely a sop, and he had effectively no influence and little ability to alter Mack and Winzingerode's plans.

Tsar Alexander I pledged three Russian armies to the allied cause, totaling 100,000 men. They were to be deployed in three stages. The first Russian army under General Mikhail Kutusov, with almost 55,000 infantry, 8,000 cavalry, and 200 guns, would march from Brody on 16 August. Kutusov's force would march by stages in six separate columns of 9,000 to 10,000 men each. All columns would arrive on the Inn, ready for operations in Germany by 16–20 October.[53] A second army under General Bennigsen, with thirty-nine battalions, eighty-five squadrons, twenty-four guns, and eleven batteries of siege artillery, was forming at Bresz and Tarnopol, but Winzingerode was unable to specify when they would be available for operations.[54] The third army, commanded by General Michaelson, was deployed on the Prussian frontier in Lithuania. Consisting of thirty-three battalions and thirty-five squadrons, Michaelson's army observed the Prussian border. It was hoped, however, that Michaelson would be able to move rapidly from Lithuania through Poland to Bohemia with the permission of the Prussian king, as the quickest route would take the army through Prussian Silesia.[55]

Alexander's firm commitment provided Mack with sufficient forces to supplement the Austrian army of supposedly 250,000 men. Archduke Charles was quite pleased at first with the Russian pledge, although the uncertainty of whether Bennigsen or Michaelson's armies would be able to arrive in a timely fashion to support Austrian military efforts was questionable. Alexander also committed Russian troops at Corfu for use in Naples in conjunction with their English allies. It appeared that Italy would be the primary theater of war, with Austrian divisions in the Tyrol and Austrian and Russian troops on the Bavarian border.[56]

Mack believed that the number of Russian forces would enable him to pursue a dual offensive into Italy and Bavaria. The hammer would still fall on Italy. The main Austrian army of 142,000 men was to drive to the Mincio River in the kingdom of Italy. A second Austrian army of 89,000 was to advance into Bavaria to the Lech, await the arrival of all Russian armies, and then proceed to the Danube with 180,000 men. A reserve of 53,000 Austrians would be deployed in the Tyrol and Vorarlberg, respectively, to support either the army in Italy or the Austro-Russian army in Germany. Upon the achievement of all objectives, the army in Italy would march through Switzerland to join with the Austro-Russian army in Germany, and a combined force of more than 250,000 would invade France.[57] Secondary operations were planned for a Russo-Swedish landing in Stralsund, aimed at ejecting the French from Hanover. An Anglo-Russian force would land in Naples and, joined by the Neapolitan army, march into central and northern Italy. Lastly, if Frederick William III decided to commit Prussia to the coalition, he would be directed to liberate Holland and then advance upon the middle Rhine.[58]

Ever the military scientist, Mack prepared timetables for the deployment and concentration of coalition forces, and determined Napoleon's own reaction time to coincide with allied operations. According to Mack, Napoleon would be unable to react to an allied advance into Bavaria for sixty-eight days. He calculated that Napoleon could not possibly transfer his army from the Channel coast with adequate logistical preparation in less than two months. Concurrently, Kutusov's advance would be completed prior to the arrival of French forces in southern Germany.[59] Cobenzl and Colloredo were pleased with the military cooperation between Austria and Russia, and confident in Mack's strategic planning.[60]

The coalition's strategic outline was politically sound, but wholly impractical. What the Tsar and Austrian emperor desired was the *status quo ante bellum* (1792). The elimination of French presence in northern Germany and Holland, the restoration of the ruling houses of northern and central Italy, and the reduction of French influence in southern Germany. Habsburg interests went further to imagining the complete return of the Austrian Netherlands (Belgium) to their empire. The Imperial wish list assumed that Napoleon would negotiate once his armies were removed from Germany and Italy. He did not, however, do this upon seizing power in 1799, when French forces suffered egregious defeat in both theaters of war. Instead Napoleon launched a counteroffensive across the Alps into Italy resulting in the defeat of the Austrian army at Marengo in 1800. Later that year General Moreau crushed the Austrian army at Hohenlinden in south Germany. Yet, Habsburg memory appeared to have faded in four years.

Mack's desire to invade Bavaria and push on to the Danube prior to the arrival of Kutusov's army can be rationalized within Austria's specific political interests in south Germany. Although Francis was Holy Roman Emperor, his influence was virtually non-existent in Germany. Prussia already dominated the north, and Napoleon had provided Baden, Württemberg, and Bavaria with alternatives. Bavaria, more than the others, posed a significant problem for Austria. Juxtaposed to the heart of the Habsburg Empire, Bavaria had the largest army in Germany exclusive of Prussia. It was a thorn in Austria's side. As recently as 1804, Francis and Maximilian IV Joseph of Bavaria quarreled over the bishopric of Passau. By striking first into Bavaria, Mack hoped to compel the elector to throw in his lot with the coalition or else.[61] This pre-emptive act would stand as an example to Württemberg and Baden.

Mack's plan was replete with assumptions. The Archduke Charles had great difficulty accepting it and presented a number of significant criticisms to his brother. Mack assumed Napoleon would not react to the concentration of troops on the Inn (the Austrian border with Bavaria), nor in Italy. He assumed Napoleon would not carry the war to the Danube. He assumed that the main Austrian army in Italy could move rapidly through northern Italy and then through Switzerland. He assumed Napoleon's counteroffensive would be fought between the Rhine and Danube and would result in his utter defeat. He did not factor the number of troops needed to reduce the Franco-Italian fortresses in the Po valley (northern Italy). He did not factor the number of troops realistically required for the reduction of French fortresses on the Rhine.[62] He relied on Napoleon being anyone other than Napoleon. His actions in the past had indicated great energy and determination to wrest the initiative from the enemy. Charles had faced Napoleon in Italy in 1797, Mack had not.

In the end Charles was right. By 13 August, while Mack was still calculating timetables, Napoleon abandoned his plan to invade England and turned his army toward Germany to meet the impending threat.

CHAPTER EIGHT

AUGUST–SEPTEMBER 1805

"NOTHING IS AS BEAUTIFUL AS MY ARMY HERE," Napoleon remarked to his stepson, Prince Eugene, from Boulogne.[1] It was a magnificent army, perhaps the finest ever assembled in Europe. The Army of Ocean Coast, as Napoleon established it in 1803, comprised some of the most experienced soldiers on the continent. Half the rank and file and all the officers and non-commissioned officers entered the army prior to 1800. Several thousand, in fact, could legitimately claim service before 1789. Many, however, were drawn from the levies of the republic and the Directory.[2] When Napoleon established the camps along the Channel coast, it was intended that these soldiers train incessantly, otherwise forgetting the simplest drills. He instructed his marshals and generals to conduct brigade and divisional maneuvers in addition to the basic manual of arms. Since the conclusion of combat on the European continent in December 1800, the French army was reorganized, reequipped, and practiced for war.[3] By the summer 1805 it was ready.

With Admiral Villeneuve at Ferrol, there remained some hope that a Channel crossing was possible. In fact, it was not, and by 12 August Napoleon faced the probable reality that he would have to delay any invasion of England to address the growing continental threat. He instructed Talleyrand to convey to Cobenzl that France did not desire war with Austria. The increasing number of Austrian troops deployed along his Italian kingdom's frontiers, however, was perceived as an act of aggression. If Austria did not withdraw their regiments to Bohemia or Hungary, war it would be. "I want to attack Austria and be in Vienna before November in order to face the Russians if they are present,"[4] he told his foreign minister. To the Austrian vice-chancellor, he clearly and unequivocally stated that he would turn from the coast to deal with the threat.

This was not the first letter of protest Napoleon had dispatched to Austria. The responses were wholly unsatisfactory, and he predicted Cobenzl's reply to the forthcoming demand would be filled with, "dilatory phrases." He told Talleyrand, "[T]hese are not my concern."[5] Words would not suffice, only action. Cobenzl intended on responding with pleasantries. Flowery language and pacific discussions were to lull Napoleon into a false sense of security. Time played to the coalition's advantage. Kutusov's army should have already been placed on the march. The longer Napoleon believed Vienna was sincerely interested in settling matters peacefully, the closer the Russian army got to Vienna. Time also enabled Austria to complete its concentration in Venetia and on the Inn. The Austrian vice-chancellor, therefore, offered his good services to mediate between France, Russia, and England.[6]

England was ill-served by its ambassador in Vienna, Sir Arthur Paget. Although Austria determined to conduct negotiations with Great Britain through Russia's "good auspices," Paget was completely unaware of events transpiring at court. On the one hand he reported to London on the state of Austrian mobilization. He was pleased with its progress. On the other hand, he was terribly frustrated by Cobenzl's offer of mediation. It was not until the very end of August that Cobenzl saw fit to inform his English ally's ambassador of all that transpired since the Russo-Austrian convention of November 1804. Only then was Paget able to write London of Austria's full commitment to the coalition.[7] Considering the desperation Pitt experienced through the end of July, an ambassador that did his job properly, gathering information and discerning the true intentions of the state to which he was assigned, would have better served him.

Unlike Pitt, Napoleon possessed an incredibly effective and competent diplomatic corps. Enormous amounts of information flowed regularly into the Foreign Ministry and to the emperor. Laforest in Berlin and La Rouchfoucauld in Vienna continued to keep Napoleon abreast of events. In the German states Didelot in Baden and Otto in Bavaria did well to relay the state of affairs in the Swabian territories. The latter ambassador, Louis-Guillaume Otto, was particularly effective in maintaining good relations with Elector Maximilian IV Joseph, but had a fine rapport with his Francophile first minister, Maximilian Montgelas. Otto's position in Munich also made his embassy particularly significant in directing and gathering intelligence on Austrian military concentrations along the Bavarian border and in the Tyrol.[8] It was through these men that Napoleon could correctly presume Cobenzl's true intentions. The information received indicated, however, that the Austrian army was not yet capable of offensive operations, and the Russian armies had not moved. Perhaps there was still time to invade England if Villeneuve acted.

Villeneuve was foremost of the mind of Admiral Cornwallis, who commanded the fleet blockading Brest. Admiral Calder failed to prevent Villeneuve and the Spanish admiral Gravina from making for Ferrol, and the minor engagement off Cape Finestre, while managing to disable two Spanish ships of the line, did not improve England's strategic situation at sea. It would have been a greater relief to know that Napoleon was conflicted, having spent years assembling an invasion army but at any moment ready to alter his plans to deal with Austria and Russia. Napoleon continued to write feverishly to Admiral Decrès, his minister of marine, through August. Napoleon's frustration with Villeneuve finally reached a breaking point. "I consider Villeneuve to not have the character necessary to command a frigate. This is a man without resolution," he told Decrès, "and without moral courage."[9] Napoleon ordered Villeneuve to Brest with no less than twenty-nine ships of the line, but he had yet to arrive. Once more Napoleon communicated to the admiral the necessity of moving quickly. Counting Ganteaume, Napoleon believed he could have fifty ships of the line to oppose the numerically inferior English fleet. "Within twenty-four hours," the emperor exclaimed to Villeneuve in a dispatch, "all is lost."[10]

Opportunity was already lost. Villeneuve and Gravina left Ferrol with their fleet on 13 August en route to Brest. Poor weather pushed them further west. By the night of 15 August Villeneuve abandoned his orders and sailed for Cadíz, being spooked by the British squadron shadowing the French admiral. Five days later he entered the Spanish port, concentrating thirty-five French and Spanish ships of the line. Admiral Collingwood pursued Villeneuve from Ferrol and arrived before Cadíz on 21 August. In less than ten days Calder's fleet joined him, making twenty-six ships of the line. Villeneuve remained at Cadíz for the next two months not liking the odds.[11]

"Monsieur Talleyrand, Minister of Foreign Relations," the letter began, "the more I reflect on the situation in Europe, the more I am resolved to act decisively." Napoleon believed nothing would come of his overtures to Austria. "They will respond with pretty phrases and will gain time. . . . I will find 100,000 Russians in Poland, fed by England . . . 15 to 20,000 English in Malta and 15,000 Russians at Corfu." The emperor continued, "I will find myself in a critical situation. My course is set."[12] On 23 August 1805, the plans were laid for the invasion of Germany and the conquest of Austria.

Marshal Alexandre Berthier wore two hats. He was the French minister of war, and the chief of staff of the army. Berthier had served with Napoleon since 1796, and he was one of the few officers who could translate his voluminous orders and disseminate them rapidly and accordingly. Berthier worked tirelessly over the preceding years, although Admiral Decrès recently bore the onus of the Emperor's frustrations. All of it changed, however, on 26 August 1805. On that day the Army of the Ocean Coast became *la Grande Armée*, the grand army of the Emperor Napoleon I.[13] Berthier would now work feverishly to set the emperor's plans in motion.

The divisions encamped in the towns along the coast for the forsaken invasion of England were organized and designated as *corps d'armée*. Seven corps were formed from the four camps, Holland, Hanover, and the interior.

Each corps was commanded by a marshal of France, with the exception of the one under General Marmont, and comprised three divisions of infantry and one of cavalry. The Army of the Ocean Coast would remain under Marshal Brune to guard the Channel coast from English raids, but its formidable numbers were reduced considerably. The Italian division at Bolougne supplemented Brune's numbers.[14] The organization of the army was thus:

I   Corps under Marshal Bernadotte in Hanover

II   Corps under General Marmont at Utrecht in Holland

III   Corps under Marshal Davout at Ambleteuse

IV   Corps under Marshal Soult at Boulogne ⌐

V   Corps under Marshal Lannes at Etaples ⎱ From the camps

VI   Corps under Marshal Ney at Etaples   ⎰ around Boulogne

VII   Corps under Marshal Augereau at Bayonne

Imperial Guard at Paris

Cavalry reserve at Boulogne and throughout France[15]

Napoleon divided the II, III, IV, V, and VI Corps into three wings—right, center, and left—and directed them to the Rhine. This grouping was made solely for speeding the march routes so as not to have 95,000 men moving along a single road. Marmont had the furthest distance to travel, being ordered from Utrecht to Mainz. Bernadotte's corps was to concentrate at Göttingen in the southern part of Hanover and await further orders.[16] Marshal Augereau's VII Corps on the Atlantic Coast would not be able to arrive on the Rhine at the same time as the other five corps. He was designated as the reserve.

Napoleon made it very clear to Berthier that march orders were to be sent forthwith. He expected his army to arrive on the Rhine in three weeks, having covered at least 300 miles. Napoleon then dispatched instructions to Italy. The combined Franco-Italian forces numbered 68,000 men, but they were dispersed throughout the peninsula. Prince Eugene, viceroy of Italy, was too young and inexperienced to defend Italy. Marshal Jourdan, his military advisor, was ill suited, having spent much of his later career on campaigns in Belgium and Germany. Napoleon chose Marshal André Massena. Massena commanded exclusively in Italy through 1799, then Switzerland. He served under Napoleon with great distinction in 1796 and 1797 and managed to prevent the capture of Zurich two years later. Prince Eugene could learn from him, and Napoleon had every confidence Massena would guard Italy as if it were his own.[17]

Napoleon capitalized upon his relationship with the German princes preceding the movement of his army from the Channel to the Rhine. Ten days earlier Talleyrand was ordered to inform the French ambassador to the

Imperial Diet at Regensberg and the German diplomatic corps in Paris that Austrian mobilization in the Tyrol was perceived as an act of aggression. He further instructed that his foreign minister relay to them, "that France, menaced on the borders of Italy, cannot arrive in time to halt the enemy there; but by passing the Rhine its troops will seek out the enemy in the heart of their state."[18] The declaration was clear to all. War would be carried to Austria by way of Germany. The matter now was to assure the German princes, particularly those of south Germany, that Napoleon would guarantee their lands and sovereignty in the coming conflict in return for their political and military support.

With this in mind Talleyrand instructed the French ambassadors at the courts of Bavaria, Württemberg, and Baden to achieve declarations of support for France from their respective courts. In the case of Bavaria, Louis-Guillaume Otto was told that he must make it abundantly clear to the elector that Napoleon "would not accept that she remain neutral."[19] Napoleon's rationale for such forceful language was founded in all that he had done to increase the lands of these states over the past years, and intended to give them greater opportunity to act outside of Vienna's grasp. As recently as 1804, Austria challenged Bavaria's right to the former bishopric of Passau.

The statements to the electors were certainly veiled threats. Napoleon, however, wanted the princes to know that support for the coming war would result in considerable rewards for his allies. In Bavaria's case Napoleon authorized Otto to pursue a military alliance as early as May 1805. The French ambassador and the Bavarian minister, Montgelas, conducted a series of negotiations over the course of four months. Vienna's attitude toward Bavaria since 1803 did not incline the elector to remain beyond the French orbit. Nonetheless, a formal alliance with France might be perceived by Austria as an act of aggression. The French army was in no position through August to offer protection from Austrian retribution.[20] It was not until reports of the construction of Austrian military camps along his frontier that Max Joseph seriously considered a Franco-Bavarian convention. For his part, Montgelas, strongly believed the alliance would be in Bavaria's best interests.

At Bogenhausen on 24 August 1805, Montgelas and Otto concluded a formal Franco-Bavarian alliance. Napoleon pledged 110,000 men to the protection of Bavaria. In return the elector committed his army of 20,000 men to the French cause and agreed to provide logistical support to the French army. Promises were also made to recognize Max Joseph's right to absorb the autonomous fiefdoms within Bavaria's borders and his elevation to king if the situation presented itself.[21] Max Joseph was terribly uncomfortable with the agreement. Montgelas strongly encourage it. Nonetheless, the Bavarian elector did not look favorably upon the coming conflict. This was reasonable considering it seemed the war would be fought on Bavarian soil.

French pressure on Baden and Württemberg and the deployment of Austrian troops in the Vorarlberg adjacent to the latter elector's southern borders placed both princes in a predicament. In an act of desperation, Frederick II of Württemberg convinced his neighbors to seek Prussian guarantees for German neutrality.[22] The Swabian princes understood that their territories had certainly been aggrandized through French intercession in 1803. The cost for the last decade of war, however, had drained their financial resources. Wars in the eighteenth century between France and Austria were often fought on battlefields in southern Germany. There was understandable fear and reluctance. The Austrian emperor could not force the princes through the Imperial Diet to pursue a *Reichkrieg* against France. None would support it, and Prussia would surely seek to block it. If war was imminent, the only German state strong enough to insure the neutrality of Germany was Prussia.

The situation was particularly complicated for the elector of Württemberg. His sister was the Tsar's mother and General Graf Winzingerode arrived at Ludwigsberg, the elector's palace, to draw the German prince into his nephew's coalition. At the same time Thiard, the French special envoy, also sought Frederick's support for a French alliance. Court factions debated both sides. This was not unique to Württemberg; the same arguments took place in Baden and Bavaria. In the end, Frederick II concluded the only way to resolve this diplomatic Gordian knot was to seek Prussian intervention.[23]

On 2 September the electors of Baden, Württemburg, and Bavaria issued a joint letter to Frederick William III, asking the Prussian monarch to intercede and declare Germany neutral.[24] This was a defining moment in the history of Prussia. The kingdom's control of north Germany and its ability to remain apart from the conflict since 1795 led to this great opportunity to extend its influence into what had always been the Habsburg realm. Frederick William III, however, had little inclination to involve Prussia in this fight. To declare Germany neutral would potentially involve his kingdom inadvertently in the war. The German princes were not seeking protection from France or Austria, respectively, but a guarantee of the sovereignty of their states and their right not to have hundreds of thousands of foreign soldiers marching on their grass.

The elector of Baden was hopeful that his states could be spared but found a great deal of pressure placed upon him by his son, Prince Ludwig, who was vehemently pro-French. In two audiences Didelot, the French ambassador, pressed home Napoleon's position. Württemberg's neutrality was a "chimera," Didelot claimed. The French army would be on the Rhine in eight days, and Württemberg's stance was understood in Paris because it was, "more exposed to the resentment of the court of Vienna if it entered into a treaty with France." Baden's status, Didelot concluded, was the contrary.[25]

While Württemberg held out for a Prussian response, Max Joseph hoped that Prussian guarantees would prevent an Austrian invasion and perhaps dissuade Napoleon from moving across the Rhine. This was a fool's hope, and Montegelas never considered it. In any case, the Prussian monarch ignored the plea. Karl Friedrich, elector of Baden succumbed to geographic realities and French promises. He concluded an alliance with France on 5 September 1805.[26] The elector committed 3,000 troops to the French cause if war broke with Austria. Although Bavaria and Baden acceded to Napoleon's demands, an open declaration of alliance would immediately place them at odds with Vienna. All of these agreements remained secret until after the Austrians invaded Bavaria. As such, the electors had to play a careful game, assuring Napoleon of their support while not challenging Austria openly. Württemberg remained steadfastly neutral until a French corps under Marshal Ney knocked at the gates of Stuttgart in October.[27]

As early as February 1805, Napoleon proposed an alliance between France and Prussia. Again in March Napoleon tried to convince Frederick William III that Russian and English designs would lead to the isolation of France and Prussia.[28] By August he instructed his ambassador in Berlin, Antoine Laforest, to offer Hanover in return for a Prussian alliance. Concerned about the potential for Prussian vacillation, he dispatched General Giraud Duroc, the grand marshal of the palace, to Berlin to press home Napoleon's proposal.[29] Frederick William was not willing to resign his kingdom to an entangling alliance with France and rebuffed the requests. Prussia's position in north Germany would be ruined and a line would be drawn in Europe between two opposing alliances. Prussia would no longer have options.[30]

Prussia's stance in the midst of this crisis and their inaction after the French occupation of Hanover in 1803 indicated to the elector of Hesse-Cassel and the landgraf of Hesse-Darmstadt, that France was a viable alternative polity in north German affairs. Indeed, Prussia's disposition to dictate conditions in north Germany since 1795 alienated the Hessian states, further working in the French favor.[31] Both Hessian states were strategically vital for Napoleon. Although the Grande Armée could simply march through France to the Rhine, moving Marshal Bernadotte's corps from Hanover required the permission of the Hessian princes. The king of Prussia, and the Hessian princes, however, were informed that the intended object of Bernadotte's march was Mainz. This city on the Rhine was in France, and the excuse given was that the imminence of war necessitated the return of the French army in Hanover.

As early as 8 September, however, Duroc wrote Napoleon and apprised him of Bernadotte's options in his march south. Napoleon did not intend Bernadotte go to Mainz, but to Wurzburg in Bavaria.[32] There Marmont's corps and the Bavarian army would join him. From Wurzburg, he wrote, they

could move by "neutral road" to Schweinfurt and Bamberg to the Upper Palitinate, thereby arriving on the Bohemian (Austrian) frontier. Otherwise the
corps would be "obliged" to march through Anspach (Prussian territory) in
order to arrive in Swabia.[33]

Not wanting to estrange Prussia, Duroc informed Frederick William III
of the request to Wilhelm I, elector of Hesse-Cassel.[34] Napoleon knew that
Frederick William would not oppose the reduction of French troops in
Hanover and would wholeheartedly support their return to France under the
guise of the coming war. The reaction of the Hessian elector, however, was
not concomitant with the Prussian monarch's views. To allow French troops
passage through his territory was a dicey affair. General Blucher, the Prussian
commander of Paderborn in Westphalia, wrote the elector, apprising him of
the French concentration at Göttingen along the Hessian frontier, before
Bignon, the French ambassador in Hesse-Cassel, met with Wilhelm to
explain.[35] The elector concluded this was the culmination of a dispute with
Napoleon concerning his refusal to eject the British ambassador of Hesse-
Cassel. He wrote Frederick William seeking guidance. The monarch replied
that he would support the elector's decision to maintain the English ambassador at Cassel, but could not offer military assistance, although whatever he
felt must be done would be supported in Berlin.[36] Wilhelm mobilized the
Hessian army and resigned himself to resisting Bernadotte until he was
forced to withdraw and seek Prussian military aid.[37] Bernadotte's true intentions were finally brought to the elector's attention by Bignon, and after brief
negotiations and no definitive action by Frederick William III the elector gave
assent to the French request.

Bernadotte's true objective of Wurzburg in the Upper Palitinate (Bavaria)
needed to remain secret; otherwise part of Napoleon's strategic plan would
be revealed. Wilhelm, however, rejected the route first proposed by Bernadotte. Instead of allowing them to proceed from Göttingen to Fulda, thence
Frankfurt and Mainz (a route that seemed too circuitous to the elector), he
demanded they move in a southwesterly direction via Marburg to Frankfurt
to Mainz.[38] Of course Bernadotte's first choice was the shortest route to
Wurzburg, but to maintain the charade the marshal had to agree to the elector's preference. French troops would march by stages through the electorate, exiting the major territories after four days. This new route directed
Bernadotte through parts of Hesse-Darmstadt.

Ludwig X, the landgraf of Hesse-Darmstadt, was reluctant to commit
himself to a formal agreement, although he was only required to provide
logistical support along with a small military contingent for the French
advance from the Rhine to Bavaria.[39] Hesse-Darmstadt benefited greatly
from north German neutrality, although half the prince's territories lay south
of the Main River. Ludwig X also received substantial territory as a consequence of the Imperial Recess in 1803. When French overtures were received

in Darmstadt, the landgraf was ill disposed to join with France and he stalled by haggling. Napoleon increased pressure as the month of August closed and finally demanded Ludwig give him a simple "yes or no."[40] The landgraf wrote Frederick William III on 3 September seeking guidance and protection. The Hessian note accompanied the joint request from Bavaria, Baden, and Württemberg. The Prussian response did not arrive in Darmstadt until 30 September, long after the landgraf was compelled to make his own arrangements, and in any case Frederick William refused to commit Prussia.[41] By mid-September the landgraf of Hesse-Darmstadt joined Baden and Bavaria in a military alliance with France.[42]

Bernadotte's corps advanced by echelon through Hesse-Cassel on 17 September 1805. The French marshal was the elector's guest for not more than three days during his corps' march. Napoleon made it clear that Bernadotte should not fatigue his corps during their march, but it seems that the marshal did not want to overstay his welcome in the electorate, and he ushered his divisions through as rapidly as possible. Moving through Hesse-Darmstadt the French corps reentered Wilhelm's county of Hanau, dominated by the city of Frankfurt. Here, Bernadotte's corps was to turn west to Mainz, but prior to arriving at Frankfurt it turned southeast and proceeded to Wurzburg, arriving before the city on 28 September. His corps covered more than 200 miles in eleven days.[43]

Throughout the march, Bernadotte kept in close correspondence with the Hessian elector, insuring that the French troops behaved properly and requisitioning was carried out with strict discipline. As part of the agreement, French supply convoys moved freely through the electorate from Hanover. When Austrian troops moved into Bavaria and the French army crossed the Rhine in September, Wilhelm found himself in the middle.[44] This was due more to Frederick William's concern that Wilhelm was too permissive in his arrangements with Bernadotte.[45] Although he permitted Bernadotte to leave Hanover, he did not appreciate finding the marshal's corps moving on Wurzburg when he expected Mainz.

All of this affected Prussia. The kingdom's position in Europe was determined by its willingness to enforce its neutrality through 1803; thereafter, Frederick William III gradually lost a great opportunity as Prussia was defined by its lack of action. This reduced its credibility when north German princes were confronted with French diplomatic and military pressures. They sought Prussian guidance, and ultimately protection, but Frederick William III refused to stray from the path he had chosen. This led the princes to make arrangements insuring their own security. This by no means placed them squarely in the French camp, but it allowed them to conclude agreements in the absence of Prussian influence.

Prussia's stance in mid-September was frustrating not only to Napoleon but to the Russians and Austrians as well. Clemens von Metternich, the

Austrian ambassador to Prussia, was constantly disconcerted by Frederick William's obstinacy. Perhaps more disturbed was Tsar Alexander I. He wrote to Count Alopeus in early August that General Michaelson's army (later Bux-howden) was to cross into Prussian territory en route to Austria. Alopeus was instructed to secure permission from Frederick William III. If the Prussian monarch perceived the Russian action as an act of war, Alopeus was to withdraw his request. Michaelson's army was ordered to move into Silesia regardless of Frederick William's decision. Alopeus was to leave Prussia if all of this led to war between the two states. Alexander told his ambassador that war with Prussia was not desired, and all would be lost. "We would have to employ all our resources to reduce Prussia."[46] If Frederick William agreed to the Tsar's request, Alopeus was to press for a formal alliance claiming the Tsar, "is ready to guarantee the reestablishment of the House of Orange in Holland, the annexation of Fulda and the possessions on the left bank of the Rhine. Thereafter England would establish a subsidy of 1.2 million for 100,000 men."[47]

Alopeus presented Alexander's request to Frederick William III on 30 August. The king flatly refused. The Prussian high command, the *Ober-kriegs-Kollegium*, discussed options. A report on the state of the Prussian army was presented to the king on 4 September. Three days later Frederick William III placed the Prussian army on a war footing. What this meant in practical terms was that standing infantry battalions were to be brought up to full strength and officers recalled from leave. The relatively new third battalions, which existed in skeletal form, remained inactive.[48] The Prussian army stood at that moment with sixty-one infantry battalions and eighty cavalry squadrons. It was not very impressive, nor did it translate into the paper strength of 80,000 men under arms. The overwhelming majority of the Prussian army was deployed in the East. No more than thirteen battalions and seven squadrons were deployed in Westphalia in western Germany.[49]

Upset at Frederick William's refusal to participate in the coalition or permit his army access to Silesia, Alexander dispatched Prince Dolgoruky to Berlin to demand it.[50] The Prussian king convened a meeting of his advisors on 19 September to discuss the crisis. Present were the duke of Brunswick, Fieldmarshal von Mollendorf, Count von Hardenberg, and Count von Haugwitz, who was recalled from retirement. The council convinced Frederick William that Prussia had only one option, full mobilization. Third battalions would be filled out, cavalry depots augmented, and logistical preparations for the campaign arranged. The army would achieve its full strength of 180,000 men over the next month, or so they expected.[51]

General von Kalkreuth, with eighteen battalions, four companies of Jaeger (light infantry), and thirty-three cavalry squadrons, was given command in Pomerania. His corps would take up a position enabling it to cover Swedish Pomerania and Russian Poland. It was Frederick William's intention that if Russian troops violated Prussian territory, Kalkreuth was to act against either Russo-Swedish forces at Stralsund or the Russians in Poland.[52] Alexander's threat elicited Frederick William's hostile reaction—not, however, to mobilize and deploy the Prussian army against France, but instead to repel a potential Russian invasion in the east. He informed the Tsar of this fact.[53]

Napoleon's ambassador and special emissary in Berlin carefully watched all of these events. General Duroc kept Napoleon keenly apprised of events at court and the state of the Prussian army. He wrote Talleyrand that mobilization was decreed under the guise of defending north German neutrality and that it was of no concern to France. The Prussian army, he assessed, was in a poor state and ill-prepared for a campaign. Its equipment, supplies, and magazines had been neglected and Prussia's lack of financial resources would prevent an alteration of these conditions in the near future.[54] Duroc's assessment was vital. Napoleon trusted the general and could plan accordingly considering Prussia's military potential. This remained foremost on his mind when determining the best route south for Bernadotte, Marmont, and the Bavarians once concentrated at Wurzburg.

As Napoleon laid the groundwork for his army's advance into Germany, Mack developed the operational plans for the Austrian armies. In a conference on 29 August, he revealed them to Francis and the Archduke Charles. The main army in Italy, consisting of 120,000 troops, would be placed under the command of the Archduke Charles. A smaller army of 34,000 troops in the Tyrol would protect his right flank. A reserve corps of 20,000 men would remain in the interior and be shifted as necessary. The army in Germany, 58,000 strong, would advance to the Iller in Bavaria and await the arrival of the Russian army.[55] Mack assumed Austria would be able to field an army in excess of 200,000 troops by September. Actual numbers were closer to 186,000, and this was achieved with great difficulty.

Despite Mack's promise to Cobenzl in the spring that he could carry out military reforms, along with preparations for war in a matter of months, the fact was otherwise. Charles worked assiduously for four years to study the reasons for Habsburg military defeat and then implement change while coping with fewer resources. Mack had less time and even less money. In April the cavalry needed more than 37,000 horses. By summer many battalions stood at half strength and the artillery only possessed 50 percent of their horses. The Hungarians proved extremely difficult in acceding to recruitment demands; as early as 1803, they resisted the call for 64,000 men over a three-year period. The army's logistics were worse. Beyond irregular pay, the soldiers lacked firearms, uniforms, and food.[56]

Charles offered an immediate critique of Mack's plans. He recommended to his brother that the Army of Germany delay its advance into Bavaria until Kutusov's army was available for joint operations. He stressed that the Army of Germany was too weak to achieve its objectives, and by the beginning of September he successfully convinced Francis to allow him to transfer 30,000 men designated for Italy to Germany.[57] Further complicating matters, the Tsar requested in July that protocol demanded a member of the Habsburg family, either an archduke chosen by the emperor or the Archduke Charles, lead the Austro-Russian army in Germany.[58] It is clear from the time and detail put into the operations in Bavaria that Mack desired to personally direct the campaign, although the main effort was supposed to be in Italy. This is understandable considering Mack served on the Rhine through 1797. In order to accede to Alexander's wishes, Francis appointed his cousin the Archduke Ferdinand d'Este commander of the Army in Germany, with Mack as quartermaster-general. Archduke Ferdinand was under the impression that his appointment was more than nominal, although he would soon be disabused of this notion.[59]

Deployment of Austrian troops proceeded through August. Archduke Ferdinand and General Mack took a post with the Army of Germany not far from the Bavarian border on 2 September 1805. Ferdinand and Mack established their headquarters at Wels. Austrian forces there initially comprised a paltry thirty battalions of infantry and thirty squadrons of cavalry.[60] The majority of the army, an additional fifty-eight battalions and 118 squadrons, excluding Ludwig's column, was to follow over the course of the next few weeks. A further forty-four battalions and ten squadrons remained in the Vorarlberg and Tyrol under General Jellacic as Mack's strategic reserve.[61] Archduke Charles remained in Vienna, preparing for his journey to Italy.

Mack's earlier assumptions were now tested. On 9 September Archduke Ferdinand d'Este and General-Quartermaster Karl Lieberich von Mack led the army across the Bavarian frontier without a declaration of war. Four days earlier Prince Karl zu Schwarzenberg arrived in Munich and demanded Max Joseph join the Third Coalition and place the Bavarian army under Austrian command. The Franco-Bavarian alliance remained secret, and the elector's attempt to seek Prussian guarantees of German neutrality further fooled the Austrians as to Bavaria's true intentions. This was not prearranged; it simply worked out this way. For a moment the Bavarian elector faltered and considered abandoning Napoleon whose army was only en route to the Rhine. Montegelas managed to persuade his master to hold to his commitments and Napoleon's promises. Max Joseph left Munich on the night of 8 September for Wurzburg knowing that the Austrian army had crossed the Inn at Scharding and Braunau. The Bavarian army was ordered to follow, leaving scant forces to conduct a withdrawal against the Austrian invasion, but by no means offer serious resistance.[62]

Napoleon's army was already marching from the Channel coast; it would take sixty-eight days to reach the Danube according to Mack's calculations. He was seriously mistaken. The French army was not passive while Austrian infantry and cavalry advanced in echelons as planned through mid-

September. On 18 September Mack took up position with the majority of his force around the city of Ulm, northwest of Munich. There he intended to observe the Black Forest and Upper Rhine. Kutusov's army was no doubt well on its way. In fact it was, but *well* would be an inappropriate term. The good Russian general was at least a month distant. When the Archduke Charles arrived at his headquarters in Italy on 20 September, Germany was on his mind. He resolved that his army's dispositions and his conduct of the campaign would be carried out with a conscious concern for events in Bavaria.

The coalition struck the first blow, or so it seemed, but Bavaria was at war with no one. There was no declaration of war, and as of 9 September Austria had blatantly violated the sovereignty of a German territory. On the day Mack established his headquarters at Ulm, the Russian ambassador to Baden, not knowing of the elector's alliance with France, tried to sway him to join the coalition. He was met with determined resistance. The elector responded by stating that Baden would pursue neutrality, and in any case there was no call for a *Reichkrieg* in the Imperial Diet or anything of the sort.[63]

The princes of the Holy Roman Empire found it difficult to openly ally with France when the Austrian army was amassing in great numbers in south Germany and the French were soon arriving on the Rhine.[64] Nonetheless, Austria's invasion allowed Napoleon to proclaim to the Diet at Regensberg that he would defend them against Austria's violation of Germany. Marshal Joachim Murat, commanding French forces on the Rhine prior to Napoleon's arrival, wrote the elector of Baden, Karl Friedrich, on 24 September. "Loyal to his promises, the Emperor and King [Napoleon], has ordered me to cross the Rhine with his army to protect the independence of the sovereign princes of Germany and to avenge the violation of their territories."[65] Imagine, Napoleon could claim the moral high ground.

Max Joseph was in Wurzburg for almost two weeks when Murat wrote the elector of Baden. His capital and much of his electorate were under Austrian occupation. Even Emperor Francis spent time in Munich at the end of September. The Bavarian prince's wait ended on 28 September when Marshal Bernadotte arrived. The Bavarian army was in good order and prepared to join Bernadotte in his march to the Danube.[66] General Marmont's II Corps left Mainz and was expected at Wurzburg within a day.

As of 24 September the corps of the Grande Armée were arrayed along the Rhine. Marshal Lannes's V Corps, the Imperial Guard commanded by Marshal Bessieres, and the cavalry reserve under Marshal Murat were camped at Strasbourg. Marshal Soult's IV Corps was further north at Speyer with Marshal Davout's III Corps to his left at Mannheim. Marshal Augereau's VII Corps traversed the French interior, hoping to reach Basel within a few weeks.[67] All of this was accomplished in far less than the sixty-eight days predicted by Mack.

To date Napoleon could count Bavaria, Baden, Hesse-Darmstadt, Nassau, and Spain among his allies. Austria, a member of the Third Coalition, could also claim England and Russia. Yet, Austria inaugurated the war before her allies were able to act. The Russo-Swedish corps had still not arrived in Stralsund. The English and Russian expeditionary forces in the Mediterranean had not landed in Naples. Coordinating the landing, combined with the revelation that King Ferdinand IV of Naples had signed a neutrality agreement with France on 21 September, complicated matters. Lastly, and perhaps most important to Mack, was the lethargic advance of the Russian army through Galicia.

The Austrian army was in force along the upper Danube facing the Black Forest. French forces arrayed along the Rhine gave Mack the impression that the ensuing campaign would be fought in Swabia, as he had foreseen. The far left under Prince Schwarzenberg, with 21 battalions and 46 squadrons, occupied the area from Singmaringen to Bieberbach to Ravensberg, with patrols extending toward Hohenzollern and Württemberg. General Kollowrat was at Ulm with 24 battalions that extended south along the Iller. At Kempten, General Auffenberg with 14 battalions and eight squadrons held the center, and to his left was General Jellacic with 19 battalions and eight squadrons at Meersburg and Lindau. The third echelon under General Werneck, with 15 battalions and eight squadrons, deployed between the Iller and Lech Rivers at Landsberg. Mack posted General Kienmayer to guard the army's right wing along the Danube, with six battalions and 16 squadrons at Ingolstadt.[68]

Mack and Archduke Ferdinand received reports of French troops on the Rhine and of Bernadotte's concentration at Wurzburg. The union of the Bavarian and French armies came as a shock both at Ulm and Vienna. The utter secrecy maintained by the Bavarian elector and Montegelas caught the Habsburgs completely unaware. Despite the rude awakening, Mack was convinced that the combined army at Wurzburg was intended to cover any coalition advance from Bohemia. The quartermaster-general thought his position quite safe as the Prussian territory of Anspach stood between the Franco-Bavarian army and the Danube. He had no notion that the Franco-Bavarian forces were in fact the left wing of the Grande Armée.[69]

CHAPTER NINE

FROM THE RHINE TO THE INN

EVEN BEFORE NAPOLEON'S ARMY REACHED THE RHINE he conceived of an enormous counterstroke that would envelope the Austrian army at Ulm. Mack had deployed far forward, and the dispositions of the French corps between Mainz and Strasbourg invited a *maneouvre sur la derriere*, a strategic envelopment. Napoleon employed this before, albeit on a smaller scale, in Italy in 1796. His first attempt was successful in that it forced the Austrian army in Piedmont to face encirclement or retreat. Napoleon desired the former, but despite his best efforts, the Austrians discovered the trap and withdrew before the maneuver was complete. The potential to attempt such again on an even grander scale was incredibly enticing. He had every confidence that his troops could complete the envelopment with such speed that Mack would be unable to escape.

The French emperor issued orders almost a week before his army arrived on the German frontier.[1] Mack had not budged from his position between Ulm and the Iller. If he held there for a few more days Napoleon believed he could steal a march east along the Danube. Hence, the appearance of a headlong advance upon Ulm was required to complete the illusion. The Grande Armée crossed the Rhine during the last days of September. By 2–3 October, the II Corps, VI Corps, Imperial Guard, and cavalry reserve (approximately 60,000 men) arrived before Ludwigsburg and Stuttgart, having covered fifty miles in three days.[2] Forming the hinge of the envelopment, Marshal Soult's IV Corps and Davout's III Corps marched on Hall and Ingelfingen, respectively. The left wing of the army was at Wurzburg, composed of Bernadotte, Marmont, and the Bavarians. They were ordered through Prussian Anspach to arrive at Weissenberg north of the Danube by 9 October.

The strategic situation seemed quite favorable for Napoleon, but France's financial situation worsened, and that had a direct and immediate impact on logistics. If the army was not properly supplied, it could not operate effectively. Furthermore, to allow the French corps to forage in German lands would only alienate the local population and the princes who were now friends of France. Napoleon could not openly proclaim to the Germans that the army of France came to save them from Austria if French soldiers took to pillaging their cities, towns, and villages. It is in this conundrum that is found the emergence of a myth. "The French army marches on its stomach."

The histories of the Napoleonic wars are replete with accounts of the incredible distances marched by French troops; they were able to achieve such feats due to their detachment from traditional supply columns and magazines. According to the myth, foraging and feeding off the countryside provided the emperor's soldiers with ample food and thus allowed them to traverse enormous distances at great speeds. It is simply not so. More appropriately, it is only partially true. Foraging did not translate into the requisitioning of food from the local populations without regard to their safety or needs. The French army found food in the German lands because they were allies of France, and Napoleon had already made arrangements with the princes.

The French treasury found itself in enormous difficulty as further demands were placed upon it in August and September. Army contractors had not been paid for services prior to the war. The government was in arrears. The Bank of France sold subscriptions—similar to bonds—backed by anticipated revenues for 1806. Previous subscriptions were already sold on revenues through 1805. The problem, however, came in two forms. First, the bonds were sold at discounted rates to "friends" of the bank. Secondly, anticipated revenues were not properly adjusted to consider wartime expenditures. The security of the investments and the ability to predict future revenue became highly questionable. As war loomed investors began to redeem their bonds for specie. Nicholas-Mollien, Napoleon's treasurer, commented, "all the symptoms of a grave and immediate crisis already appeared before Napoleon left for Germany."[3] Under these circumstances army contractors refused to provide services unless payment was made in advance and in specie.[4] There was no more to be had.

Indications of a crisis appeared well before 1805. Marshal Bernadotte in Hanover did not have the benefit of sustaining his army from French revenue, but was required, as was his predecessor Marshal Mortier, to draw from the cities and provinces of the occupied electorate. The situation became so desperate that Bernadotte requested permission to sell the city of Minden to the elector of Hesse-Cassel and use the funds to pay his troops. Napoleon adamantly refused and told Bernadotte to levy taxes upon farmers who lived on the lands formerly owned by the elector of Hanover (George III of England).[5]

The question then was how to pay contractors and raise revenue, all the while paying out to investors? The answer was found in the sale of *domaines nationaux,* formerly known as *biens nationaux,* or state land. Since 1790, the French government sold land confiscated from the Roman Catholic Church or émigré nobles. By the time of the Consulate, the practice of selling these lands remained, but in less substantive form. The Concordat and Napoleon's amnesty to French emigrant nobles reduced the amount of land available for such sales. In their place the French government possessed enormous amounts of land as a consequence of the Treaty of Lunéville. The French government came to possess the former lands of the German princes with formal recognition of French annexation of the left bank of the Rhine. Beginning in 1803, these lands were occasionally placed on the auction block to raise revenue. In autumn 1805, as the demand for funds became critical, the French treasury sold increasing amounts of real estate at discounted prices. The result was a windfall for the French government and a wonderful bargain for purchasers.[6] It did not resolve the financial crisis, but it provided some liquidity to an increasingly depleted French treasury.

Once the army reached the Rhine, they would be supplied with biscuits and bread for four days.[7] From that point on it was up to Napoleon to insure that the corps would find adequate supplies in Germany. Nothing should be left to chance. On 25 August, in his letter to Max Joseph affirming their alliance, Napoleon requested the elector have 500,000 biscuits prepared at Wurzburg and Ulm. If he would be so kind as to pay for this, the emperor would reimburse him.[8] Article 6 of the Franco-Bavarian convention provided that the French army could requisition in electoral territory. Water, shoes, uniforms, and muskets were also needed, and should be available in sufficient numbers at Strasbourg, Landau and Spire.[9]

Rations distributed on the Rhine were intended to carry the army into Württemberg. The marshals were instructed to avoid using the biscuits except in an emergency, preferring to initially consume the bread. Foraging was only to take the form of requisition by voucher, to be paid later. In orders given on 20 September, Napoleon made it quite clear that they could gather supplies from predetermined regions but "acknowledge by vouchers in due form whatever you may take from the country of princes friendly to France."[10] The standard ration in the French army included one and a half pounds of bread, a half pound of meat, and either an ounce of rice or two ounces of dried fruit.[11] Bread would keep their bellies full, but the rest would have to be acquired along the route of march. The army, however, did not possess the four days' supply of bread and biscuits the emperor ordered. Bread was in short supply when they arrived on the Rhine, and the ability of the Rhenish cities to provide the quantity desired was insufficient. What was available was taken, and at times the marshals pursued a "first come, first serve" attitude, taking as much as possible without regard for the other corps.[12]

Marshal Bernadotte did not find the situation any better in Wurzburg. Although Napoleon requested that Max Joseph have ready a half million biscuits, the city had few resources available to provide such quantity. Two weeks prior to Bernadotte's arrival, Napoleon demanded 300,000 biscuits; it was not done.[13] Max Joseph had delayed in Munich, hoping for a miracle, and it appears no order was given until the Bavarian elector fled to Wurzburg the second week of September. Once there he provided for his own army before preparing for the French. Bernadotte's and Marmont's combined corps exceeded the number of soldiers in the elector's entire army. Bernadotte could not draw supplies during his march through Hesse-Cassel, although that elector allowed the French marshal to maintain supplies and communications through his territory. Bernadotte was distressed once at Wurzburg. There was an abundance of ammunition but few supplies and no money to purchase provisions. The impending arrival of Marmont's corps became logistically problematic.[14]

The elector of Baden was initially excluded from forced obligations of this sort, accepting the maintenance of his 3,000 man auxiliary force. Napoleon found supplies woefully inadequate upon arriving at Strasbourg. He requested that Karl Friedrich permit the French army to requisition supplies within his electorate.[15] Carl Josef Oehl, privy councilor and high commissioner to the elector, left for Imperial headquarters in Strasbourg to coordinate French requisitions in Baden.[16] Berthier pledged French troops would not be in the electorate for more than two days, but in that time provisions and shelter were required. Oehl likened the advance of the Grande Armée to ants, and worried that they would exhaust the countryside. It was of the utmost importance, therefore, that he expend all his energy to insure that all that was needed was provided, thereby reducing any possibility of excesses committed by hungry soldiers.[17] The French army behaved generally well during its march through Baden, with minimal incident. The city and University of Heidelberg requested exemption from French requisitions. Napoleon affirmed the request for the university, but not the city.[18]

There is no question that quartering and provisioning the tens of thousands of French troops burdened the population of Baden. It was a most unpleasant task, but it was directed and conducted with the cooperation of the local authorities in the name of the elector. IOUs abounded. Ratstatt provided 25,000 rations of bread in twelve hours. Heidelberg produced 40,000 rations of biscuits, 20,000 rations of meat and 10,000 pairs of shoes.[19] These supplies sufficed to carry the army into Württemberg, but no formal alliance had yet been established with that German prince.

It became critical for Napoleon to either secure an agreement from Frederick II or let his army loose on the countryside. Negotiations with the elector of Württemberg continued through September and up to the moment Marshal Ney's corps arrived before Stuttgart. Napoleon guaranteed the elector's territorial sovereignty, to support mediatization of the lands of Imperial counts and knights within his borders, and to promote his elevation to king.[20] The elector was truly in a bind, as Mack's army at Ulm was directly upon Württemberg's border and Austrian cavalry patrols regularly forayed into his territory looking for the French. Thus, Napoleon would have to move a bit closer if he desired Wurttemberg's support. In any event, the French emperor informed his marshals that upon arriving at Stuttgart and Ludwigsburg they would find bread and supplies. "Give Marshal Lannes to understand what difficulties he will experience in providing the 100,000 rations of bread," Napoleon wrote, "that in this matter the well known zeal and abilities of Marshal Lannes are of great confidence."[21]

If speed was Napoleon's primary weapon, then the time spent foraging would play against it. Considering the average distance marched by French troops was eighteen miles a day, foraging would have been a difficult affair. Napoleon therefore arrived with all haste at Ludwigsburg on the night of 2 October. He had left Strasbourg the previous morning, not stopping to pay a visit to the reluctantly cooperative elector of Baden. Marshal Ney was before Stuttgart, and his patrols were ranging throughout the electorate toward Ulm. Napoleon wanted Frederick II to know that if it was fear of the Austrians that kept him from a formal alliance, he no longer had anything to fear. If the elector were, in fact, more favorably disposed to Austria than France, the presence of a French army before his capital would serve to change his mind. Nothing could be left to chance. In letters to his brother Joseph, and the Empress Josephine dated 1 October, he spoke of Württemberg as a willing ally.[22]

It appears that Frederick II was hedging his bets. It was perhaps the wisest move he could make. On 1 October he wrote Emperor Francis that the presence of more than 70,000 French troops on his soil placed him in a difficult situation.[23] When Napoleon arrived he was treated to banquets and operas while Didelot conducted negotiations. "I am very content with the Elector of Württemberg and in general the spirit of Germany," Napoleon wrote Cambacérès, his arch-chancellor. "My junction with the Bavarians is made. I have done the same with the troops from Württemberg and Baden," he continued. "Timing is superb, my columns are proceeding in a grand march, and the month of *véndemiaire* [October] will not pass without truly great events."[24]

On 5 October Württemberg officially joined the French alliance. Napoleon pledged to rid the electoral territories of Austrian troops and to procure an indemnity for damages caused by Austrian forces. In return Frederick II would provide 8,000 to 10,000 men and 1,000 cavalry. The electoral city of Ludwigsburg and the capital of Stuttgart were to be free of French troops.[25] More pressing than the contribution of 10,000 Württembergers to the French war effort was a subsidiary agreement establishing supply contracts in the elector's territories. The French army was able to draw provisions from Würt-temberg without having to scour the countryside. The corps thus attained ample supplies that would easily carry them into Bavaria.[26]

Further north Bernadotte, Marmont, and part of the Bavarian army left Wurzburg on 30 September for the Danube via Prussian Anspach.[27] Napoleon resolved that Prussian territory would be violated in the name of expediency and strategic necessity. Writing Max Joseph, Napoleon explained that in the course of operations in south Germany during the war of the Second Coalition, French troops traversed Anspach without causing much concern in Berlin. Napoleon assumed such would be the case again. He continued, saying that if Prussian forces in Anspach were in sufficient strength and determined to prevent the passage of the army, "[W]e will lose nothing at this point."[28]

Bernadotte still faced the difficult task of furnishing the most basic supplies for his corps, Marmont, and the Bavarians. He reported that his troops had less than two days' worth of grain to make biscuits, but hoped to purchase what was needed in Anspach with vouchers.[29] The three corps advanced upon the Prussian territory in separate columns, and while a Prussian major and the local officials informed Bernadotte that Prussian neutrality must be respected, the French marshal and his forces continued on their way. The Prussian military governor, General Tauenzein, was in Bayreuth with his small division and not capable of reacting to this blatant violation. Nonetheless, Bernadotte was refused provisions. The Prussian administration and population was most uncooperative. The four days traversing Anspach were clearly uncomfortable, and the marshal remained concerned about adequate supplies.[30]

The violation of Prussian neutrality sent King Frederick William III into an uncharacteristic rage. Prussia found itself caught between Alexander's threats and Napoleon's actions. Metternich, the Austrian ambassador in Berlin, proffered to Franz Colloredo, the Austrian minister, that news of Alexander's earlier ultimatum to violate Prussian neutrality by marching Buxhowden's army from Poland through Silesia reached Napoleon's ear through Laforest and/or Duroc. Upon learning this information he determined that the violation of Hohenzollern territory would occur after the Russians had done so in Silesia.[31] Napoleon completely misread the situation. Alexander balked, halting Buxhowden's movement until he met personally with Frederick William. Bernadotte and Marmont, however, did not delay and committed an unthinkable sin against Prussia. At least that is how Frederick William III saw it. Curiously enough, while French actions enraged the king, news that Bavarian troops were among the French corps infuriated him.[32] In the end, French violation of Prussian territory moved Frederick William III toward the Russian camp. He decided to occupy Hanover in response and entertain Alexander's overtures when the Tsar arrived in Berlin in October. Yet, he was not fully convinced to depart from Prussia's neutrality.[33]

Napoleon's decision to move the corps through Anspach was both a military and a diplomatic decision. Clearly he did not consider Frederick William's potential reaction too seriously, otherwise he would not have given the orders. Prussian mobilization and Frederick William's vitriolic response to the violation of Anspach proved a dangerous combination. Yet, Duroc's information allayed fears of the Prussian army marching against the Grande Armée's rear. Furthermore, the current deployment of the Prussian army insured that they could not pose a significant threat to the French armies in Germany for some time.

As it stood in September 1805, the majority of the Prussian army was encamped in the east. There were thirty-nine battalions and sixty-five squadrons in east and west Prussia, with an additional forty battalions and seventy-five squadrons in Prussian Poland. An observation corps of fifteen battalions and twenty squadrons was in upper Silesia, and another of eighteen battalions and thirty-three squadrons in Pomerania. This deployment reflected Frederick William's desire to protect north German neutrality against Russian armies moving through Poland, and Russian and Swedish expeditionary corps in the Baltic. The only Prussian forces in western Germany were those in garrison in Anspach, Bayreuth, the central provinces, and a larger Westphalian corps of thirteen battalions and seven squadrons. A reserve army of forty-four battalions and fifty-five squadrons were in the Mark (Brandenberg) and Magdeburg.[34]

There are several issues to examine here. The number of battalions and squadrons is misleading. This is one of the central problems when discussing Prussian military potential in 1805. Although the Prussian army was substantial on paper, it was not at full strength in September or, for that matter, October 1805. In an article assessing Prussian military power through 1806, Dennis Showalter observed that the Prussian army was a "front-loaded military system."[35] When one looks at the Prussian army in its wars of the eighteenth century, it is critical to note that it never entered a conflict as a reaction force. This was so in 1740, 1756, and 1792. The Prussian army was never forced to mobilize in reaction to an already existing threat. As such it entered conflicts at full strength, having ample time to prepare for their respective campaigns. In 1805 this was not the case.

The Prussian army was ill prepared for war in the fall of 1805, and Duroc's September assessment was correct. The canton, reserve, and furlough system was designed to keep military expenditure at a minimum and did much to retard the pace of mobilization in 1805.[36] This is where historians are confronted by the difficulty of separating perception from reality. To all parties outside Prussia, its military reputation and potential made it a significant factor. The reality was otherwise, but which of the parties knew the true condition of the army outside of Prussia? For that matter, it is clear that among the court camarilla there was dissension over Prussia's response.

Frederick William III summoned Duroc and Laforest to Potsdam and vilified them, threatening to expel them from the kingdom. It was Karl von Hardenberg, the Prussian co-foreign minister who convinced the king to moderate his anger and first demand an explanation.[37] Hardenberg, however, was among those at court pushing the king toward the coalition. Although his status was diminished in September by the appointment of his pro-French foil, Christian von Haugwitz, as co-foreign minister, Frederick William received council from both. Similarly, Johann Lombard, a cabinet councilor, sided with Haugwitz and did not desire to "rush headlong" into a confrontation with France. He wrote Hardenberg in mid-October as tensions were building, asking him to consider the implication of pushing Prussia toward war. Lombard was quite concerned with the court's decision to occupy Hanover in retaliation for Anspach. He told Hardenberg that the occupation of Hanover was essentially a declaration of war against France. "If we must fight," he said, "what can we do with only 35 battalions?"[38] It appears that Hardenberg accepted Lombard's logic and requested from Laforest that French troops be withdrawn from Hanover prior to the arrival of Prussian forces.[39]

Lombard's characterization of Prussian army strength at thirty-five battalions indicates members of the court were well aware of their military shortcomings. A week or so earlier, the Duke of Brunswick met with Prussian military leadership to discuss options. It was agreed that the electors of Hesse-Cassel and Saxony would be asked to commit troops to future Prussian military endeavors.[40] On paper the strength of the Prussian army and its allies was impressive, but mobilization was slower than expected, and orders for redeployment applied only to the reserve army in the Mark.[41] Some of the army's battalions were dedicated to a Lower Saxon Corps to be eventually deployed between Erfurt, Eisenach, and Saalfeld. Most of the army, however, remained in Pomerania, East Prussia, and Prussian Poland.[42]

All of this came to Napoleon's attention as the Grand Armée bore down on the Danube. The movement of his corps through Swabia and Anspach was completely successful. Once the illusion of a headlong advance upon Ulm was made, Napoleon ordered Lannes, Murat, and Ney to skirt north of the Danube and cross the river further down between Elchingen and Donauworth. By 8 October Imperial headquarters was established at the latter city, accompanied by Soult's corps.[43] Mack had 66,000 infantry and 9,000 cavalry in Bavaria, and refused to acknowledge Napoleon was not going to oblige him with a frontal assault. During his discussion with Francis earlier, the quartermaster general went as far as to propose sending a column through Switzerland, along Lake Constance, to outflank Napoleon![44]

Archduke Ferdinand, the nominal commander of the Austrian army in Germany, was fully aware of the situation. He understood that an advance from Württemberg compelled Mack to keep forces in place at Ulm; all the while Bernadotte was moving against the Danube bridges at Ingolstadt and Neustadt. He felt somewhat relieved by the arrival of additional forces, courtesy of Archduke Charles in Italy, but desperately awaited news of the Russian army.[45] Mack finally realized Napoleon's true intentions on 6 October and began to draw his forces closer to Ulm, concentrated between Gunzburg and Memmingen. They were in no position to reinforce Kienmayer, holding Ingostadt and Neuberg on the Danube with scant forces. The Austrian general withdrew against overwhelming numbers, giving up the Danube bridges and falling back upon Austrian reserves near Augsburg. Kienmayer's movements were unknown to Mack, and much of his army was moving northeast from Memmingen toward the Lech. There were still quite a few battalions in the Vorarlberg and Inner Austria, although Jellacic's large column was ordered up as well.[46]

Napoleon arrived on the Danube between Dillingen and Ingolstasdt with 180,000 men. On 7 October he resolved to cross the river and swing part of his army around Mack's right flank, pushing them against Ulm. Murat, Lannes, Ney, and Soult were ordered from Donauworth to Augsburg, then west, cutting Mack and Ferdinand off from Austria and Kutusov's army. Ney divided his corps moving along both banks of the Danube, with Lannes further south toward Zusmarshausen. Soult marched to Augsburg and Landesberg, and Murat covered the gap between the two corps. The first major encounter with Austrian forces occurred at Wertingen. General Werneck's division was the furthest forward. En route to Donauworth he discovered Lannes's corps before him. The combination of Lannes's infantry and Murat's cavalry overwhelmed Werneck's battalions; bloodied, they withdrew toward Ulm. Ney also made quick work of Austrian detachments at Gunzburg.[47]

Soult continued unmolested against Memmingen, where he chased Austrian forces from the town. He then shifted north toward Ulm. Marmont's corps moved into line with Lannes's as he moved on Ulm. The trap was closing. To the east, Davout, Bernadotte, and the Bavarians advanced against Keinmayer, who was now falling back upon Munich. Bernadotte received intelligence that the Russians were arriving at Braunau on the Bavarian border. Napoleon immediately sent the three corps to cover the Isar River at Munich and to prevent Kutusov from coming to Mack's aid.[48] Five days after crossing the Danube, Napoleon caught an Austrian army in his net.

By 10 October half the Austrian army was in and around Ulm. The walled city straddled the Danube. Although it was abundantly clear to Mack and Ferdinand that the French were on the right (south) bank in force, the question remained whether they had any significant strength on the left (north) bank. Two options lay before the stymied Quartermaster General: attempt to break out toward the Tyrol, or go north across the Danube to Bohemia. At this moment Marshal Soult's corps had not completed its movement toward Memmingen. Napoleon certainly believed Mack would take the shortest route, withdrawing to the Tyrol, with Jellacich covering the retreat. Mack and Ferdinand, however, decided the longer route to Bohemia would be better, as there would be less resistance. On 11 October General Schwarzenberg sortied from the city with 25,000 troops. He met Dupont's isolated French division before Haslach. The French general withdrew in good order after suffering heavy casualties. Instead of capitalizing upon their victory, Schwarzenberg turned about and marched his troops back to Ulm. The following day Napoleon sent all of Ney's corps, accompanied by half of Lannes's corps, across to the north bank.[49]

Mack and Ferdinand retained the largest portion of their army on the north bank, and on 13 October General Werneck, with 13,000 men, tried once more to break out. He moved northeast of the city on the road to Noerdlingen. Werneck's advance provided Ferdinand the opportunity to break out himself. He had enough of Mack. Leading twelve squadrons of cavalry, the Archduke rode out of Ulm to join Werneck. Napoleon quickly dispatched Murat with two cavalry divisions and one infantry division. They pursued Ferdinand vigorously. Short of Noerdlingen, Werneck found himself isolated and hard-pressed. He surrendered to Murat on 18 October. Ferdinand, however, refused to place himself in French hands and with his cavalry escaped through Anspach to Bohemia. Napoleon prohibited Murat from following the archduke through Prussian territory, telling him, "I have already quarreled enough with this power over the first passage."[50]

Much of the lethargy present in the Austrian camp was the product of divided command. Between 11 and 14 October, Mack held several war councils. The confusion over command led to heated arguments over options. Whereas Napoleon was coordinating the movement of 180,000 men in Bavaria, Mack could not control his small army at Ulm.[51] In the end "too many cooks" prevented the Austrian army from escaping.

Lannes and Marmont, with part of the cavalry reserve, moved in from the east. Marshal Ney moved along the north bank to seal off the city. A final Austrian attempt to keep the noose from tightening was defeated at Elchingen on 14 October. That same day Marshal Soult entered Memmingen and sent his advanced guard north toward the beleaguered city. General Jellacic, perhaps the most fortunate, extricated his division to the Vorarlberg before Soult closed the trap. Mack was alone. By 16 October French cannon opened fire on Ulm. Mack began negotiations in earnest, pledging to surrender the city by 25 October if the Russians did not march to their relief. He lost his nerve, however, and surrendered the city and the remnants of his army, some 23,000 men, on 19 October.[52]

Napoleon's victory in Bavaria was complete. Less than three weeks passed from the moment the Grande Armée crossed the Rhine on 30 September until the seizure of Ulm on 19 October. Mack's humiliating defeat did not eliminate Austria from the coalition. News of the surrender did not reach Vienna until 24 October. Despair is perhaps the best word to describe the scene as recounted by British ambassador Sir Arthur Paget.[53] The shock of Mack's complete and abject defeat soon faded as Prussian intervention seemed imminent. Tsar Alexander was in Berlin trying to speed Prussia's accession to the coalition. Clemens von Metternich, the Austrian ambassador, wrote Colloredo of his interview with the Russian monarch. Alexander was none too concerned with Mack's fate. "Your reverses are no doubt unfortunate," he told Metternich. "[I]t is only one misfortune to repair and twenty thousand men do not form the Austrian power."[54]

Napoleon understood Mack's surrender did not mean the end of the war. General Kutusov's army of 50,000 men was at Braunau, and Kienmayer's Austrians managed to extricate themselves from Bavaria in the face of Bernadotte's rapid advance upon Munich. Prussia, however, gave Napoleon grave concern. Frederick Wiilliam's reaction to the violation of Anspach was completely unexpected. Duroc's appraisal of the situation in Berlin and all information coming to Imperial headquarters indicated that there was movement in Prussia. Duroc observed that the Prussian king's cabinet was "unanimously" against France, and Russian influence was gaining ground. Yet, he followed his remarks by saying that for all Alexander's influence, Frederick William III determined not to commit Prussia to war. He wanted peace and would demand only those terms that would truly secure peace in open negotiations with Napoleon.[55] The emperor could no longer count on Prussian passivity. Frederick William permitted Buxhowden's army passage through Silesia, and the Russians and Swedes landed substantial forces at Stralsund.

Napoleon penned the Prussian king from Munich, seeking to diffuse the situation. He told Frederick William that he was unaware that the movement of French forces through Anspach would have elicited such a reaction in Berlin. Moreover, the emperor innocently claimed the Treaty of Basel provided for such latitude, and, in any case, during the two previous wars French troop movements through Anspach had not been met with protest from Berlin. To illustrate his honest intentions, Napoleon explained that his forces did not pursue Archduke Ferdinand into Prussian territory, and the king should consider this an act of good faith.[56] It is unclear if Napoleon's allusion to the Treaty of Basel simply implied that the Prussian territory lay south of the Main River and was therefore not officially considered neutral. His contention that Anspach was traversed in the last two wars with no seeming reaction by Berlin was incredibly weak. In any case, Frederick William and his cabinet were taking a long, hard look at Prussia's response.

Napoleon rarely left anything to chance. In anticipation of a potential threat to France's Rhenish frontier he had ordered the formation of four reserve corps on the Rhine at the outset of the campaign. These corps were composed primarily of National Guard, with several regiments of regulars to bolster their ranks. The two largest were the II Reserve Corps under Marshal Lefebvre at Mainz and the III Reserve Corps under Marshal Kellerman at Strasbourg.[57] By the end of October these corps were taking shape, and Prussian forces in Westphalia were minimal. The deployment of the Lower Saxon Corps, however, potentially threatened the Grande Armée's line of communications, even with the approach of Marshal Augereau's VII Corps, who was within a week of the Rhine.

Napoleon also contended with the English threat to the French coast. He did not abandon the Boulogne camp or the others along the Channel coast. At the end of August he ordered Marshals Davout, Soult, and Ney to leave one of their line regiments in camp, along with ten of their third battalions. Under Marshal Brune, a further nine third battalions from assorted regiments of the Grande Armée and three Italian regiments, which were part of the Army of the Ocean Coast, reinforced these units. In all this provided some 30,000 troops for the defense of Boulogne, not counting the forces deployed in Holland.[58]

Most French regiments in 1805 had three battalions; the first two were combat battalions and the third served as a depot or training battalion. Those detached to the Channel coast or remaining in the interior were not incorporated into the army as they moved to the Rhine. Throughout the autumn of 1805, Napoleon employed the third battalions as ready reserves, combining them into provisional regiments forming conscript divisions. This was an incredibly efficient use of manpower to meet an unanticipated threat to the Empire. Although these battalions were initially deployed on the Channel coast, Napoleon directed them at the end of September to the Rhine. There they were sent to either Mainz or Strasbourg where the reserve corps were formed under Marshals Lefebvre and Kellermann, respectively.

Both marshals were ordered to the Rhine on 21 September, where they were charged with the defense of the French frontiers. Lefebvre's corps at Mainz was composed of two divisions totaling fifteen third battalions from the regiments of the Grande Armée, including those currently with Brune's army on the coast. Similarly, Kellermann's corps was divided into two divisions, but hosting nineteen third battalions. These battalions were not at full strength, but it was anticipated, based upon Napoleon's decree, that they would soon reach their full compliment with the arrival of active conscripts of the years XIV and XV, supplemented by conscripts of the reserve for the years X, XI, XII, and XIII. All totaled Napoleon anticipated 40,000 troops eventually deployed on the Rhine.[59]

Annual conscription under the Consulate was fixed at 30,000 men for the active army with an additional 30,000 for the reserve.[60] Therefore, those designated for the reserve corps on the Rhine were drawn from the current conscription classes, as well as from the reserves of the previous four years. These men ranged from 20 to 25 years of age and had rudimentary military training.[61] By calling upon the active and reserve conscripts, Napoleon could be assured that they would arrive at their depots relatively quickly, thereby filling the ranks and establishing a reasonable defense of the Rhine if needed. Indeed, Lefebvre and Kellermann provided a ready reserve to reinforce the Grande Armée if needed. In this situation the reserve system was essential to Imperial defense. In actuality the number of conscripts in these corps never exceeded 25,000 men.[62]

While the Rhine was watched, Napoleon directed the formation of another reserve corps along the Atlantic coast. Napoleon wanted to guard against a landing in the Gironde or the Vendée. General Gouvion was given command of six regiments of the line, some 5,000 men, and ordered to assemble at Poitiers. There he would receive a further 5,000 conscripts of the year XIV to bolster his ranks.[63] A reserve division was also established in Piedmont under General Menou to reinforce Imperial troops in Italy, although they numbered less than 5,000 men.[64]

Menou's reserve in Piedmont protected the Ligurian coast, but there were insufficient forces available to cover the coastline into Tuscany. The kingdom of Etruria (Tuscany) was a Napoleonic satellite. Its queen, Maria-Louisa, was the daughter of Carlos IV of Spain.[65] As France and Spain were allied, and Etruria a Bourbon kingdom, Napoleon insisted Spain contribute 2,000 to 3,000 troops for its defense. Moreover, Napoleon demanded they send a second contingent of 15,000 men to Boulogne in order to free up 6,000 French there for service on the Rhine. The Spanish were not forthcoming and negotiations were intense. By the first week of October, however, a small division was assembled under the command of General O'Farrill, and they began their march to France and thence Italy. The contribution of 15,000 men was tabled.[66]

The Imperial forces allocated for defense of the coasts, the Rhine, and Italy were supplemented further with the addition of French National Guard battalions. On 15 September Napoleon called up National Guard companies in thirty-three French departments and all departments in Belgium. Napoleon was very particular, mobilizing only the elite companies of the National Guard battalions in those departments. These companies were organized into converged battalions and distributed among seven reserve divisions, each constituting 5,000 to 6,000 men. Reserves were concentrated along the eastern frontiers of France from the Channel to the Mediterranean. Similar orders were given to the Italian departments in Piedmont and Liguria.[67] Although National Guard battalions were not intended for use on campaign, the creation of the seven reserve divisions provided another line of defense on the French frontier. It also freed a number of line battalions for duty closer to the theaters of war.

This was critical. Napoleon wanted to reinforce his army in preparation for their march on Vienna. He also needed to strengthen his position in southern Germany if Prussia declared war. Marshal Augereau's VII Corps finally crossed the Rhine on 26 October. The electors of Baden and Württemberg and the landgraf of Hesse-Darmstadt had yet to provide their military contingents required by treaty. They were reluctant to do so until the campaign in Bavaria was decided. If it had turned poorly for Napoleon, they could easily explain their agreements with France as signed under duress. Napoleon prodded Karl Friedrich of Baden and Frederick II of Württemberg, but his attitude toward Ludwig X, the Landgraf of Hesse-Darmstadt, was decidedly hostile. He told Talleyrand, "[H]e must give me 3,000 men or the landgraf will forever renounce my protection."[68] With Napoleon's decisive victory, the German princes were forthcoming. Only Max IV Joseph kept to his terms, considering Napoleon liberated his electorate six weeks after Mack's army chased him from Munich.

As it stood by the third week of October, Napoleon prepared to advance into Austria, but was quite conscious of the Prussian threat. Furthermore, while combat in Bavaria was already decided, the campaign in Italy had not yet begun. Then there was Admiral Villeneuve, who at last report was still in Cadíz. There were too many loose ends. The French emperor shifted his corps toward the Inn, while Marshal Massena advanced against the Archduke Charles on the Adige River. For his part, Villeneuve finally sailed out with his fleet to engage Nelson off Cape Trafalgar. The war was far from over.

CHAPTER TEN

NOVEMBER 1805

ADMIRAL VILLENEUVE HAD BEEN IN CADÍZ for two months. If Napoleon was angered by Villeneuve's lack of aggressiveness in July, his loitering in the Spanish port infuriated him. As the Grande Armée marched to the Rhine, Napoleon sent new orders to the admiral directing the combined fleets into the Mediterranean. The arrival of British troops at Malta, along with the reinforcement of the Russian contingent at Corfu, was read as a precursor to an invasion of Naples. General St. Cyr, with his dispersed corps, would be hard pressed to hold his position in central Italy against a concerted allied effort. Furthermore, the presence of the main Austrian army in Venetia meant Marshal Massena would have his hands full, and unable to support St. Cyr. Villeneuve's mission, therefore, was to sail from Cadíz with Admiral Gravina, reach Cartagena where the fleet would be joined by a Spanish squadron, and then proceed to Naples, where he would disembark troops and disrupt British activity in the central Mediterranean. The fleets would then resupply at Toulon and continue to operate from that port. Napoleon had lost all patience with Villeneuve. He told Admiral Decrès that Admiral Rosily would replace Villeneuve as soon as he arrived at Toulon.[1]

Napoleon's discontent with Villeneuve festered, and two days after writing Decrès, he dispatched Admiral Rosily to Cadíz—no doubt believing it would be another two months if he had to wait for Villeneuve to summon enough courage to leave the comfort of the Spanish port.[2] The emperor was unaware Nelson's fleet watched the harbor and was in equal numbers. Both fleets had thirty-three ships of the line, but England maintained the qualitative advantage. Regardless, Napoleon seemed to believe that the Franco-Spanish fleet could elude Nelson and make for Cartagena. He thought the addition of the Spanish squadron would provide the admiral with sufficient numbers to challenge the pursuing British fleet. Villeneuve received Napoleon's orders on 27 September but found few of his colleagues eager to chance an engagement. On 11 October Rosily arrived in Madrid, and

Villeneuve realized his days as commander of the combined fleets would soon be at an end. Not wanting to be relieved without attempting action, Villeneuve and Gravina sailed from Cadíz on 19 October.[3]

Nelson's brigs and frigates posted close to the harbor reported the enemy fleet had departed. The British admiral was somewhat disconcerted, as he recently had sent off six ships to Gibraltar. He faced Villeneuve with only twenty-seven ships of the line. At noon on 21 October, Nelson attacked the Franco-Spanish fleet off Cape Trafalgar. Cutting their line in two, his ships maneuvered around the latter half of the line under Gravina and destroyed it piecemeal. Villeneuve in the vanguard turned about but was unable to reach his Spanish comrade in time. His own squadron became separated and the French admiral found himself facing superior forces. By four o'clock Villeneuve engaged the British and was compelled shortly thereafter to strike his flag. Gravina escaped by some miracle. A squadron of four French ships, separated from Villeneuve in the afternoon, also made it to sea as the battle drew to a close. They were subsequently intercepted and captured two weeks later. Nineteen of the thirty-three ships of the combined fleet were lost. The British lost none, but Nelson fell, mortally wounded.[4]

Napoleon received news of Trafalgar from Admiral Decrès three weeks after the battle. He replied, "[T]his changes nothing."[5] Indeed, it had no bearing on events in central Europe. The victory in Bavaria was more immediate, and the campaign in Italy crucial. Once the emperor turned from the Channel at the end of August he did not look back. Victory for England, however, did not translate into victory for their continental allies. In the last days of October Napoleon redeployed his army in Bavaria, and Marshal Massena began his offensive against the Archduke Charles.

The situation in Italy was not as desperate as it had been in August. Charles's army significantly outnumbered Massena, but toward the end of September negotiations between France and the kingdom of the Two Sicilies (Naples) culminated in a treaty of neutrality. Ferdinand IV vowed to prohibit the coalition from landing forces in his kingdom, and he forbid the use of his ports by coalition ships. In return, Napoleon would withdraw St. Cyr's troops from the ports, to be replaced by the Neapolitan army. French forces would be removed one month after the treaty's ratification.[6] St. Cyr's redeployment by October's end would bolster the security of the Kingdom of Italy. Moreover, O'Farrill's Spanish division was expected to arrive sometime in November.[7]

Marshal André Massena arrived in Italy to find Marshal Jourdan, his predecessor, and Prince Eugene, viceroy of Italy, had already provisioned the fortresses and insured the army was properly supplied. The Army of Italy comprised six French infantry divisions, one Italian infantry division, and three cavalry divisions. Its possessed approximately 48,000 men under arms and prepared for campaign. This did not include St. Cyr's 20,000 men still in Naples.[8] French regiments in Italy had not the benefit of the extensive training that the divisions of the Grande Armée experienced at Boulogne, but their quality and experience were similar to their compatriots. Veterans abounded, many of them having served in Italy since 1799.[9] Massena, therefore, found the army in good condition, and logistical support was far superior to anything Napoleon contended with in Germany. The only matter of concern was that he faced an Austrian army almost twice his number led by a very competent general, and although the divisions in Italy remained dispersed, much of Charles's army was concentrated.

On 23 September Napoleon ordered Massena to assemble his army at Verona, cross the Adige, and take the offensive.[10] The emperor expected to be across the Rhine the following week and wanted Charles occupied in Italy. Napoleon was well aware Charles's forces were present in greater numbers. He confidently proclaimed to Prince Eugene, "60,000 men in Italy is a third more than I ever had. Austrian boasts cannot deceive my old soldiers. The Austrians have only 70,000 men . . . a rabble that cannot compare to my troops."[11] Charles had more than 70,000 men, but they were stretched along the Adige and into the Tyrol. The main army was camped at Padua under General Heinrich Bellegarde, with a smaller corps (*abteilung*) under General Josef Hiller in the Tyrol, which maintained communications with Auffenberg and Jellacic in the Vorarlberg.[12] The distance from Padua to Ulm was roughly 200 miles "as the crow flies."

Upon his arrival in Italy, the archduke found the army in poor condition. Though his was supposedly the main army, food, clothing, weapons, wagons and all necessary equipment went to Germany. The quartermaster general wanted to insure his forces in Bavaria were well supplied. After all, they were taking the field before the army in Italy. Charles's command exceeded 90,000 men, but 10,000 were in the Tyrol and 7,000 in garrison at Venice. Archduke Ludwig's 30,000 men forming in Inner Austria were originally designated to Italy, but Charles convinced his brother Francis to redirect them to Germany. Making matters worse, battalions stood at fifty percent of their required strength. Charles estimated he could not adequately field more than 60,000 men but eventually gathered more.[13]

Unaware of Charles's predicament, Massena needed more time to muster his forces. He wrote the archduke on 29 September requesting hostilities not commence without a six-day notice. Charles replied that no official state of war existed between France and Austria, therefore he could not accede to the marshal's petition. Shortly thereafter, however, Charles reconsidered and agreed to the convention.[14] He was terribly concerned about events in Germany and about severe shortages affecting the army. "Already regiments have water and bread for only three days," he wrote his uncle, "and I am told our magazines contain less than 15 days supply. We have need for 60 ovens.

Mack has said 30 would suffice and we have found in this country neither ovens nor bakers."[15]

During the first week of October, Charles and Massena moved their divisions forward. The French army converged on Verona as the emperor recommended. He intended on carrying the city and establishing himself on the east bank of the Adige with the river to his right and the mountains to his left. The position would allow him to advance against Charles with his flanks secure. As his object was to pin the archduke, this would hopefully keep his attention focused. Charles was cognizant of Massena's disposition, but he was not quite sure whether Massena intended to come straight on or perhaps pass over the Adige further down at either Arcole or Albaredo as Napoleon had done in 1796. Massena led a division at that battle and was keenly aware of his options. Charles contended then with both strategic and operational dilemmas. The threat of a French flank march could be dealt with by a judicious allocation of forces; the fate of the army in Germany, though, was out of his hands.

Napoleon ordered Massena to commence operations as the Grande Armée moved through Swabia. Six days later the marshal informed the archduke that their truce would end as of 14 October. Although Massena was in constant correspondence with Napoleon via Switzerland, Charles was left without information from Germany for some time. The French emperor called upon his Swiss allies to proclaim their neutrality and prevent the use of their territory by Austrian troops.[16] Charles remained without news from Germany for five days. A captured dispatch written between 7 and 8 October told him that Napoleon was advancing from the Rhine to the Danube and probing toward Munich. This heightened his fear that Mack would be destroyed in Bavaria, leaving the Russians to defend the road to Vienna. He finally received word by 17 October, confirming his worst fears. The French were pouring across the Danube and Munich had fallen. Mack and Ferdinand were cut off and planning a breakout north to Bohemia. In a letter to his uncle, Charles conveyed, "Napoleon has good reason to say Mack is nothing more than a charlatan."[17]

Anticipating disaster, the archduke deployed his army in consideration of either coming to the aid of the army in Germany or withdrawing upon Vienna. His right wing under Hiller remained fixed in the Tyrol and maintained solid communications with the army in Germany. Charles detached General Davidovich to guard the Adige crossings from Arcole to Albaredo to his left. He allocated a substantial number of cavalry squadrons toward the lower Adige and Venice. In his center between Verona and Caldiero he placed the bulk of his army under generals Bellegarde and Argenteau. They covered the main road that would carry the army, if needed, to Inner Austria.[18] Charles abandoned any intention of offensive operations. There would be no glorious march to Milan, advance into Switzerland, and union with the Austro-Russian army on the Rhine.

The city of Verona sat on the west bank of the Adige within the Kingdom of Italy. On the opposite bank sat the smaller town of Veronetta. Massena determined to storm Veronetta and seize the heights above the town, establishing a bridgehead for his army to debouch onto the east bank and advance against Charles's position along the Verona-Vicenza road. In the morning hours of 18 October the stalwart marshal led the assault across the bridge, carrying the town and the heights by the afternoon.[19] Charles held his position for the following week, unclear if the French assault was merely a diversion. Three French divisions had attempted to push across the river, one at Pescatina and the other two at Albaredo. It forced the archduke to refrain from counterattacking at Veronetta, leaving most of his 60,000 men around Caldiero, believing that he might find himself trapped between the Adige and a *manouevre sur la derriere.*

Massena had intended all of this. As his orders were to keep Charles occupied, he need not attack if the archduke neither counterattacked nor withdrew. Instead the marshal prepared to move all but two of his divisions across to the east bank of the Adige via Verona-Veronetta. He advanced headlong against the Austrian positions before Caldiero. For his part Charles was confident in his position, and desperately awaited news from Germany. On the night of 24 October Hiller passed along a demoralizing communiqué: Mack had surrendered at Ulm. Charles took stock of the general situation and sent off a report to his brother the emperor. His army in Italy was "the last force of the Austrian monarchy." The army in Germany had been destroyed. Its remnants were divided, some with Kutusov's Russians, no more than 55,000 men, and 15,000 to 16,000 in the Tyrol.[20]

Charles spent the night prefiguring the quickest route from Venetia to Inner Austria. He instructed his generals to prepare a withdrawal to the Brenta, Piave, Livenza, and Tagliamento rivers. They would then move on the Isonzo and continue their march into Austria. General Bellegarde was given the rear guard at Caldiero.[21] Charles understood that the distance from his current position to Vienna was double that from Bavaria to the Austrian capital.[22] His intended route was the same one his army took in 1797, having been forced from Italy by General Bonaparte. Unfortunately for the archduke, Massena received similar word of Mack's capitulation on 26 October and determined to strike at the Austrian army in anticipation of its withdrawal. For the next three days Massena's divisions pushed Austrian outposts back from the hills northwest of Caldiero and eventually cleared the road in advance of Charles's position.[23] The archduke realized that Massena would not permit him to leave Italy unmolested. The French marshal committed to battle before Caldiero, and the archduke obliged, needing to hurt Massena in order to effect his own retreat.

Heavy skirmishing between the two armies on 29 October preceded the greater battle the following day. Massena concentrated 23,400 infantry and

4,700 cavalry on the plane a mile west of Charles's position. Facing him the archduke deployed Bellegarde and Argenteau's columns, some 44,000 infantry and 6,500 cavalry. Massena's intention was to direct another 6,600 infantry and 1,000 cavalry under General Verdier on the west bank, and to cross the river by boat in the early morning and arrive on Charles's flank. Charles had a strong position, with the foothills of the Alps to his right, the town of Caldiero toward his center, and General Nordmann with a small division holding the left toward the river. General Davidovich with 10,000 men still guarded the Adige from Arcola to Albaredo. Massena kept him in place by detaching a cavalry brigade to demonstrate on the other bank.[24]

The battle of Caldiero began at ten o'clock in the morning. Verdier's division had not completed its crossing when it was engaged and thrown back across the Adige. Davidovich made a reconnaissance in force downstream to forestall any French attack. Finding no French other than cavalry, he pushed on, causing Verdier to consolidate his forces by early afternoon. Massena's flank attack never materialized. He launched two divisions against the Austrian center, and although initially successful they were repulsed by determined counterattacks. Massena tried to turn Charles's right. His regiments managed to reach the hills on the archduke's flank, but Charles maintained substantial reserves and was able to stem the French assault. In the end Massena lacked the numbers to press home his tactical advantages, and they were ultimately beaten back. Massena withdrew to his morning position and the battle drew to a close. Charles admitted suffering 5,000 casualties. Massena claimed 2,000, but it was most likely equal to Austrian losses.[25]

Undeterred by the battle's results Massena renewed his attack the next day. Verdier's division crossed the Adige during the night and advanced upon Charles's left. Massena's divisions in the center were sent forward to divert the archduke's attention. Unfortunately, Massena's desire to continue the battle was not reciprocated by his men. They were terribly fatigued. Verdier found little support for his advance and soon came under enormous pressure from two Austrian divisions. Operations ceased after five hours of combat and the Austrians, likewise fatigued, withdrew to their lines.[26]

When on the following day Massena sent a cavalry division to probe Charles's lines, he found the Austrian army had departed, leaving a rear guard to cover the road. Efforts to dislodge the small Austrian contingent failed after fierce resistance. General Frimont, commanding Austrian troops, had given the archduke a day. Charles had no concern for Massena. He wrote his brother on 3 November relaying the events of Caldiero, and more importantly that his army was already on the march for Vienna.[27] General Hiller took his division north to join with the Archduke John at Innsbruck. From there the generals intended on either finding their way to Vienna or, if blocked, uniting with the main army. Charles dispatched Davidovich to Venice to reinforce the garrison. Not long after, St. Cyr arrived with part of his army and placed the city under blockade. The general's other division remained in the Papal States, joined by an Italian brigade, and observed the Neapolitan frontier.[28] Unaware of Massena's attack and Charles's withdrawal, Napoleon redeployed his corps in anticipation of a possible Russian counteroffensive.

Kutusov arrived at Braunau on the Inn two weeks before Charles's battle at Caldiero. To describe the march of the Russian army from Brody to Braunau as lethargic would be charitable. Mack counted far too much on the Russians saving the day. Upon arriving at Vienna, Kutusov's army was strung out, with his cavalry and artillery in the last columns. As the rapidity of the French advance became clearer in the first days of October, Kutusov mounted his infantry on wagons and moved with all speed to the Bavarian border. Bernadotte first received intelligence of Kutusov's approach on 12 October from Austrian prisoners. He dispatched an officer to spy on the road to Braunau. Upon his return he reported that no more than two Russian regiments were present, along with the remnants of Kienmayer's Austrians.[29] By 17 October the marshal estimated 30,000 Russians were concentrated on the Inn, but that they lacked any artillery or cavalry. Bernadotte apprised the emperor that a second Russian army (Buxhowden) of 40,000 men was approaching Vienna.[30] Napoleon took every precaution to prevent the introduction of Russian forces into Bavaria by moving his corps to Munich and pushing Davout and Bernadotte toward the Austrian border.

Kutusov had no intention of advancing into Bavaria under existing conditions. Although General Kienmayer's corps, currently under Meerveldt, was present in force and there were 60,000 Russians and Austrians on the Inn, the Russian general refused to do more than reconnoiter French positions. He probed Passau, which remained under Bavarian control even after the Austrian invasion in September. There he found General Deroy's Bavarian division recently arrived to relieve the city. Kutusov's scouts reported Bernadotte and Davout's corps to his front. The number of French moving toward the Inn increased dramatically as Napoleon concentrated Marmont, Lannes, Soult, and Murat around Munich by 25 October. Ney at Ulm was directed to the Tyrol upon the approach of Augereau's VII Corps, currently crossing the Rhine.[31]

Francis traveled to Wels some miles to the east and discussed Austria's options with the Russian general. Kutusov determined not to stand at Braunau only to suffer the same fate as Mack. He informed Francis that he was withdrawing toward Vienna with Kienmayer's column, where he hoped to find Buxhowden. Kutusov also anticipated the introduction of the Prussian army into the conflict. He preferred to offer battle when the odds were slightly better and in his favor. Tsar Alexander arrived in Berlin on 25 October to move things along. The Russian monarch seemed far more interested in speeding the Prussian army into the field than he did his own.

The situation in northern Germany improved considerably through October. General Ostermann-Tolstoi arrived at Stralsund with 16,000 Russians on 8 October. Gustav IV Adolf had already assembled 12,000 Swedish troops there, although only 10,000 were available for the field army.[32] The Swedish king finalized subsidy negotiations with Pitt and arrived in Stralsund to take command of his army. He spent more time organizing his forces than moving them. Tolstoi concluded a military convention with the duke of Mecklenberg-Schwerin on 25 October, allowing for the passage of Russian troops from Pomerania to Hanover. In less than a week the Russian expeditionary force established its headquarters at Schwerin, no more than two days from the Hanoverian frontier.[33] Within a matter of days the Swedish army finally joined their Russian allies.

Duroc's assessment of the situation in Prussia indicated there was little chance Frederick William would do more than perhaps occupy Hanover in retaliation. Hardenberg's request that General Barbou, commanding 3,000 French in Hanover, withdraw prior to the introduction of Prussian troops into the electorate, indicated apprehension at Frederick William's court.[34] Indeed, Metternich reported to Colloredo that the negotiations between the Prussians, Russians, and Austrians in Berlin were exasperating. Count Haugwitz challenged each and every proposal. "Prussia is only accustomed to work when it is clearly for her own benefit," the ambassador proclaimed. "Europe would disappear before her eyes if it depended on her efforts to save it."[35] Prior to allied negotiations Napoleon concluded Duroc had done all he could in the Prussian capital, and he recalled him to Imperial headquarters. Laforest was left to observe the situation in Berlin.

The duke of Brunswick, commander in chief of the Prussian army, drew up two military memoranda and presented them to the king and his cabinet for their consideration. He laid out Prussia's military options, and predicted Napoleon's based on the position of Austrian and Russian forces in the Tyrol and on the Inn. Brunswick believed Napoleon would not advance on Vienna with 40,000 Austrians in the Tyrol, 50,000 in Italy, and 75,000 Russians and Austrians to his front.[36] He concluded that the French emperor could not possibly advance upon Vienna without leaving 40,000 men to guard his flank against Archdukes Charles and John. Moreover, with the Prussian army assembling in Franconia (central Germany), Napoleon had two choices: he could either march against the Prussians, leaving the Austrians and Russians to threaten his flanks; or he could advance against the Russians and Austrians, who would merely retreat down the Danube drawing the French from Bavaria and leaving south Germany open to a Prussian offensive.[37]

It appears that by all accounts the Prussian military leadership was absolutely convinced that Napoleon would not advance on Vienna with the Prussian army to his rear and a Russo-Swedish army in Hanover. Even the perceptive Colonel Gerhard von Scharnhorst (the future father of Prussian military reforms), who was on staff in Westphalia, noted to his friend Major

Knesbeck that Napoleon would be forced by events in north Germany to protect himself.[38] All of this of course was based on assumptions that Napoleon was going to take to his bed when he realized his actions had stirred Prussia.

Brunswick seemed less aware of the state of the Prussian army by the beginning of November than Napoleon. By October's end the Lower Saxon Corps, which was to form the core of the army, was still assembling. Prince Hohenlohe's corps in Prussian Poland was redeployed to Erfurt as the left wing of the new army, but it was only now marching through Saxony. Brunswick counted 10,000 to 12,000 Saxon auxiliaries to bolster Hohenlohe's numbers. In the meantime, a smaller corps prepared to secure Hanover, while General Blucher in Westphalia awaited the arrival of the Hessian elector's army.[39]

Brunswick's assessment of Napoleon's options failed to consider a third choice. Napoleon could afford to dispatch 40,000 men to separate Charles and John from Vienna, while allocating another 40,000 to guard Bavaria against Prussia when he had more than 200,000 in Germany under his command. The French emperor could call upon his reserve corps at Mainz and Strasbourg to reinforce Marshal Augereau's VII Corps and the German contingents. In short, Napoleon understood time was not on his side, and he pushed his corps into Austria at the moment Brunswick presented his conclusions to Frederick William III.

One of Napoleon's greatest assets was centralization of command. The coalition significantly overawed France in terms of troops and resources, but the events of October–November illustrated the lack of coordination among the allies. Kutusov and the Austrians believed that Prussia's commitment to the coalition would result in the introduction of Prussian troops into Bohemia via Saxony. At no time in the autumn of 1805 did the duke of Brunswick or Frederick William III ever consider this possibility. Tsar Alexander never demanded it during his negotiations in Berlin. Military operations were addressed directly, but Brunswick's proposals were accepted at the conclusion of discussions.[40] Decisions were made then in Vienna based upon false assumptions.

General Count Maximillian Latour, Charles's successor as president of the *Hofkriegsrat*, presented Francis I with a report on the state of coalition forces. He believed that despite the defeat in Bavaria, sufficient forces remained in the field. (See table on page 128.)

Latour's assessment was in fact correct. The combined Austro-Russian armies exceeded 300,000 men. When one includes the potential addition of 180,000 Prussian troops, the total strength rises to almost a half million. Napoleon could claim no more than 350,000 men, including his army in Italy. The Archduke Charles wrote his brother Josef that the emperor [Francis] was, unfortunately, surrounded by men who were either "idiots or scoundrels,"

AUSTRO-RUSSIAN FORCES 3 NOVEMBER 1805[41]

	Austria				Russia	
	Battalions	Squadrons	Infantry	Cavalry	Infantry	Cavalry
Army on the Inn	35	40	21, 989	4,073	37,700	11,000
At Vienna	22	7	13,356	571		
En route					85,552	40,808
Bohemia	22	7	18,502	3,140		
Tyrol	47	36	22,279	3,305		
Italy	162	86	93,293	8,585		
Total	305	181	169,419	19,674	123,252	51,808

always inclined to interpret events in a "good light."[42] It was this rosy assessment that became the prop and support of the coalition into November. Napoleon understood the danger if the allied armies united, but he was not prepared to accommodate them. Movement in Prussia concerned him more than the progress of Buxhowden's army in Bohemia. The French emperor dealt with the matter by pushing the Grande Armée into Austria on 30–31 October.

Unlike the logistical nightmare that nearly befell the French army in Swabia, Napoleon invaded Austria with an abundance of food, clothing, and ammunition. Augsburg was transformed into an enormous supply center. Max Joseph also abided by his agreements with Napoleon, who at this point could do no wrong as far as the elector was concerned. Bavarian grain flowed, and bakeries produced for the army. Napoleon benefited from the handsome harvest in southern Germany and was able to acquire sufficient foodstuffs due to the season. Thousands of pairs of shoes were distributed, replacing those worn during the rapid march over the past six weeks. Upon arriving at Braunau Napoleon found large stores of food and ammunition abandoned by the Austrians and Russians in their haste. This windfall was distributed as well. In order to keep the army in good supply as they advanced down the Danube toward Vienna, Napoleon established a large magazine at Passau where barges could easily transport supplies for the army's substantial needs.[43]

Fed, shod, and properly supplied, the corps of the Grande Armée moved into Austria. Marshal Ney's VI Corps advanced upon Innsbruck to prevent Archduke John from threatening communications in Swabia. General Marmont moved from Salzburg toward Leoben and Graz to cut Archduke Charles off from Vienna. Marmont arrived at Leoben on 7 November while Charles was still in Venetia. Bernadotte formed the reserve, whereas Davout, Soult, Lannes, and Murat composed the main body directed upon Linz. Napoleon created a new Franco-Dutch corps under Marshal Mortier by combining divisions at Passau and adding another along the way. He was tasked with clearing the north bank of the Danube in order to permit the unmolested transit of supply barges down river. Napoleon also wanted a flank guard in case Archduke Ferdinand reappeared from Bohemia.[44]

From his headquarters at Lambach, roughly 100 miles from Vienna, Napoleon proposed to the Austrian emperor a complete cession of hostilities. It is unclear whether he was sincere, but as time was not on his side, there seems to be little other explanation. At best, the offer was conducted with the intention of ending hostilities before the other Russian armies arrived and prior to Prussia's accession to the coalition. His proximity to Vienna no doubt lent confidence that the Austrians would eagerly negotiate, as he was closer to Vienna now than he had been in 1797. At that time General Bonaparte, with a much smaller army, was at Leoben, some 120 miles from the Austrian capital, and they eagerly agreed to sign an armistice.

General Ignaz Gyulai was dispatched by Francis to entertain negotiations. He was instructed to stall Napoleon as long as possible until the Prussians were fully committed and Buxhowden's army was further along.[45] The Austrians would not agree to an armistice, but instead wanted to continue operations during the course of negotiations. Napoleon would have none of it. He ended negotiations from Linz, some 80 miles from Vienna, and told Francis that as he abided the Tsar's interests, they had nothing in common. "This war is for Russia a war of whimsy," Napoleon scolded, "it is for Your Majesty and for me a war which absorbs all our means, all our sentiments, all our faculties." Napoleon complained Gyulai had not been authorized to conclude an armistice. When Francis was serious about peace, Napoleon said, he would be most receptive.[46]

Francis's determination to stay the course was not propagated by Tsar Alexander, as that monarch was in Berlin, but by Cobenzl and the like. It was further encouraged by news that a convention between Prussia and the coalition was forthcoming. On 3 November the Treaty of Potsdam was concluded between Prussia, Austria, and Russia. Short of openly declaring for the coalition, Frederick William agreed to present Napoleon with an ultimatum: accept Prussian mediation or Prussian guns. The terms of mediation called for the restoration of territory as established in the Treaty of Lunéville, restoration of the king of Sardinia to Piedmont, and restoration of Parma and Genoa. Sensing victory in their grasp, the treaty also demanded the independence of Holland and Switzerland, and the extension of Austrian territory from the Adige to the Mincio rivers, cutting into the Kingdom of Italy. Finally, Napoleon must abandon his Italian throne.[47] Metternich recalled later that the Prussians did not willingly submit to the alliance, but that it took three full days of hard negotiations before Haugwitz found the terms acceptable to present to Frederick William.[48] Prussia's commitment to the cause was most welcome. Tsar Alexander departed Frederick William's palace at Potsdam on 5 November. He bade farewell to the Prussian monarch before Frederick the Great's tomb.[49]

Now that the specifics were hammered out, it was left to England to close the deal. One of Frederick Williams's conditions upon acceding to the treaty provided that England cover the entire cost of fielding an army.[50] The former foreign minister, Lord Harrowby, was enlisted to travel to Berlin and make appropriate arrangements. He had permission to offer 2.5 million pounds for 150,000 to 200,000 troops. Lord Mulgrave, the sitting foreign minister, further instructed Harrowby to insure that any arrangements made by the continental powers take into consideration English interests.[51] Mulgrave had not soon forgotten the difficulty Alexander caused over Malta. Upon Harrowby's arrival in Berlin and presentation of the treaty, he proceeded to question numerous clauses of the convention, including Britain's position on Holland and Hanover.[52] Discussions with Hardenberg continued through the end of the month. Harrowby's visit did nothing to alter Napoleon's plans as he was already in Vienna when the British minister first arrived in Germany.

Napoleon was not terribly troubled by Austrian foot-dragging as his army bore down on Vienna. Perhaps they would be more amenable to negotiations if French troops were closer to the Austrian capital. On 8 November, Sir Arthur Paget reported from Vienna that panic had set in among the general population, Cobenzl and the government had departed the previous evening, and the Emperor Francis was also headed north to Moravia, where he intended to join the Tsar and Buxhowden's army.[53] Everyone assumed Napoleon would take the capital. Kutusov was at St. Polten forty miles west. Although the remnants of Kienmayer's command, now under General Meerveldt, had moved in unison with Kutusov, the Austrian general split his column from the Russian army on 4 November and withdrew from Steyr toward Leoben to await the Archduke Charles. Marmont, however, pursued Meerveldt and in successive engagements reduced his numbers to 2,000 men, forcing him into Hungary.[54] Kutusov continued his retreat and crossed the Danube on 9 November at Krems, desiring to join the Tsar and Buxhowden in Moravia. Marshal Mortier was on the north bank of the Danube with half his corps when Kutusov arrived at Krems. Wanting to discourage Mortier's pursuit, Kutusov pounced upon the weak corps at Durrenstein and inflicted heavy losses upon it. The Russian general then held his position along the Danube for two days.[55]

Napoleon continued his advance, spearheaded by Murat's and Lannes's corps, undeterred by Kutusov's minor victory. On 12 November they entered Vienna. An Austrian detachment under General Auersperg was left to destroy the mile-long bridge spanning the Danube. Murat and Lannes tricked Auersperg and the Austrian troops, claiming an armistice had been achieved. While the befuddled soldiers tried to confirm the story, French troops moved across the bridge, capturing it intact. This enabled Napoleon to launch his army into Moravia without delay.[56] The emperor arrived in Vienna on 14 November along with Soult's corps. Napoleon believed he could catch Kutusov at Krems before he moved to unite with Buxhowden. Sensing a trap, the wily Russian general led his columns on a quick march toward Znaim, closer to the Tsar's army.

Again Napoleon sent Murat north to cut off the Rusian general, with Lannes's and Soult's corps and the cavalry. The next day his advanced guard engaged Austrian troops around Hollabrun. Kutusov's advanced guard arrived not long afterward, and a rather confused engagement between the two continued into the night. Prince Bagration, with a Russian division, was directed to hold the French long enough for Kutusov to escape with the army. Bagration's rear guard fought tenaciously and gave his superior more than a day. On 19 November Kutusov and Buxhowden united south of

Olmutz. With the remnants of several Austrian divisions, the coalition's army totaled more than 85,000 men.[57] The Grande Armée, however, pursued the Austrians and Russians with such speed that they were now dispersed: Murat's 40,000 men were in Moravia, Bernadotte's 20,000 men were deployed to block Archduke Ferdinand in Bohemia, and Davout and Mortier were in Vienna. Napoleon and the Imperial Guard were at Brunn, but he understood that this was a precarious position.

At the moment Napoleon entered Vienna the Archduke Charles reached the Isonzo River. Archduke John had fled Innsbruck ten days earlier upon the approach of Marshal Ney's corps. Both Charles and John found themselves in a poor position to continue on to the Austrian capital. Marmont— already at Leoben and Graz—blocked the route. Certainly Charles's army outnumbered Marmont's by more than three to one, and John's was roughly equal his number. Napoleon knew well that if the archdukes were determined to push on to Vienna, Marmont would be overwhelmed. He instructed the general that his purpose was to observe Charles's movement, but not encourage an engagement.[58] The French army was in no position to contend with the main austrian army southwest of Vienna and the Russians to the northeast. Neither archduke, however, was in any state of mind to push through, nor were they aware of these facts. Charles thought the prudent course was to shift his retreat to the southeast into Hungary and the fortress at Körmend. There he would find precious supplies. The army could rest and refit while the archduke could assess their situation. On 26 November John managed to weave his way through the various French divisions spreading through Carinthia and link up with his brother. Together they headed away from Vienna.[59]

Massena aided Charles's retreat into Hungary by halting his pursuit the day after the archduke crossed the Isonzo. He sent detachments to secure Trieste and the Carinthian passes against John's divisions, making contact with Ney's corps now in the south Tyrol.[60] St. Cyr still had Venice under siege, and Prince Eugene was organizing forces in the Italian interior. The situation in Italy, however, was not entirely rosy. On 20 November an Anglo-Russian expeditionary force landed in Naples. The September treaty between Ferdinand IV and Napoleon was a ruse. By acceding to it the Neapolitan monarch was able to remove St. Cyr's army from his kingdom. General Maurice Lacy and General James Craig commanded the Russian and British expeditionary forces respectively. Combined they fielded more than 20,000 men, exclusive of the Neapolitan army. St. Cyr had left General Reynier with one French and one Italian division in the Papal States; otherwise there were no French troops in central Italy. Fortunately for Napoleon, allied intelligence was lacking, and instead of advancing immediately Lacy and Craig took time to discuss operations. Their advance north did not proceed until the second week of December. By that time the war was already decided.[61]

CHAPTER ELEVEN

AUSTERLITZ, PRESSBURG, AND PRUSSIA

WHEN TSAR ALEXANDER AND HIS ENTOURAGE left Potsdam on 5 November for Moravia they passed through Saxony, stopping at Dresden to call on the elector, Friedrich-August. There was little enthusiasm on the Saxon prince's part for the visit of such a dignitary. Since the mid-eighteenth century, Saxony became an unwillingly appendage of Prussia. Although Saxony was one of the oldest Imperial electorates, its army was no match for its Austrian and Prussian neighbors. Saxon troops fought with the Prussians in the 1790s against Revolutionary France and the elector capitalized upon the Peace of Basel to extricate himself from the conflict. Nonetheless, Saxony was considered a Prussian ally whether the Saxons wanted to be drawn into Prussian politics or not. Friedrich-August did not complain about the decade of peace that followed Basel, and he enjoyed north German neutrality. In that time Napoleonic France and the electorate normalized relations.

During the spring of 1805 when Clemens von Metternich was posted to Berlin he visited with the elector and encouraged him to join the coalition. Friedrich-August politely declined, claiming his lands fell within the neutrality zone. This excuse was an expedient. Friedrich-August acquired some lands from the Imperial Recess in 1803, but lost his bid on Erfurt to Prussia. Frederick William III managed to trump him again in the Saxon duchies. Prussian mobilization, the violation of Anspach, and the Treaty of Potsdam changed all of this. Saxony was expected to fully participate in military operations by committing half the Saxon army as an auxiliary and allowing Prussian troops passage to Franconia.[1]

The duke of Brunswick demanded that 10,000 to 12,000 Saxon troops march to Erfurt and unite with Prince Hohenlohe's army. Together they would form the left flank of the Prussian army in its advance into Bavaria. Hohenlohe arrived in Dresden on 11 November, shortly after the Tsar's departure. He informed the elector that his regiments had already moved into Saxony and were going to camp north of the Saxon capital before continuing on to Erfurt. Friedrich-August had few options. He mobilized eighteen battalions and twenty squadrons, but took his time deploying them. By the first week of December the Saxons were still in Saxony. Despite military preparations the elector did not expel the French ambassador Durant, but explained to him Saxony's precarious position.[2]

Strong-arming Saxony was a Prussian pastime, but it did not compensate for the clear deficiencies in Prussia's military system. When Duroc reported to Napoleon in September that the army was in a poor state, he was referring to its logistics and mobilization system. The Prussian army was still not fully capable of campaigning although partial mobilization was decreed two months prior and full mobilization one month earlier. Elements of the Lower Saxon corps finally moved from Hildsheim into Hanover on 10 November. General Barbou, the French commander, had no more than 3,000 men, and yet the enormous time and energy required to dedicate sufficient forces to the French-occupied electorate taxed Prussia. As of 25 November the Prussian army deployed 60,000 infantry and 16,000 cavalry from Westphalia to central Germany. An additional 20,000 infantry and 6,000 cavalry were held in reserve, with 27,000 infantry and 7,000 cavalry posted as a corps of observation in Silesia.[3]

Wilhelm I, elector of Hesse-Cassel was as perturbed by events in north Germany as Friedrich-August of Saxony. Frederick William III had been no help in the past months, and his demands for the mobilization of the Hessian army was most disconcerting. The firm historical relationship between the two states, however, meant that Wilhelm would honor his obligations more actively than the Saxon elector. On 22 October he decreed full mobilization and took post at Paderborn with General Blucher's Prussians.[4] His neighbor, Ludwig X, landgraf of Hesse-Darmstadt, was in a most unenviable situation. Having signed a military alliance with Napoleon in September, he reluctantly raised 4,000 troops as part of the military convention. Within weeks of the violation of Anspach and the Treaty of Potsdam, the Prussians demanded Ludwig place his army at Prussia's disposal. The landgraf balked initially, but when Prussian troops crossed the border and occupied upper Hesse at the end of November, the landgraf withdrew to his capital at Darmstadt and disbanded his army.[5] The duke of Brunswick did not include the landgraf's army in his war plans. As the prince's September convention with Napoleon was known, Prussia's request and subsequent occupation of Hessian territory may well have been done to neutralize him.

Coalition forces in north Germany were substantial enough to compensate for the Hessian prince's actions. Prussian operational plans called for the advance of the main army, under the duke of Brunswick, from Hildsheim to Bamberg in Bavaria. Prince Hohenlohe's Prusso-Saxon corps assembling at

Erfurt was directed to the Prussian territory of Bayreuth, skirting the Bohemian frontier and covering the left flank of Brunswick's army. A Prusso-Hessian corps comprising part of the Prussian contingent with the army of Hesse-Cassel was to cover the right flank of the main army. A second corps, under General Kalkreuth, was to observe the central Rhine and guard the right of the Prusso-Hessian corps in case of a French advance from Mainz. In Hanover the combined Russo-Swedish-Anglo-Hanoverian army was to move upon Holland from Hanover. General Tolstoi, commanding Russian forces in Hanover, went to Berlin on 26 November to coordinate operations.[6]

The Hanoverian electorate was thoroughly occupied by coalition forces at the end of November. General Barbou locked himself up in the fortress of Hameln, surrounded by 7,000 Russians. Tolstoi's army was reinforced by Russian contingents that landed at Lubeck. He now had 19,000 infantry and 2,300 cavalry in north Germany extending east to Nienburg. The Swedish army in Germany hosted a further 8,600 infantry and 1,800 cavalry. It was only at Lauenberg, however, on the Mecklenberg frontier. The Prussian contingent occupied Celle and the city of Hanover.[7] The timely arrival of Anglo-Hanoverian troops at Bremen and Verden further increased coalition forces in north Germany. Once the electorate was secured and coalition forces united, they intended to march on Holland.

On 13 November Frederick William III sent off a gravely reluctant Count Haugwitz to Vienna where he was to present Prussian demands to Napoleon. Haugwitz's hesitance and trepidation concerning his mission was strongly influenced by a conversation he had with the duke of Brunswick prior to his departure. The duke commented that the main Prussian army would not be in position until 6 December and could only conduct defensive operations by 15 December if Napoleon refused mediation.[8] Haugwitz understood and was subsequently in no hurry to arrive in Vienna. He wrote Hardenberg from Prague that his journey was delayed because he was suffering from severe diarrhea. He then commented sardonically that this worked in his favor, as he could get a better appreciation for the Austria position prior to his meeting with Napoleon.[9]

Laforest managed to remain in Berlin despite the hostile environment. He kept Talleyrand abreast of military and political developments. Haugwitz spoke to the French ambassador prior to leaving for Vienna and made it clear that Prussia's current course was not his own. He blamed his colleague Hardenberg. The conversation enabled Laforest to relay some pertinent information regarding Haugwitz's mission to Vienna.[10] Talleyrand received Laforest's dispatch on 20 November at Vienna and immediately forwarded it to the emperor at Brunn. Napoleon told Talleyrand he would not return to Vienna to meet the Prussian minister. He must question Haugwitz on Prussia's intentions and make it clear that if Prussia wanted war, that is all well, but if it truly wanted peace its recent actions had not indicated such.[11]

Undeterred by Haugwitz's journey to Vienna or by the news of allied armies in Germany, Napoleon dealt with more immediate matters. In part this was simply due to distance, and in part this was due to the uncertainty of Prussian policy. Napoleon had the wherewithal to address the threat to Holland and the Rhine. Already the reserve corps at Mainz and Strasbourg were filled with conscripts and National Guard, and Marshal Brune still commanded an army along the Channel coast. On 8 November, upon receiving news of the Treaty of Potsdam, Napoleon formed the Army of the North at Juliers. Composed of six divisions—two from Brune's army, two from Holland, one from Mainz, and the other from Strasbourg—he anticipated its strength at 30,000 men. A week later he gave Marshal Lefebvre command. "The King of Prussia has assured me that he wants to strictly protect his neutrality," he told Lefebvre, "I have the right to do the same."[12]

The disposition of French forces along the Rhine included the Army of the North at Juliers, the II Reserve Corps between Mainz and Landau, and the III Reserve Corps between Weisembourg, Strasbourg, and Huningen. On the upper Rhine both reserve corps mustered 19,000 infantry and 3,000 cavalry. The II Reserve Corps's cavalry depots were along the Meuse River in Belgium, closer to Juliers, providing the Army of the North with an additional 3,000 cavalry if needed. Marshal Brune's army on the Channel was concentrated at Boulogne and hosted almost 13,000 men. The overwhelming majority of soldiers assigned to these corps were conscripts with little if any experience; only Brune's troops were once part of the great army poised to invade England. Napoleon could boast of 70,000 men from the Channel to the Rhine, but their ability to halt a concerted allied offensive into Holland was questionable.[13] Of course, Marshal Augereau's VII Corps was at Ulm after crushing Jellacic in the Vorarlberg, and the Baden and Württemberg contingents, along with the Bavarians, were also present in south Germany. One should not also forget Marshal Ney's VI Corps was in the Tyrol. For all his boldness, Napoleon preferred not to fight in Germany, but to decide the war in Moravia, yet he had sufficient forces to defend the Rhine and hold in south Germany.

The Prussian foreign minister's reception was cold when he arrived in Vienna. Talleyrand occupied Haugwitz for some time. Impatient, the minister traveled to Brunn to meet with the French emperor. Their discussion was purposely brief, and Napoleon refused to entertain serious matters until after he engaged the Russo-Austrian army now at Olmutz. As the French emperor was keenly aware of Haugwitz's mission, he could afford to delay him. The subject of mediation would be discussed after the fate of his campaign was decided. If Napoleon found defeat on the battlefield, no doubt he would have entertained Prussian mediation. If, however, he won, then Haugwitz and Prussia would find themselves in a "pretty pickle."

Tsar Alexander was eager for battle. The French army was overextended, and there were no more than 60,000 French troops dispersed in Moravia.

With a combined Austro-Russian army of 89,000 at Olmutz, the situation seemed favorable. On 27 November Alexander, Francis, and their staffs determined to launch a counteroffensive; only Kutusov offered words of caution.[14] Anticipating an engagement Napoleon called all available corps to Brunn, where on 30 November he marched east with elements of three corps (I, IV, V), Oudinot's elite division, the cavalry reserve, and the Imperial Guard. On 1 December he sent for Marshal Davout around Vienna to make with all haste to the battlefield some forty miles away. Napoleon, however, did not exhibit the confidence seen two months earlier during his march to Ulm. In a letter to Talleyrand on 30 November, he wrote, "There will probably be a serious battle with the Russians tomorrow. . . . Write to Paris, but do not speak of a battle; it would be too disturbing to my wife; I do not want to alarm her. I am in a strong position. I regret that it will be costly, and with little purpose."[15] Napoleon was less concerned about causing Josephine excessive anxiety than about the possibility of explaining a defeat.

The battle of Austerlitz, 2 December 1805, is clearly one of the most brilliant victories in the annals of military history.[16] It was hard-fought and the outcome was far from certain. Odds favored the Tsar. Napoleon deployed his army over a five-mile front behind the Goldbach stream. Lannes's and Soult's corps covered the northern half of the field, from the Brunn-Olmutz road to the pond around the hamlet of Kobelnitz some three miles distant. Further south, Napoleon posted a single division from Soult's corps to defend the flank from Tellnitz to Kobelnitz, more than two miles in length. The emperor expected Davout to arrive from Vienna some time in the morning and reinforce his right. Napoleon placed Bernadotte (I Corps), Murat's cavalry, and the guard in reserve behind his center and left astride the Brunn-Olmutz highway.[17]

The allied army advanced in five columns upon the Pratzen Heights overlooking Napoleon's position. The Russian Imperial Guard was camped around Imperial headquarters at Austerlitz, and Prince Bagration was expected to arrive in the early morning. The two consulted the new quartermaster-general of the combined armies, Franz Weyrother. After observing Napoleon's position he concluded that the weakness lay on the French right. Weyrother proposed three of the five columns debouch from the heights in oblique order and smash the scant French forces deployed there. The fourth column would hit the center, and the fifth and Prince Bagration would pin the French left. The Russian Imperial Guard would remain in reserve on the heights. In all, the allies intended to hit Napoleon's right with almost 40,000 men and thereby turn his flank, cutting him off from Vienna.

Napoleon had no preconceived plan but would await developments. The battle commenced in the early morning. Fog obscured the French position and caused confusion among the allied columns debouching from the Pratzen. Shortly after nine o'clock in the morning, as the fog cleared, the

Russian columns hit Soult's lonely division between Telnitz and Sokolnitz Castle. Unfortunately for the Russians, the morning confusion prevented the columns from moving in unison, and their attack fell upon the French in waves. Their assaults were repulsed with heavy loss, and by ten o'clock lead elements of Davout's corps arrived to shore up the line. The marshal miraculously had marched the distance from Vienna to Austerlitz in a night. He was unable to bring his entire corps to the emperor's aid, but his one infantry and one cavalry division held the flank against determined Russian attacks. Throughout the morning, 12,000 French kept 40,000 Russians at bay.

Kutusov commanded the allied center on the heights. The fourth column under General Kollowrat was disposed to advance against the French center at Puntowitz. Kutusov, however, was one of the few allied generals who did not perceive Weyrother's plans as conceived of genius. He delayed Kollowrat until the allied flank attack developed. Tsar Alexander came up at nine and demanded Kutusov release the Austrian general. Obeying his sovereign, the allied center advanced from the Pratzen, leaving the Russian Imperial Guard as the sole reserve. Alexander and Francis observed the attack. Napoleon watched from his position on the Santon, a prominent hill on his far left. He had little information from Davout, and although he knew the marshal's corps was three miles from the field at five in the morning, he had yet to hear of developments on his right. Upon seeing Kollowrat's column move against Soult, he ordered the marshal to meet him head-on. Here the odds were almost equal and by eleven the two divisions of IV Corps cracked the allied center.

Prince Bagration advanced against Napoleon's position along the Brunn-Olmutz highway. He was perhaps one of the best generals in the allied army. His fierce resistance at Hollabrunn two weeks earlier had saved Kutusov. The Russian prince led 13,000 men against an equivalent number of French under Marshal Lannes. Furious fighting raged throughout the morning, with neither side gaining the advantage. This, however, worked well for the French emperor. As Bagration and Lannes were locked in combat on the left, and Soult was engaged in the center, a mile-long gap appeared in the allied line between Kollowrat and Bagration. Seizing the moment, Napoleon directed his reserves, including Bernadotte's I Corps, Murat's cavalry, Oudinot's elites, and the Imperial Guard, into the breach.

At noon, Alexander and Francis watched with horror as more than 20,000 French infantry and cavalry scaled the heights. The Russian Imperial Guard, some 13,000 strong, was thrown against the French columns. After an hour of determined combat, the Russian Guard was forced from the field. The two emperors fled to avoid capture. Napoleon followed his victory on the Pratzen by shifting his forces to finish off Kollowrat and fall upon the three Russian columns facing Davout. By three o'clock it was all over. Panic dictated action, and the Russian army routed. Prince Bagration led the only contingent that withdrew in good order. Napoleon's victory was complete. The Grande Armée suffered 7,000 casualties, compared to 25,000 allies killed and wounded.

Napoleon sent Murat in pursuit of the allied army the next morning. He wrote the bishops of France calling for victory *Te Deums*. He informed Talleyrand that negotiations with the Austrian ambassador Stadion at Brunn, which had been proceeding for some weeks, were at an end. The conditions Napoleon had offered prior to Austerlitz were no longer valid. The next day he told his foreign minister the Austrians were negotiating an armistice and asked him inform Haugwitz, still at Brunn, to meet him in Vienna. "I will speak to you at Brunn of my intentions," he said, "[P]resume nothing."[18]

Francis I headed to Teschen with the remnants of his army. There had been 16,000 Austrians at Austerlitz, of whom almost 6,000 were casualties. Archduke Ferdinand had advanced from Prague upon Brunn, but was intercepted and defeated en route by General Wrede's Bavarian division. Marshal Ney eliminated the few Austrian holdouts in the Tyrol, while General St. Cyr annihilated an Austrian column that moved into Venetia with thoughts of relieving Venice. On the day of Austerlitz, the Archduke Charles finally arrived at Körmend in Hungary with 155 battalions and 96 squadrons, some 80,000 men. The Austrian emperor understood he no longer had any options. On 6 December Prince Liechtenstein concluded an armistice with Napoleon. Tsar Alexander and his army were required to leave Austria. Moravia and half of Bohemia would remain under French military occupation, along with the Tyrol, upper and lower Austria, Carinthia, and Styria. The Archduke Charles was required to hold his position in Hungary, and peace negotiations would commence at the earliest convenience.[19] News of the battle and the subsequent armistice negotiations reached the archduke by 6 December. With 13,000 ill and Marmont and Massena to his rear, he was relieved operations seemed to be at an end.[20]

Over the next week Napoleon authorized his foreign minister to establish formal political alliances with Bavaria, Württemberg, and Baden. On 10 and 11 December respectively, representatives from Bavaria and Württemberg acceded to these agreements. On 12 December in Vienna, a treaty was concluded with Baden. Napoleon did not seek greater sacrifices of his German allies, but worked with all speed to solidify his position in Germany. The promises made to Max Joseph in August, and to Karl Friedrich and Frederick II in September and October, were to be fulfilled. These treaties provided that Napoleon would seek the elevation of Bavaria and Württemberg from principalities to kingdoms. Baden would be enlarged to a grand-duchy. These princes would absorb all lands belonging to Imperial counts and knights within their territories. France recognized and guaranteed the sovereignty and independence of these kingdoms, and they pledged themselves to a permanent continental alliance. Napoleon would demand these things of Francis I, who was still Holy Roman Emperor.[21]

Count von Haugwitz waited in Vienna amid the furious diplomatic activity. Napoleon let him cool for more than a week. Indeed, Haugwitz used the time well to recalibrate his message. The Prussian minister decided that offering an ultimatum under current circumstances was ludicrous. He would therefore propose something else. In the meantime the Prussian army assembled at Erfurt. Several weeks earlier, at the end of November, Austrian and Russian military attachés proposed that the Prussian army advance into Bohemia rather than Bavaria. The king held discussions at Potsdam on the issue. On 3 December, unaware of events transpiring in Moravia, it was decided that Prince Hohenlohe's Prusso-Saxon corps and the advanced guard of the main army under General Blucher in Bayreth would move into Bohemia and unite with Archduke Ferdinand's forces around Prague. On 11 December news of the armistice reached Berlin and the Prussian army was halted.[22]

The armistice severed the coalition. Prior to receiving Haugwitz's report on events, Hardenberg tried to convince Frederick William that Austria would never leave the Russian alliance, therefore Prussia should continue on its course. The day Haugwitz's dispatch arrived, Hardenberg again argued the army should march into Bohemia.[23] Frederick William, however, decided otherwise. The Prussian army was halted, not that it had moved a great deal since mid-November. Brunswick and the main army were in the Saxon duchies, Hohelohe and the Saxons between Gera and Zwickau in Saxony. Wilhelm I, elector of Hesse-Cassel was with his army at Fulda, while the Prussian contingent was at Hersefeld.[24] The question remained, what of the Russians? General Bennigsen's army was currently in Silesia, and Tolstoi had 20,000 troops in Hanover. If war continued without Austria what was Prussia's position? Haugwitz provided the answer when he finally met with the French emperor and offered congratulations on the incredible victory. He then proceeded to negotiate a treaty of friendship and alliance between the two states.

Napoleon offered Haugwitz Hanover. It was not given explicitly, but the treaty provided Prussia take possession of the electorate in order to "preserve the sovereignty of the king of England's states in Germany."[25] The convention called for an offensive-defensive alliance and for the cession of Anspach to Bavaria, and Cleves and Neufchatel to France. Frederick William was also required to recognize Max Joseph as king of Bavaria.[26] Three weeks were granted to ratify the treaty. Napoleon desired to split Prussia from Alexander's influence. Hanover was the prize. He had no intention of allowing the electorate to return to the English monarchy. Furthermore, Napoleon used it to encourage Frederick William to remove Russian and Swedish troops from north Germany.[27]

Despite Hardenberg's protests, Frederick William was pleased to see Haugwitz upon his return to Berlin. Within days, the Prussian monarch accepted Napoleon's proposals in principle. He wrote Friedrich-August, elector of Saxony, and thanked him for his support and informed him that discussions between the French emperor and Haugwitz indicated a peaceful resolution of the crisis was forthcoming.[28] Hardenberg commented sardonically to Lucchesini, the Prussian ambassador to Paris, that Prussia has been forced from their system of neutrality into an alliance.[29] The minister was not far from the mark. Although the treaty took another month to ratify, Napoleon succeeded in playing upon Frederick William's pacific nature, and he turned Prussia into an accomplice.

French negotiations with Austria continued through the month of December. Until peace was firmly established Napoleon contended with Charles's army at Körmend. Writing Massena, he told him to make a quick march to the capital if Charles moved north against Vienna. He instructed Berthier to gather the corps toward Vienna and dispose them toward Hungary.[30] Charles had not moved toward the city, but in fact, remained camped at Körmend with detachments in the surrounding towns. On 22 December the archduke wrote Francis that the monarchy was lost if peace was not soon established.[31] His brother took heed. At Pressburg, the day after Christmas, Prince Liechtenstein and Talleyrand concluded a treaty of peace.

The Treaty of Pressburg could not be described as generous or moderate. Napoleon reduced Austrian power significantly by stripping it of lands in Italy, in Germany, and along the Adriatic coast. Francis abandoned Venice and its territories to the Kingdom of Italy, and recognized annexations of all other Italian states to the Italian kingdom. He accepted the royal elevation of the electors of Bavaria and Württemberg and would recommend the Imperial Diet in Germany do the same. The new kingdom of Bavaria was enlarged with the inclusion of the former Austrian lands of the Vorarlberg, Tyrol, and Salzburg. Württemberg and Baden would incorporate Habsburg possessions in Swabia. Most importantly, Francis agreed to pay 40 million francs in indemnities to France.[32]

It took the Austrian emperor only a few days to consider the draft. On 1 January 1806 the war was officially at an end. Tsar Alexander returned to Russia after the December armistice. Negotiations with Napoleon were conducted through 1806. The Tsar, however, proved as difficult in settling affairs with France as he had been in his talks with Pitt the previous spring. Although a draft treaty was finally settled six months later on 20 July 1806, Tsar Alexander ultimately rejected it. He had the luxury of distance, something Austria and Prussia did not. This affected operations in Hanover and Naples.

General Craig and his Russian counterpart General Lacy received word of Austerlitz on 7 December while in Naples. This was followed by reports of the armistice. Both gentlemen waited for further orders. On 2 January 1806 General Lacy announced to Ferdinand IV that the Anglo-Russian expeditionary force would withdraw from the kingdom.[33] By the end of January, the allied forces had departed, leaving the Neapolitan army to face Napoleon's wrath. More than 40,000 French and Italian troops were assembled in central Italy under Marshal Massena. On 8 February they crossed the Neapolitan border, and within six weeks the kingdom had a new king, Joseph Bonaparte, eldest brother of the French emperor.[34]

The Russian army evacuated Hanover by January. The English and Hanoverian forces followed suit. Gustav IV Adolf, however, refused to abandon the electorate and concentrated his army around Lauenberg.[35] He was enraged when on 15 February 1806 Frederick William III annexed Hanover.[36] Napoleon's offer of the electorate in December became Prussian policy two months later. The Swedish king read this as betrayal, although he had never truly trusted the timid king of Prussia. From February through April 1806, it seemed as if Prussia and Sweden would go to war. Cooler heads eventually prevailed, and Gustav Adolf withdrew to Stralsund.[37] In May, however, Frederick William found himself in an undeclared war with England over Hanover. William Pitt was not alive to see it. He had died of illness the month before. Charles James Fox, Pitt's parliamentary nemesis, was left to clean up the mess. He had never supported the war with Spain, and with Britain's naval victory he had the luxury of entering negotiations with the French emperor in March, despite the situation on the continent.[38]

In Vienna Francis I dispensed with Cobenzl and Colloredo. It was only fitting that they accept responsibility for marginalizing the Archduke Charles, elevating Mack, and pursuing an alliance with Russia. Count Philip von Stadion, the Austrian ambassador to Russia, replaced Cobenzl in January as vice-chancellor. Two weeks after ratifying the Treaty of Pressburg, Francis invited Charles to assume the mantle of *Generalissimus*, supreme commander of Habsburg forces. The archduke accepted. Poor General Mack was repatriated to Austria shortly after his capture at Ulm. Napoleon had no use for him. Upon his return to Vienna, he was arrested and court-martialed. The purging of the Austrian court also cleansed the emperor of any responsibility for the debacle.

Napoleon handsomely rewarded the princes who supported him. Since his days as a young lieutenant, he never forgot those who aided him in times of trouble. Max Joseph was king, and his lands doubled. The new king cemented his alliance with Napoleon by agreeing to the marriage of his daughter Auguste-Amelia to Prince Eugene, Napoleon's stepson. Frederick II, king of Württemberg, was forgiven for his initial reluctance to support France, and he was compensated well. Karl-Friedrich of Baden was now one of the premier princes of the Holy Roman Empire. For the erstwhile landgraf of Hesse-Darmstadt, Napoleon excused his actions under the circumstances and made it known to him that he needed to adjust court politics accordingly.[39] Napoleon's German policy and the subsequent aggrandizement of

German states led to the dissolution of the Holy Roman Empire, approved by the Imperial Diet in the summer of 1806. It was replaced by the Confederation of the Rhine, with France as the protector and guarantor of the independence and sovereignty of the German states.

Godoy and Carlos IV were the least pleased of Napoleon's allies. Victory for Spain meant victory over England. Napoleon's success against the continental powers did nothing for the Spanish kingdom. Its fleet was shattered at Trafalgar, and Napoleon demanded troops for Europe. The Spanish economy was in shambles, and Ouvrard's adventurous project only brought wealth to the bankers and merchants. Some silver found its way to France, but none to Spain. The revenue from overseas trade in 1805 dropped by 99 percent compared to the funds collected in 1804.[40] No lands were granted for a decade of support, and Carlos's brother Ferdinand IV was in exile in Sicily.

For Napoleon the conclusion of the war established France as the master of western and central Europe. War remained with Russia and England, but Austria was weakened and incapable of further resistance. Prussia was now an ally of circumstance. The emperor's luck extended to his finances. The run on the Bank of France and the enormous deficits carried by the state placed the Empire on the verge of bankruptcy at the moment it controlled half of Europe. News of Austerlitz was a relief in Paris, but it did not restore confidence in the bank's financial stability. Napoleon returned to Paris at the end of January and proceeded to root out those responsible.[41] The emperor was in some cases fortunate; the war paid for itself and provided a windfall in contributions and Austrian war indemnities. The receiver-general for the Grande Armée presented Napoleon with a report on these funds through January 1806. More than 18 million francs were collected from Habsburg lands in Swabia and Austria. This excluded the 40 million francs required by the Treaty of Pressburg. Revenue came in the form of specie, bills of exchange, and bank notes. English merchandise seized in conquered territory was sold, along with goods held by the Austrian government. In all, France boasted more than 75 million francs. Deducting the cost of war in Germany, and French debt to the German states—roughly 27 million francs—Napoleon's war was extremely lucrative, netting almost 50 million francs in profits.[42]

Napoleon did not want a continental war. Nonetheless, he pushed the envelope of Prussian good will in Hanover, and broke his agreements with Austria that had been firmly established at Lunéville. If he did not want a European war, his actions dictated otherwise. Pitt, however, desperately desired a continental war. As he had rightly predicted, the formation of the coalition compelled Napoleon to turn his attention from the Channel coast. England was saved at Austria's expense. Tsar Alexander escaped no greater harm than the loss of 30,000 soldiers, a price he could certainly afford. One must consider, however, that the victories at Ulm and Austerlitz were products of an unwanted war and were made possible by successful French diplomacy during the Consulate. Napoleon did not have the luxury of time to prepare for the campaign. His success, in part, must be attributed to his pursuit of favorable relations with the German princes since assuming power. Their perception of the French ruler was placed within the context of historical relations with France and juxtaposed to the radicalism of the Revolutionary governments that preceded him. Spain, too, saw alliance with France within the scope of the Bourbon Family Compacts. Napoleon's victory then was not simply achieved on the battlefield, but similarly won at the negotiating table before his armies marched.

NOTES

Chapter 1: Napoleon

1. Paul Schroeder, *Transformation of European Politics* (Oxford: 1994), provides a thorough examination of the foreign policies of the monarchies of Europe. On the decline of the Holy Roman Empire, see John Gagliardo, *Reich and Nation: The Holy Roman Empire as Idea and Reality, 1763–1806* (Bloomington, IN: 1980).

2. Carl von Clausewitz, *On War*, Book 3, Chapter 1, 177.

3. The five governments were 1789, Estates General to National Assembly; 1792, the birth of the Republic; 1794, Thermidorean Reaction; 1797, Coup of Fructidor; 1799, Coup of 18 Brumaire. One could also include the Reign of Terror as a separate entity, and argue that this list is too brief.

4. On the Coup of 18 Fructidor, see Georges Lefebvre, *The French Revolution: Volume 2: 1793 to 1799* (New York: 1964) 197–199.

5. Schroeder, *Transformation of European Politics*; Harold Parker argues that Napoleon was constantly changing his self-image and that his own associations with historical figures were, either in part or completely, purposeful lies. See Harold Parker, "Napoleon's Changing Self-Image to 1812: A Sketch," *Consortium on Revolutionary Europe Proceedings* (1983): 449–450.

6. Harold Parker had led the way in the past thirty years with several examinations of Napoleon's personality, beginning with "The Formation of Napoleon's Personality: An Exploratory Essay," *French Historical Studies* 7 (1971): 6–26, which is largely Freudian in its approach. Parker also wrote "Napoleon's Changing Self-Image" in 1983, and "Napoleon Reconsidered: An Invitation to Inquiry and Reflection," *French Historical Studies* 15 (spring 1987): 142–156.

7. Several of the major works that explored Napoleon's youth and the formation of his personality are Arthur Chuquet, *La jeunesse de Napoleon* (Paris: 1897); Jean Colin, *L'education militaire de Napoleon* (Paris: 1900); Frederick Masson and Guido Biagi, *Napoleon innconu: papiers inedit*, 2 vols. (Paris: 1895); Harold T. Parker, "Napoleon and French Army Values: The Early Phases," *Proceedings of the Annual Meeting of the Western Society for French History* 18 (1991): 233–242; cf. Parker, "The Formation of Napoleon's Personality."

8. The debate over the use and application of psychology in history remains active. Cf. Fred Weinstein, "Psychohistory and the Crisis of the Social Sciences," *History and*

Theory 34, 4 (1995): 299–319; and Thomas Kohut, "Psychohistory as History," *American Historical Review,* 91, 2 (1986): 336–354.

9. Refer to Michael Broers, *Europe under Napoleon* (London: 1996) and Louis Bergeron, *France under Napoleon* (Princeton: 1981). Both argue that Napoleon's method of governance was that of an enlightened monarch. Martyn Lyons reflects on Napoleon as the inheritor of the Revolution in *Napoleon Bonaparte and the Legacy of the French Revolution* (New York: 1994).

10. Dorothy Carrington, *Napoleon and His Parents* (New York: 1990), provides a wonderful examination of the trials and tribulations of the Bonapartes from before the birth of Napoleon until after his father's death. The litigious conflicts are well documented here, and they are discussed with a critical eye. The biography of Napoleon by Geoffrey Ellis also refers to the vendetta and the brutal nature of Corsican society. See Geoffrey Ellis, *Napoleon* (London: 1997), 10. Carrington has convincingly dismissed the myth of the vendetta and its relationship to the Bonaparte family. Harold Parker noted that in examining the nature of Corsican life there remains the problem of differentiating between those who lived in the towns and cities on the coast, and those who lived in the mountains. See Harold Parker, "Napoleon Reconsidered: An Invitation to Inquiry and Reflection," *French Historical Studies* 15 (1987): 146.

11. Parker, "Napoleon's Personality," 9–10.

12. Ibid., 12.

13. Carrington, *Napoleon and His Parents,* 188, 194.

14. The following articles provide a solid examination of Corsica and the Enlightenment: Thadd Hall, "Corsica and Its World," *Consortium on Revolutionary Europe Proceedings* (1987): 49–55; Thadd Hall, "Jean-Jacques Rousseau and the Corsican Connection," *Studies on Voltaire and the Eighteenth Century,* 267 (1989): 199–215; Thadd Hall, "The Development of Enlightened Interest in Eighteenth Century Corsica," *Studies on Voltaire and the Eighteenth Century* 64 (1968): 165–185; Thadd Hall, "Thought and Practice of Enlightened Government in French Corsica," *American Historical Review* 74, 3 (February 1969): 880–905.

15. Jean Tulard, *Napoleon: The Myth of a Savior* (New York: 1977), 27, argues that Napoleon knew little of Montesquieu and Diderot, that he was "ignorant of much of Voltaire's writings," and that he knew few of Rousseau's works. Carrington, *Napoleon's Parents,* 180, says quite the opposite, particularly that he did read Montesquieu; Colin, *Education militaire,* 111; Spencer Wilkenson, *The Rise of General Bonaparte* (Oxford: 1930), 3–4.

16. See Lee Kennett, *The French Army in the Seven Years' War* (Durham, NC: 1967).

17. Marc Raeff, "The Well-Ordered Police State and the Development of Modernity in Seventeenth and Eighteenth Century Europe: An Attempt at a Comparative Approach," *American Historical Review* 80 (December 5, 1975): 1221–1222.

18. See Kennett, *French Army,* specifically Chapter 6, "Personnel: The Corps of Officers"; and Sam Scott, *The Response of the Royal Army to the French Revolution* (Oxford: 1978): 19–26.

19. See particularly A. Colin, "La réaction aristocratique avant 1789: l'example de l'armée," *Annales,* 29 (1974): 23–48, 505–534. The concept of an aristocratic revolution prior to 1789 has become a part of the historiographical discussion on the origins of the French Revolution. Refer to William Doyle, *The Origins of the French Revolution* (Oxford: 1980).

20. David Bien, "The Army in the French Enlightenment: Reform, Reaction and Revolution," *Past and Present,* 85 (1979): 74–81.

21. Scott, *Response of the Royal Army,* 190–206.

22. Parker, "Napoleon and French Army Values," 283; David Bien, "The Army in the Enlightenment," 68–69.

23. Harold Parker, *The Cult of Antiquity and the French Revolution: A Study in the Revolutionary Spirit* (New York: reprint 1964), 18–19; Chuquet, *Jeunesse Napoleon,* 103–104.

24. Parker, *Cult of Antiquity,* 25.

25. Ibid., 48.

26. Bien, "The Army in the Enlightenment," 71.

27. Chuquet, *Jeunesse Napoleon,* 85; Twelve military schools were established in 1776 by the minister of war St. Germain and approved by Louis XVI.

28. Voltaire, *Philosophical Dictionary,* vol. 5, part I, 200.

29. Ibid., vol. 5, part II, 99; Montesquieu, *Oeuvres complètes* (Paris: 1964), 536–539; John Lynn, "Toward an Army of Honor: The Moral Evolution of the French Army, 1789–1815," *French Historical Studies* 16 (spring 1989): 153.

30. Voltaire, *Dictionary,* vol. 7, part II, 164.

31. Carl von Clausewitz, *On War,* Book 3, Chapter 5: Military Virtue (Princeton: 1976), 187–189.

32. Parker, "French Army Values," 235.

33. Peter Gay, *The Enlightenment: The Rise of Modern Paganism* (New York: 1995), 74, 107–109.

34. Carol Blum, *Rousseau and the Republic of Virtue* (Ithaca: 1986), 40–41. Blum asserts that the eighteenth century perception of Roman virtue was merely a stereotype/generalization and simplification of this complex concept. Parker, *Cult of Antiquity,* argued earlier that all of the revolutionary leaders had misinterpreted the classical texts specifically regarding glory and opportunity.

35. A. Colin, "Le reaction aristocratique avant 1789: l'example de l'armee," *Annales* 29 (1974): 87.

36. Scott, *Response of the French Army,* 6.

37. Chuquet, *Jeunesse Napoleon,* 103–104; Colin, *Education militaire,* 111; Wilkenson, *Rise of Bonaparte,* 4.

38. See Masson, *Napoleon iconnu,* for Napoleon's early readings and observations.

39. Parker, "Napoleon's Personality," 12; but more so Parker, "Napoleon's Changing Self-Image," 451–452.

40. Quoted in Carrington, *Napoleon's Parents,* 109.

41. Again refer to Parker, "Napoleon's Changing Self-Image," which addresses Napoleon's construction of a public image.

42. Carrington, *Napoleon's Parents,* 99. His brother was Yves Alexandre de Marbeuf.

43. Napoleon's other brothers, Louis and Jerome, came of age after the French Revolution had begun, although both entered the military—Louis the army and Jerome the navy.

44. Tulard, *Napoleon,* 37–39.

45. Refer to the following series of articles on Corsica during the French Revolution: Thadd E. Hall, "Corsica and Its World"; Dorothy Carrington, "The Achievement of Pasquale Paoli (1755–1799) and Its Consequences"; John Defanceschi, "Le Corse et la Revolution française: La Rêve brisé"; John McErlean, "Between Paoli and Bonaparte:

Philippe Masseria, An Anglomaniac in Corsica, 1789–1793"; Harold Parker, "The Broken Dream"; all in *Consortium on Revolutionary Europe Proceedings* (1986): 48–95.

46. Parker, "Napoleon's Self-image," 452–453, fn. 22, 463.

Chapter 2: France and Spain

1. Edward White, "The French Revolution and the Politics of Government Finance, 1770–1815," *Journal of Economic History* 55, 2 (June 1995): 236–237.

2. The best articles on Revolutionary and Napoleonic finance, in addition to the source cited above, are Michael Bordo and Eugene White, "British and French Finance during the Napoleonic Wars," in Michael Bardo and Forrest Capie, eds., *Monetary Regimes in Transition* (Cambridge: 1994), 241–273; Micahel Bordo and Eugene White, "A Tale of Two Currencies: British and French Finance During the Napoleonic Wars," *Journal of Economic History* 51, 2 (June 1991): 303–316; and Jean Gabaillard, "Le financement des guerres napoleonniennes et la conjoncture du Premier Empire," *Revue Economique* 4 (1953): 548–572.

3. Bordo and White, "Tale of Two Currencies," 308.

4. André Corvisier, ed., *Histoire militaire de la France,* 2 vols. (Paris: 1988), II, 315–316; and Bordo and White, "British and French Finance," 250–251.

5. Bordo and White, "British and French Finance," 247.

6. Frederick Schneid, *Soldiers of Napoleon's Kingdom of Italy* (Boulder: 1995), 24; on the other satellite states, see Owen Connelly, *Napoleon's Satellite Kingdoms* (New York: 1965); Simon Schama, *Patriots and Liberators: Revolution in the Netherlands, 1780–1813* (New York: 1992).

7. Nicholas Mollien, *Mémoires d'un ministre du trésor public, 1780–1815,* 4 vols. (Paris: 1845), I, 366.

8. Ibid., I, 407–408.

9. Ibid., I, 416.

10. Schama, *Patriots and Liberators,* 446.

11. John Lynch, *Bourbon Spain, 1700–1808* (London: 1994), 367.

12. Jeremy Black, *From Louis XIV to Napoleon: The Fate of a Great Power* (London: 1999), 111, 132; Piers Macksey, *The War for America 1775–1783* (Lincoln, NE: reprint 1993), 262.

13. For the Spanish and French campaigns in 1793–1795, see Ramsay Weston Phipps, *Armies of the First French Republic: Volume III: Armies of the West and Armies of the South* (London: 1931), 151–216.

14. M. de Clerq, *Recueil des Traités de la France: Tome I: 1713–1802,* 10 vols. (Paris: 1880), I, 245–249.

15. André Fugier, *Napoleon et l'Espagne: 1799–1808,* I (Paris: 1930), 26–27.

16. The best sources concerning the Spanish economy at this time are Jacques A. Barbier, "Peninsular Finance and Colonial Trade: the Dilemma of Charles IV's Spain," *Journal of Latin American Studies* 12, 1 (1980): 21–27; Jacques A. Barbier and Herbert S. Klein, "Revolutionary Wars and Public Finances: The Madrid Treasury, 1784–1807," *Journal of Economic History* XLI, 2 (June 1981): 315–339; on silver mining, see Carlos Marichal and Matilde Souto Mantecón, "Silver and Situados: New Spain and the Financing of the Spanish Empire in the Caribbean in the Eighteenth Century," *Hispanic American Historical Review* 74, 4 (1994): 587–613.

17. John Sherwig, *Guineas and Gunpowder: British Foreign Aid in the War with France, 1793–1815* (Cambridge: 1969), 25n.

18. Fugier, *Napoléon et Espagne*, 16–17; de Clercq, *Recueil des Traités*, I, 246.

19. Macksey, *The War for America*, 274–275.

20. Jacques A. Barbier, "Indies Revenues and Naval Spending: The Cost of Colonialism for the Spanish Bourbons, 1763–1805," *Jahrbuch fur Geschichte von Staat, Wirtschaft und Gesellschaft Lateinamerikas* 21 (1984): 173–174; John D. Harbon, *Trafalgar and the Spanish Navy* (Annapolis: 1988), 171–172. The title is misleading as the majority of Harbon's book examines the reconstruction of the Spanish navy during the eighteenth century; cf. Alfred T. Mahan, *The Influence of Sea Power on the French Revolution and Empire, 1793–1812*, 2 vols. (London: reprint n.d.).

21. Carlos Secco Serrano, *Godoy: El hombre y el politico* (Madrid: 1978), 126. Serrano attributes the quote to Spanish historian Jesus Pabón, *Las ideas y el sistema napoleónicos* (Madrid: 1944).

22. Fugier, *Napoleon et l'Espagne*, I, 3; Lynch, *Bourbon Spain*, 382–383.

23. Ibid., 386.

24. France accounted for 25 percent of Spanish imports prior to 1792, of which a substantial amount was reexported to the Americas. Javier Cuenca Esteban, "Statistics of Spain's Colonial Trade, 1792–1820: Consular Duties, Cargo Inventories and Balances of Trade," *Hispanic American Historical Review* 61, 3 (1981): 412–413.

25. John Fisher, "Imperial Response to 'Free Trade': Spanish Imports from Spanish America, 1778–1796," *Journal of Latin American Studies* 17 (1985): 47–48.

26. Fugier, I, *Napoleon et l'Espagne*, 24; The 1780 League of Armed Neutrality was created by Catherine II (the Great) of Russia with Sweden and Denmark, and later the Holy Roman Empire and Prussia, to enforce the right of neutrals to trade. It was a reaction to the Royal Navy's strong-arm tactics in seeking to halt trade with France and Spain. The league was quite successful, and a thorn in England's side. Paul Schroeder, *Transformation of European Politics 1763–1848* (Oxford: 1994), 25, 38, 46; Macksey, *War for America*, 377.

27. See Manuel de Godoy, *Principe de la Paz, Memorias*, 2 vols. (Madrid: 1956), volume 1.

28. De Clerq, *Recueil des Traités*, 245–249.

29. Ibid., 287–292.

30. Ibid.

31. Steven T. Ross, *Quest for Victory: French Military Strategy, 1792–1799* (New York: 1973), 106; Schroeder, *European Politics*, 163; The Neapolitan squadron consisted of four ships of the line. It was attached to the Spanish fleet until 1795, then to the English fleet. Virgilio Ilari, Piero Crociani, and Ciro Paoletti, *La Guerra della Alpi (1792–1796)* (Rome: 2000), 197; Mahan, *Seapower*, I, 211–216.

32. Simon Schama, *Patriots and Liberators: Revolution in the Netherlands 1780–1813* (New York: 1977), 278–279; Ross, *Quest for Victory*, 107–108.

33. Sherwig, *Guineas and Gunpowder*, 82–83.

34. Mahan, *Seapower*, I, 221–229,

35. Esteban, "Colonial Trade," 409; Lynch, *Bourbon Spain*, 367.

36. Barbier, "Peninsular Finance," 24–25.

37. See article 18 of San Ildefonso, de Clerq, *Recueil des Traités*, 290; cf. Serrano, *Godoy*, 136 on Directory's assessment of the Spanish alliance by 1799.

38. Serrano, *Godoy*, 136.

39. Emilio La Parra López, "Les changements politiques en Espagne après Brumaire," *Annales historiques de la Révolution française* 4 (1999): 695–696.

40. Ibid., 697–699.

41. Ibid., 700–701.

42. Ibid., 699.

43. Ibid., 695; Barbier and Klein, "War and Public Finance," 333; Brian R. Hammett, "The Appropriation of Mexican Church Wealth by the Spanish Bourbon Government—The 'Consolidación de Vales Reales.' 1805–1809," *Journal of Latin American Studies* I, 2 (November 1969): 91; John Fisher, "Commerce and Imperial Decline: Spanish Trade with Spanish America, 1797–1820," *Journal of Latin American Studies* 30 (1998): 466–468.

44. La Parra López, "*Politiques en Espagne*," 703–704.

45. Ibid., 709; de Clerq, *Recueil des Traités*, I, 411–413.

46. Ibid., I, 420–423. The treaty was signed 29 January 1801.

47. Napoleon I, *Correspondance de Napoleon Ier*, 32 vols. (Paris: 1858–1862), VII, No. 5335, Napoleon to Talleyrand 4 February 1801, 3. The French contingent was led by General Charles-Victor Leclerc. He commanded the Corps d'Observation de la Gironde. His corps arrived at Cuidad Rodrigo after the Spanish invasion. See also No. 5530, Napoleon to Leclerc 13 April 1801, 123.

48. Emilio Beccera de Beccera, "El Ejercito Espanol desde 1788 hasta 1802," *Revista de historia militar* 28, 56 (1984): 133; Godoy, *Memorias*, I, 323–326.

49. Napoleon, *Correspondance*, VII, No. 5604, Napoleon to Talleyrand, 15 June 1801, 170–171.

50. de Clerq, *Recueil des Traités*, I, 421–424.

51. Napoleon, *Correspondance*, VII, No. 5604, Napoleon to Talleyrand, 15 June 1801, 171.

52. Ibid., VII, No. 5605, Napoleon to Berthier, 15 June 1801, 171–172.

53. Godoy, *Memorias*, I, 327.

54. Ibid., I, 326.

55. Napoleon, *Correspondance*, VII, No. 5630, Napoleon to Talleyrand, 10 July 1801, 190–192; No. 5691, Napoleon to Talleyrand, 15 August 1801, 226–227.

56. Andreas Muriel, Carlos IV, 2 vols. (Madrid: 1956), II, 242.

57. Ana Maria Schop Soler, *La relaciones entre España y Rusia en la época de Carlos IV* (Barcelona: 1971), 85. Letter cited in full, in Appendix VII, Godoy to the queen, 11 October 1801, 161–162.

Chapter 3: Spain, France, and War with England

1. Andreas Muriel, *Carlos IV*, 2 vols. (Madrid: 1956), II, 254–255.

2. Jacques A. Barbier, "Peninsular Finance and Colonial Trade: The Dilemma of Charles IV's Spain," *Journal of Latin American Studies* 12, 1 (1980): 29.

3. Ibid., 31.

4. Javier Cuenca Esteban, "Statistics of Spain's Colonial Trade, 1792–1820: Consular Duties, Cargo Inventories and Balances of Trade," *Hispanic American Historical Review* 61, 3 (1981): 409; Barbier, "Peninsular Finance," 24.

5. Andre Fugier, *Napoleon et l'Espagne*, 2 vols. (Paris: 1930), I, 199.

6. Ibid., I, 195.

7. R.B. Mowat, *The Diplomacy of Napoleon* (London: 1924), 140–141.

8. Ibid., 141.; M. de Clerq, *Recueil des Traités*, 23 vols. (Paris: 1880), II, 62.

9. John Fisher, "Commerce and Imperial Decline: Spanish Trade with Spanish America, 1797–1820," *Journal of Latin American Studies* 30 (1998): 465.

10. De Clerq, *Recueil des Traités*, I, 484–491.

11. Fugier, *Napoleon et l'Espagne*, I, 186.

12. Ibid., 188.

13. Ibid., 196–197; Carlos IV to Godoy, 7 May 1803.

14. Jacques Chastenet, *Godoy: Master of Spain, 1792–1808* (London: 1953), 118; Godoy, *Memorias*, I, 385.

15. Fugier, *Napoleon et l'Espagne*, I, 203.

16. Ibid., I, 203–204; Carlos Secco Serrano, *Godoy: El hombre y el politico* (Madrid: 1978), 144.

17. Ana Maria Schop Soler, *La relaciones entre España y Rusia en la época de Carlos IV* (Barcelona: 1971), 88. Count de Noroña was dispatched to St. Petersburg and Ivan Matveevich Muravev arrived in Madrid.

18. Fugier, *Napoleon et l'Espagne*, I, 205. The discussion was held 31 May 1803 in Paris. Noroña proposed armed neutrality to Tsar Alexandre I on 6 May 1803.

19. Ibid., 205.

20. Ibid., 207–209.

21. Serrano, *Godoy*, 142; Schop, *Relaciones con Rusia*, 116–117.

22. Fugier, *Napoleon et l'Espagne*, I, 204.

23. Ibid., 203–204.

24. Paul Bailleau, *Preuen und Frankreich von 1795–1807, Diplomatische Corresponden-zen*, 2 vols. (Leipzig: 1887), I, 152–154. Haugwitz to Friedrich Wilhelm III, 4 June 1803. The letter, written four days after Haugwitz's communication with Valencia, does not discuss Spain, but only north Germany. Furthermore, his other letters to the king during the summer of 1803 discuss Malta, Naples, and other European issues, but again do not mention Spain.

25. Napoleon, *Correspondance de Napoleon I*, 32 vols. (Paris: 1858–1862), VIII, No. 6801, Napoleon to Mortier, 9 June 1803, 350, Napoleon congratulates Mortier on his swift occupation of Hanover. See Chapter 5.

26. Godoy, *Memorias*, I, 384. Godoy uses harsher language to characterize Beurn-onville.

27. Ibid., 388.

28. Ibid., 388.

29. Napoleon, *Correspondance*, VIII, No. 6942, Napoleon to Talleyrand, 26 July 1803, 416.

30. Fugier, *Napoleon et l'Espagne*, I, 218. Fugier comments in a footnote that Napoleon merely used mobilization as a pretext to pressure Spain, considering he waited two months before concerning himself with it.

31. Napoleon, *Correspondance*, VIII, No. 6942, Napoleon to Talleyrand, 26 July 1803, 416; Douglas Hilt, *The Troubled Trinity: Godoy and the Spanish Monarchs* (Tuscaloosa, AL: 1987), 146.

32. John Sherwig, *Guineas and Gunpowder: British Foreign Aid in the War with France, 1793–1815* (Cambridge: 1969), 145. Figures for the Russian subsidy equivalent to that of 1798 are found on page 111.

33. Napoleon, *Correspondance*, VIII, No. 6980, Napoleon to Berthier, 3 August 1803, 442. The 10th Hussars and two battalions of the 105th Line were to be "*complétés sur le pied de paix.*"

34. Ibid., No. 7004, Napoleon to Talleyrand, 13 August 1803, 456–457.

35. Ibid., No. 7007, Napoleon to Talleyrand, 14 August 1803, 458–461.

36. Ibid., No. 7007, Napoleon to Talleyrand, 14 August 1803, 458–461, and No. 7008, Napoleon to Talleyrand, 16 August 1803, 461–463.

37. Ibid., No. 6814, Napoleon to Berthier, 14 June 1803, 352–353.

38. Ibid., No. 6980, Napoleon to Berthier, 3 August 1803, 442. On 15 August General Carra St. Cyr, commanding the camp at Bayonne, had only 5,443 men and 872 horses present under arms. Fugier, *Napoleon et l'Espagne,* I, 220–222.

39. Nicholas Mollien, *Mémoires d'un Ministre du Trésor Public, 1780–1815,* 4 vols. (Paris: 1845), I, 408, 416.

40. T.C. Hansard, *The Parliamentary Debates from the Year 1803 to the Present Time* (London: 1812), III, Hawkesbury to Frere, 2 June 1803, 61–62.

41. Fugier, *Napoleon et l'Espagne,* I, 225, 228, for Frere's report to Godoy and the state of French forces on 2 September 1803, given at 15,723 effectives divided among one light infantry regiment, nine line, five regiments of cavalry, and eighteen cannons. This was essentially corps strength.

42. Serrano, *Godoy,* 144.

43. Quoted in Hilt, *The Troubled Trinity,* 149.

44. Napoleon, *Correspondance,* VIII, No. 7113, Napoleon to the king of Spain, 18 September 1803, 538–540.

45. Hilt, *The Troubled Trinity,* 150–151; cf. Chastenet, Godoy, 120 *passim.*

46. Hansard, *Parliamentary Debates,* III, Frere to Hawkesbury, 12 September 1803, 67–68.

47. Godoy, *Memorias,* I, 391.

48. DeClerq, *Recueil des Traités,* II, 83–84.

49. Ibid., II, 84.

50. Hansard, *Parliamentary Debates,* III, Hawkesbury to Frere, 24 November 1803, 69.

51. Ibid., refer to copies of diplomatic notes from Frere to Hawkesbury including translated correspondence from Cevallos to Frere, particularly those inserted after the debates of 24 and 28 January 1805 and 2, 4, and 6 February 1805.

52. Hall, *British Strategy,* 112.

53. Yves Bottineau, *Les Bourbons d'Espagne: 1700–1808* (Paris: 1993), 350; John Lynch, "British Policy and Spanish America, 1763–1808," *Journal of Latin American Studies* 1, 1 (1969): 16.

54. Geoffrey de Grandmaison, *L'Espagne et Napoleon,* vol. I, *1804–1809* (Paris: 1908), 2–3; Lynch, "Spanish America," 16; John Lynch, *Bourbon Spain* (London: 1994), 369.

55. Grandmaison, *Espagne,* 4.

56. Lynch, *Bourbon Spain,* 405; De Clerq, *Recueil des Traités,* II, 117–119. The naval convention was concluded on 4 January 1805 in Paris.

57. Hansard, *Parliamentary Debates,* III, 339–343.

58. Ibid., III, 367–371.Grandmaison, *Espagne,* 6–7.

59. Grandmaison, *Espagne,* 6–7.

Chapter 4: Napoleon and Germany, 1792–1803

1. Robert Billinger, "Good and True Germans: The Nationalism of the Rheinbund Princes, 1806–1814," in Heinz Durchhardt and Andreas Kunz ed. *Reich oder Nation? Mitteleuropa 1780–1815* (Mainz: 1998), 110; cf. Peter Wilson, *The Holy Roman Empire 1498–1806.* An outstanding discussion of the Imperial institutions and their history. Easily accessible to the novice and invaluable to the expert.

2. Peter Wilson, *War, State and Society in Württemberg, 1677–1793* (Cambridge: 1995), 239.

3. Karl Roider, *Baron Thugut and Austria's Response to the French Revolution* (Princeton: 1987), 94–95; T.C.W. Blanning, *The French Revolutionary Wars, 1787–1802* (Lon-

don: 1986), 58–59, 61–63, 95; Blanning states that the Diet only recognized a state of war in March 1793, but by that time Imperial territory had already been violated by French troops the previous autumn.

4. Max Jahns, "Zur Geschischte der Kriegsverfassung des Deutschen Reiches," *Prußische Jahrbücher*, 39 (1877): 487. The constitution of the Holy Roman Empire provided for the military organization of the German states. They were organized into regional military circles called *Kreise*. The Swabian, Franconian, and Rhenish *Kriese* were the primary contributors to the early *Reicharmee*. Eventually all *Kriese* provided troops.

5. For a complete account of the campaigns of the Revolution along the Rhine see Blanning, *The Revolutionary Wars*, and the classic Ramsey Weston Phipps, *The Armies of the First French Republic and the Rise of the Marshals of Napoleon I, Volume II: The Armées de la Moselle, du Rhin, de Sambre-et-Meuse, de Rhine-et-Moselle* (London: 1929).

6. Billinger, "True Germans," 111.

7. Mathias Bernath, "Die Auswärtige Politik Nassaus 1805–1812: Ein Beitrag zur Geschichte des Rheinbundes der politischen Ideen am Mittelrhein zur Zeit Napoleons," *Nassauische Annalen* (1952): 168.

8. *Traité de paix conclu á Bâle*, 5 April 1795, and *Convention particulère á Bâle*, 17 May 1795, in M. De Clerq, *Recueil des Traités de la France*, 23 vols. (Paris: 1880), I, 232–236, 242–244.

9. *Traité de paix signé á Bâle*, 7 November 1795, Ibid., 264–266.

10. Bernath, "Politik Nassaus," 108; Billinger, "True Germans," 111; Paul Sauer, *Napoleons Adler über Württemberg, Baden und Hohenzollern: Südwestdeustchland in der Rheinbundzeit* (Stuttgart: 1987), 25–26.

11. *Suspension d'armes*, 7 September 1796, with Bavaria and Convention with the Franconian *Kries*, De Clerq, *Recueil des Tratés*, I, 299–300.

12. *Traité de paix conclu á Campo-Formio*, 17 October 1797, in ibid., 335–343; John Gagliardo, *Reich und Nation: The Holy Roman Empire as Idea and Reality* (Bloomington, IN: 1980), 189.

13. Ibid., 188; H.A.L. Fisher, *Studies in Napoleonic Statesmanship: Germany* (Oxford: 1903), 29. Fisher stated that "Basel was avenged at Campo-Formio."

14. Tuscany was a possession of the extended Habsburg family and not an integral part of the monarchy.

15. Marcus Junkelman, *Napoleon und Bayern: von den Anfängen des Königreiches.* (Regensberg: 1985), 56.

16. Agreements between France, Baden, and Württemberg in de Clerq, *Recueil des Traités*, I, 283–287, 292–299; and Sauer, *Adler über Württemberg, Baden und Hohenzollern*, 26.

17. Sydney Biro, *The German Policy of Revolutionary France: A Study in French Diplomacy during the War of the First Coalition*, 2 vols. (Cambridge: 1957), II, 959–960; Linda Frey and Marsha Frey, "The Reign of Charlatans Is Over: The French Revolutionary Attack on Diplomatic Practices," *Journal of Modern History* 65 (December 1993): 735–738.

18. Sauer, *Adler über Württemberg, Baden und Hohenzollern*, 26.

19. Ibid., 42.

20. Roider, *Baron Thugut*, 261. Roider argues that Thugut did not believe that peace would be possible in the long run, but he was not sure when Austria would be strong enough to reverse the outcome of Campo Formio.

21. Jahns, "Kriegsverfassung," 488. Austria demanded a Quintuplum, some 33,000 troops from Bavaria, Württemberg, and Baden. The constitution of the Holy Roman Empire included specific military contributions by the German states. The emperor could, however, require the princes to raise any number of troops above the minimum provided for in the constitution. A Quintuplum was five times the requisite. The presence of an Austrian army was sufficient to gain tacit political support for the war, but the British had to subsidize the German princes to help them raise the troops. See John Sherwig, *Guineas and Gunpowder: British Foreign Aid in the Wars with France, 1793–1815* (Cambridge: 1969), 128–129; cf. Peter H. Wilson, *German Armies: War and German Politics, 1648–1806* (London: 1998), 298–326, for a detailed discussion of military contributions and the Imperial war effort.

22. Sauer, *Adler über Württemberg, Baden und Hohenzollern*, 31–32.

23. Frey and Frey, "Reign of Charlatans," 727 passim.; and Roider, *Baron Thugut*, 280.

24. Sauer, *Adler über Württemberg, Baden und Hohenzollern*, 29; and Eduard Driault, "Bonaparte et les Recès Germanique de 1803," *Revue historique* 100 (1909): 56; Sherwig, *Guineas and Gunpowder*, 130–131. Curiously, Sherwig refers to these German troops as mercenaries hired to assist Austria.

25. Junkelmanm, *Napoleon und Bayern*, 55.

26. Ibid., 57.

27. Karl Klüpfel, "Die Friedensunterhandlungen Würtembergs mit der französischen Republik: 1796–1802," *Historische Zeitschrift* 46 (1881): 406–407. More recently, Sauer, *Napoleons Adler*, 25–28. The neutrality agreements between France, Wurttemberg, and Baden were nullified with Austrian occupation of these states in the fall of 1796. Yet the princes were compelled to comply with Imperial policy.

28. Bernath, "Politik Nassaus" 110. Gagern embarked on this project beginning in 1797.

29. Karl Ottmar Freiherr von Arentin, *Heiliges römisches Reich, 1776–1806*, 2 vols. (Weisbaden: 1967), vol. I, 370.

30. Ibid., I, 370.

31. Napoleon Bonaparte, *The Confidential Correspondence of Napoleon Bonaparte with His Brother Joseph*, 2 vols. (New York: 1856), 52, Napoleon to Joseph, 20 January 1801.

32. Hugh Ragsdale, "Russian Influence at Lunéville," *French Historical Studies* 5 (1968): 281; cf. Roederick E. McGrew, *Paul I of Russia: 1754–1801* (Oxford: 1992), 315. McGrew believes Napoleon wanted a Russian representative present at Lunéville. Ragsdale, on the other hand, believed Napoleon was more interested in the threat posed to Austria of having a Russian negotiator present. The latter argument seems more in line with Napoleon's character.

33. Hugh Ragsdale, *Russian and the Mediterranean, 1797–1807* (Chicago: 1970), 128.

34. Ibid.

35. Roider, *Baron Thugut*, 359; Gunther Rothenberg, *Napoleon's Great Adversaries, the Archduke Charles and the Austrian Army, 1792–1814* (Bloomington, IN: 1982), 65; Oskar Criste, *Erzherzog Carl von Österreich*, 3 vols. (Vienna: 1912), II, 174–175

36. For the full text of the treaty see *"Traité de paix définitif conclu á Lunéville le 9 février 1801. . .,"* de Clerq, *Receuil des Traités*, I, 424–429.

37. Ibid., I, 425–426.

38. After 1802 the *Hoch und Deutschmeister* was Archduke Charles, brother of Francis II. Gagliardo, *Reich und Nation*, 193.

39. Eduard Driault, "Bonaparte et les Recès Germanique de 1803," *Revue historique* 100 (1909): 51.

40. Ibid., 49.

41. Gagliardo, *Reich und Nation*, 193.

42. Eberhard Weis, "Bayern und Frankreich in der Zeit des Konsulats und des Ersten Empire (1799–1815)," *Historische Zeitschrift* 237 (1983): 574.

43. Napoleon, *Correspondence de Napoleon I*, 32 vols. (Paris: 1858–1862), VII, No. 5796, Napoleon to Max Joseph, 11 October 1801, 284–285.

44. The articles of Lunéville presented for ratification to the Imperial Diet are found in Karl Beumer ed., *Quellensammlung zur Geschichte der deutschen Reichsverfassung im Mittelalter und Neuzeit*, 2 vols. (Tübingen: 1913), I, 228.

45. Driault, "Recès Germanique de 1803," 282.

46. Napoleon, *Correspondence*, VII, No. 6143, Napoleon to Duke of Wurttemberg, 496–497.

47. Harold Deutsch, *The Genesis of Napoleonic Imperialism* (Cambridge, MA: 1938), 52–53.

48. Ibid., 58. The passage is cited from Cobenzl's correspondence of 6 July 1802.

49. Biro, *German Policy of Revolutionary France*, II, 948; Paul Schroeder, "The Collapse of the Second Coalition," *Journal of Modern History* 59 (June 1987): 248.

50. Schroeder, "Second Coalition," 289–290.

51. Philip Dwyer, "The Politics of Prussian Neutrality, 1795–1805," *German History* 12, 3 (1994): 360.

52. McGrew, *Paul I*, 311–312; Hugh Ragsdale, "A Continental System in 1801: Paul I and Bonaparte," *Journal of Modern History* 42, 1 (March 1970): 76–77

53. Napoleon, *Correspondence*, VII, No. 6019, Napoleon to Talleyrand, 427–428; Napoleon, *Correspondence with Joseph*, 60, 11 March 1802. Napoleon reported that Alexander I is "inclined" to join with France in European affairs.

54. de Clerq, *Receuil des Traités*, I, 467–475.

55. Dwyer, "Prussian Neutrality," 360–362; Brendan Simms, *The Impact of Napoleon: Prussian High Politics, Foreign Policy and the Crisis of the Executive, 1797–1806*, (Cambridge: 1997), 68.

56. Dennis Showalter, "Hubertusberg to Auerstädt: The Prussian Army in Decline?" *German History* 12, 3 (1994): 323.

57. Simms, *Impact of Napoleon*, 83–83; Ragsdale, "Paul I and Bonaparte," 80–81; McGrew, *Paul I*, 314. Although George III was both king of England and elector of Hanover, the latter state was not a British possession. It was treated separately by the king, and Parliament had little interest in his affairs there as long as they did not conflict with Parliament's interests. Cf. Guy Stanton Ford, *Hanover and Prussia, 1795–1803, A Study in Neutrality* (reprint New York: 1967), see Chapters VII and VIII.

58. de Clerq, *Recueil des Traités*, vol. I, 464–467.

59. Deutsch, *Napoleonic Imperialism*, 56.

60. Junkelman, *Napoleon und Bayern*, 58; Deutsch, *Napoleonic Imperialism*, 60–61.

61. Ibid., 218.

62. Driault, "Recès Germanique de 1803," 279.

63. These were the ecclesiastic electorates of Mainz, Trier, and Cologne, and part of the secular electorate of the Palatinate.

64. Jahns, *Kriegverfassung*, 489.

65. The entire Recess can be found in Beumer, *Deutschen Reichsverfassung,* I, 509–531; on the emperor's response, Gagliardo, *Reich und Nation,* 193

66. Ibid., 195.

67. Driault, "Recès Germanique de 1803," 309.

68. Junkelman, *Napoleon und Bayern,* 62–63.

69. Bernath, "Politik Nassaus," 114.

70. Article 31 of the *Reichsdeputations-Hauptschluß* grants electoral titles to the princes of Baden, Württemberg, and Hesse-Cassel; Beumer, *Deutschen Reichsverfassung,* I, 519; Weis, "Bayern und Frankreich," 576. Weis argues that this made France the guarantor of the new system in Germany.

Chapter 5: Napoleon, Prussia, and German Politics, 1803–1805

1. See Chapter 4, "Napoleon and Germany 1792–1803," for the collapse of the Second Coalition, and Chapter 2, "Napoleon and Spain," for the Spanish invasion of Portugal in 1801; on the Prussian occupation of Hanover in 1801, see Guy Stanton Ford, *Hanover and Prussia, 1795–1803: A Study in Neutrality* (New York: reprint 1967).

2. Napoleon, *Correspondance de Napoleon Ier,* 32 vols. (Paris: 1858–1862), VIII, No. 6629, Instructions, 12 March 1803, 243–247; P. Bailleu, *Preußen und Frankreich von 1795–1807, Diplomatische Correspondenzen,* 2 vols. (Leipzig: 1887), II, Duroc, Compte de ma mission á Berlin, 20–27 March 1803, 127–132.

3. Peter H. Wilson, *German Armies: War and German Politics, 1648–1806* (London: 1998), 310.

4. M. de Clerq, *Recueil des Traités de la France,* 2 vols. (Paris: 1880), I, *Traité de paix conclu à Bâle* (Prussia), 5 April 1795, 232–235; *Convention particulière pour la neutralization de certains territoires,* 17 May 1795, 242–244; *Traité de paix signé à Bâle* (Hesse-Cassel), 28 August 1795, 262–266; *Traité conlcu à Berlin pour l'établissement d'une ligne de neutralité dans le nord de l'Allemagne,* 5 August 1796, 279–280; *Article additional au traité de neutralité pour l'accession des Princes de la Maison du Saxe* (Saxon Duchies), 311–312; Philip Dwyer, "The Politics of Prussian Neutrality, 1795–1805," *German History* 12, 3 (1994): 351–358; Wilson, *German Armies,* 321–326; Ford, *Hanover and Prussia,* 100.

5. Dwyer, "Prussian Neutrality," 359–360; Dennis Showalter, "Hubertusberg to Auerstädt: The Prussian Army in Decline?" *German History* 12, 3 (1994): 322–323.

6. Husgh Ragsdale, "A Continental System in 1801: Paul I and Bonaparte," *Journal of Modern History* 42, 1 (March 1970): 80–81; On Denmark see, Ole Feldbæk, *Denmark and Armed Neutrality 1800–1801* (Copenhagen: 1980); Herbert Lundh, *Gustaf IV Adolf och Sveriges Utrikespolitik 1801–1804* (Uppsala: 1926), 13–17; Sten Carlsson, *Den Svenska Utrikes politikens Historia, III: 1792–1844* (Stockholm: 1954), 64–68; Curt Jany, *Geschichte der preuischen Armee vom 15 Jahrhundert bis 1914,* 4 vols. (Osnabrück: 1967), III, 384-386.

7. Ford, *Hanover and Prussia,* Chapters VII and VIII deal with this subject in detail, 265–268 for analysis of occupation.

8. See Chapter 4, "Napoleon and Germany"; Edouard Driault, "Bonaparte et les Recès Germanique de 1803," *Revue historique* 100 (1909): 5; John Gagliardo, *Reich and Nation: The Holy Roman Empire as Idea and Reality* (Bloomington, IN: 1980), 193. Paul Schroeder, *The Transformation of European Politics, 1763–1848* (Oxford: 1994), 233–234.

9. André Bonnefons, *Un Allié de Napoléon, Frédéric-Auguste, Premier Roi de Saxe et Grand-Duc de Varsovie, 1763–1827* (Paris: 1902), 110. For the complete settlement of

the Imperial Recess 1803, see Karl Beumer, ed., *Quellensammlung zur Geschichte der Deutsche Reichverfassung im Mittelalter und Neuzeit*, 2 vols. (Tübingen: 1913), I, 229–251. On Hesse-Cassel's territorial interests, see Phillip Losch, *Kürfürst Wilhelm I, Landgraf von Hessen: Ein Fürstenbild aus Zopfzeit* (Marburg: 1923), 237.

10. Losch, *Kürfürst Wilhelm I,* 236–237; Rainer von Hessen, *Wir Wilhelm von Gottes Gnaden: Die Lebenserinnerungen Kürfürst Wilhelms I von Hessen 1743–1821* (Frankfurt: 1996), 323. Talleyrand was notorious for demanding money before he considered a state's interests.

11. Simon Schama, *Patriots and Liberators: Revolution in the Netherlands 1780–1813* (New York: 1992), 452.

12. von Hessen, *Wir Wilhelm von Gottes Gnaden,* 325; Losch, *Kürfürst Wilhelm I,* 236–238.

13. Philip Dwyer, "Two Definitions of Neutrality: Prussia, the European State-System and the French Invasion of Hanover in 1803," *International History Review* 19, 3 (August 1997): 524.

14. Thomas Stamm-Kuhlmann, *König in Preußens großer Zeit: Freidrich Wilhelm III der Melancholiker auf dem Thron* (Berlin: 1992), 180–185, addresses the debate among the Prussian cabinet ministers over what course to take.

15. Patricia Kennedy Grimstead, *The Foreign Ministers of Alexander I: Political Attitudes and the Conduct of Russian Diplomacy, 1801–1825* (Berkeley: 1969), 88–89.

16. Ibid., 95.

17. Ibid., 95–96; F. Martens, *Recueil des Traités et Conventions conclus par La Russie avec les puissances étrangères,* 14 vols. (St. Petersburg: 1875), VI, 313–315.

18. Ibid., VI, 308–310.

19. Ibid., VI, 313; Dwyer, "Definitions of Neutrality," 529–531; Ford, *Hanover and Prussia,* 288–289.

20. Martens, *Recueil,* VI, 309, Haugwitz to Alopeus, March 1803, "he [Frederick William III] no longer wants to speak of this occupation, and I withdrew my proposal."

21. Bailleu, *Preußen und Frankreich,* II, 127–132, No. 94, *Duroc, Compte de ma mission á Berlin,* 20–27 March 1803 and 159–161, Frederick William III to Haugwitz, 6 June 1803.

22. Napoleon, *Correspondance,* VIII, No. 6809, Napoleon to Mortier, 9 June 1803, 350–351; Ford, *Hanover and Prussia,* 309; Randal Gray, "Mortier," in David Chandler ed., *Napoleon's Marshals* (New York: 1987), 315–316; Karl Friedrich Brandes, "Hannover in der Politik der Grossmachte, 1801–1807," *Forschungen zur brandenburgischen und preußischen Geschichte* LI (1939): 249–250.

23. Russo-Prussian negotiations continued through June 1803. Alexander began to press for action beginning in June, but it was too late to prevent French occupation. Martens, *Recueil des Traités,* VI, 316–318.

24. Napoleon, *Correspondance,* VIII, No. 6742, Napoleon to Berthier, 13 May 1803, 313–314, for route to Hanover; No. 6777, Napoleon to Berthier, 31 May 1803, 333, on the conduct of the march and occupation; Losch, *Kürfürst Wilhelm I,* 242.

25. Ibid., No. 6867, *Arréte,* 27 June 1803, 379.

26. Bailleu, *Preußen und Frankreich,* II, 153, Haugwitz to Frederick William III, 4 June 1803.

27. Napoleon, *Correspondance,* VIII, No. 6821, Napoleon to Berthier, 16 June 1803, 357; No. 6822, Napoleon to Berthier, 16 June 1803, 358; and No. 6629, Instructions, 12 March 1803; and No. 6821, Napoleon to Berthier, 16 June 1803, 357–358.

28. Although Napoleon initially did not desire the occupation of towns in these duchies along the trade route, he changed his mind by early 1804. Leopold von Ranke, *Einhändige Memoiren des Saatskanzlers Fürsten von Hardenberg*, 5 vols. (Leipzig: 1877), II, 77; Napoleon, *Correspondance*, VIII, No. 6865, Napoleon to Berthier, 27 June 1803, 378.

29. Bailleu, *Preußen und Frankreich*, II, Haugwitz to Frederick William III, 152–154; Simms, *The Impact of Napoleon*, 84–85.

30. Landgraf Wilhelm IX became Elector Wilhelm I of Hesse-Cassel as affirmed at the Imperial Recess in February 1803.

31. Bailleu, *Preußen und Frankreich*, II, Frederick William III to Lucchesini, 19 June 1803, 171. The Prussian king wrote of his fear that the English would retaliate by blockading the estuaries, which they did during the summer of 1803.

32. Ibid., *Bericht* Lucchesini, 9 June 1803, 163.

33. Ibid., *Bericht* Lucchesini, 25 June 1803, 173.

34. Ibid., Frederick William III to Napoleon, 13 July 1803.

35. Napoleon, *Correspondance*, VIII, No.6956, Napoleon to the king of Prussia, 29 July 1803, 424–426.

36. Ibid., Napoleon to king of Prussia, 29 July 1803, 424–426. The letter was a response to Frederick William's complaints of French violations of the Hanseatic ports; found in Bailleu, *Preußen und Frankreich*, II, Frederick Wilhelm III to Napoleon, 7 July 1803, 179–181.

37. Lady Jackson ed., *The Diaries and Letters of Sir George Jackson*, 2 vols. (London: 1872), I, 142–143, 11 June 1803. Jackson was the brother of the English ambassador to Prussia, and he often acted in the capacity as *chargé d'affaires* in his brother's absence.

38. Ibid., I, 16 June 1803, 144 and 31 July 1803, 150.

39. On French loans, see Losch, *Kürfürst Wilhelm I*, 243; Hessen, *Wir Wilhelm*, 332.

40. Feldbæk, *Denmark and Armed Neutrality*, 205–206; Ole Feldbæk, "Denmark in the Napoleonic Wars: A Foreign Policy Survey," *Scandinavian Journal of History* 26, 2 (June 2001): 90–91; C.D. Hall, "Addington at War: Unspectacular but Not Unsuccessful," *Historical Research* LXI (1998): 313.

41. Herbert Lundh, *Gustaf IV Adolf och Sveriges Utrikespolitik 1801–1804* (Uppsala: 1926), 190.

42. W.H. Zawadzki, "Prince Adam Czartoryski and Napoleonic France, 1801–1805: A Study in Political Attitudes," *Historical Journal* XVIII, 2 (1975): 255; and Grimstead, *Foreign Ministers of Alexander*, 106.

43. Martens, *Recueil des Traités*, VI, 337, 341–345, 350–351.

44. Raymond Carr, "Gustavus IV and the British Government, 1804–1809," *English Historical Review* LX, 236 (1945): 36–44; Carlsson, *Utrikes Politiken*, III, 79–82

45. C.D. Hall, "Addington at War," 314–315.

46. Carr, "Gustavus IV and the British Government," 43–47; John Sherwig, *Guineas and Gunpowder: British Foreign Aid in the Wars with France 1799–1815* (Cambridge: 1969), 163–164.

47. Gustaf Björlin, *Sveriges Krig I Tyksland* åren *1805–1807* (Stockholm: 1882), 20, 26–27.

48. Carlsson, *Svenska Utrikes Politiken*, III, 91.

49. Martens, *Recueil des Traités*, VI, 355; Ranke, *Hardenberg*, II, 82–83; Carlsson, *Svenska Utrikes Politiken*, III, 90–92; Observation of military preparations in Pomerania and Hanover and the Prussian response can be also be found in John Holland

Rose, ed, *Selected Dispatches from the British Foreign Office Archives Relating to the Formation of the Third Coalition against France, 1804–1805* (London: 1904), No. 32, Sir J.B. Warren to Lord Harrowby, 12 October 1804, 50–52, and No. 33, 19 October 1804, 52–53.

50. Martens, *Recueil des Traités*, VI, 352; Jackson, Jackson Diaries, I, 29 October 1804, 241–243.

51. Ibid., 353; Rose, *Selected Dispatches,* No. 48, Marquis Camden to Lord Gower, 7 December 1804, 74–76.

52. Bonnefons, *Un Allié de Napoléon*, 117–119.

53. Although the Rumbold affair had yet to occur, the reluctance of the Hessian princes to travel to Mainz was related to Napoleon's policy in north Germany. Losch, *Kürfürst Wilhelm*, 246–247; Napoleon's letters of concern for the princes' health are found in Napoleon, *Correspondance*, X, No. 8067, Napoleon to the elector of Hesse-Cassel, 2 October 1804, 1, and No. 8068, Napoleon to the Landgraf of Hesse-Darmstadt, 2 October 1804, 2.

54. Martens, *Recueil des Traités*, VI, 358.

55. Ibid., II, *Déclaration d'alliance intime entre Russie et l'Autriche contre France*, 25 October 1804, 397.

56. Ibid., VI, 359.

Chapter 6: Austria, Italy, and the Mediterranean

1. Steven Ross, *Quest for Victory: French Military Strategy, 1792–1799* (Cranbury, NJ: 1973), 250, 261–262; Gunther E. Rothenberg, *Napoleon's Great Adversary: The Archduke Charles and the Austrian Army, 1792–1814* (Bloomington, IN: 1982), 54, 56–62.

2. M. DeClerq, *Recueil des Traités de la France,* 10 vols. (Paris: 1880), I, 421–429.

3. Manfred Rauchensteiner, *Kaiser Franz und Erzherzog Karl* (Munich: 1972), is a solid, brief history of the emperor and his brother.

4. Rothenberg, *Napoleon's Great Adversary,* 66–75. Rothenberg's work is the best source available in English on the subject of the Austrian army during the Revolutionary and Napoleonic Eras.

5. Adolf Beer, *Die Finanzen Oesterreichs im XIX. Jahrhundert* (Prague: 1877), 391; Oskar Regele, "Karl Freiherr von Mack und Johann Ludwig von Cobenzl. Ihre Rolle im Kriegsjahr 1805," *Mitteilungen des Österreichischen Staatsarchivs* XX, 1 (1969): 148.

6. Rothenberg, *Napoleon's Great Adversary,* 69–71.

7. Helmut Hertenberger and Franz Wiltschek, *Erzherzog Karl: Die Sieger von Aspern* (Graz: 1983), 132.

8. Ibid., 131; Rothenberg, *Napoleon's Great Adversary,* 75–76; Rauchensteiner, *Kaiser Franz und Erzherzog Karl,* 67–68.

9. F. Martens, *Recueil des Traités et Conventions conclus par La Russie avec les puissances étangérès,* 10 vols. (St. Petersburg: 1875), II, 397–400.

10. Arthur Paget, *The Paget Papers, 1794–1807,* 2 vols. (New York: 1896), II, Paget to Hawkesbury, 23 June 1803, 92.

11. DeClerq, *Recueil des Traités,* II, *Acte de médiation,* 19 February 1803, 1–56; Paul Schroeder, *The Transformation of European Politics, 1763–1848* (Oxford: 1994), 232–233.

12. DeClerq, *Recueil des Traités,* II, *Acte de médiation,* Chapter 20, Title 1, Article 2, 49; *Traité d'alliance défensive,* 76–82.

13. Ibid., I, *Traité de paix . . . conclu á Lunéville,* 9 February 1801, 424–429. The Habsburgs of Italy were promised French support for territorial compensation in

Germany. The treaty also provided that the Batavian (Dutch) Republic and the Helvetian (Swiss) Republic would remain independent of France.

14. Virgilio Ilari, Piero Crociani, and Ciro Paoletti, *Storia militare dell'Italian Giacobina: dall'armistizo di Cherasco alla pace di Amiens, (1796–1802),* 2 vols. (Rome: 2001), I, 143–144; E. Driault, *La Politique extérieure du premier Consul 1800–1803* (Paris: 1910), 118–119, 128–131; Schroeder, *Transformation of European Politics,* 239.

15. DeClerq, *Recueil des Traités,* I, 431–432; Ilari et al., *Storia militare dell'Italian Giacobina,* II, 1165–1166.

16. DeClerq, *Recueil des Traités,* I, 611–612. Convention between France and the Holy Roman Emperor recognizing the prince of Parma as the king of Etruria.

17. Virgilio Ilari, Piero Crociani, and Ciro Paoletti, *Bella Italia Militar: Escerciti e Marine nell'Italia pre-napoleonica (1748–1792)* (Rome: 2000), 11–19.

18. Virgilio Ilari, Piero Crociani, and Ciro Paoletti, *La Guerra della Alpi (1792–1796)* (Rome: 2000), 17.

19. Ibid., 174.

20. Ibid., 174–175.

21. Ibid., 176–178.

22. Ibid., 211.

23. Ibid., 306–309; Ilari et al., *Storia militare dell'Italian Giacobina,* I, 21–24.

24. Lèonce Krebs and Henri Moris, *Campagnes dans les Alpes pendant la Révolution,* 2 vols. (Paris: 1891), II, 375–378. Reprint in full of Carnot's orders to Napoleon.

25. Ilari et al., *Storia militare dell'Italian Giacobina,* I, 307–317.

26. Driault, *La Politique extérieure,* 118–119.

27. Napoleon, *Correspondance de Napoléon I,* 32 vols. (Paris: 1858), VII, No. 5934, *Discours,* 26 January 1802, 371–373.

28. Virgilio Ilari, Piero Croaciani, and Ciro Paoletti, *Storia militare del Regno Italico, 1802–1814,* 2 vols. (Rome: 2002), I, 9–12; E. Driault, *Napoléon en Italie, 1800–1802* (Paris: 1906), 76–79; Owen Connelly, *Napoleon's Satellite Kingdom* (New York: 1965), 1–2, 24.

29. Schroeder, *Transformation of European Politics,* 239.

30. Driault, *La Politique extérieure,* 136.

31. Regele, "Mack und Cobenzl," 142–143.

32. Lee Eysturlid, *The Formative Influences, Theories, and Campaigns of the Archduke Carl of Austria* (Westport: 2000), 34.

33. DeClerq, *Recueil des Traités,* I, 304–306; Ilari et al., *Storia militare dell'Italia Giacobina,* I, 319.

34. Ibid., II, 727.

35. Ibid., II, 764.

36. Rothenberg, *Napoleon's Great Adversary,* 36.

37. Ilari et al., *Storia militare dell'Italia Giacobina,* II, 765–818.

38. Ibid., II, 1165–1166; DeClerq, *Recueil des Traités,* I, *Traité de paix. . . ,* 28 March 1801, 432–433.

39. Ibid., I, 434–435; Ilari, et al., *Storia militare dell'Italia Giacobina,* II, 1166.

40. Napoleon, *Correspondance,* VII, No. 5507, Napoleon to Berthier, 5 April 1801, 105–106.

41. Ibid., VIII, No. 6763, Napoleon to Berthier, 23 May 1803, 324–325; Ilari, et al., *Storia militare dell'Italia Giacobina,* II, 1166; Ilari, et al., *Storia militare del Regno Italico,* II, 7–8.

42. Oscar Browning, "Hugh Elliot at Naples, 1803–1806," *English Historical Review* XIV (April 1889): 210–213.

43. Ibid., 211; Piers Mackesy, *The War in the Mediterranean, 1803–1810* (reprint Westport: 1981), 3–8.

44. Ibid., 21–27.

45. Ibid., 36–37.

46. Ibid., 12–15.William Flayhart, *Counterpoint to Trafalgar, the Anglo-Russian Invasion of Naples, 1805–1806* (Columbia: 1992), 4, 7–8, 11–15.

47. DeClerq, *Recueil des Traités*, I, 588–589.

48. P. Coquelle, "L'ambassade du Maréchal Brune á Constantinople (1803–1805)," *Revue d'histoire diplomatique* 8 (1904): 53–58.

49. Napoleon, *Correspondance*, VIII, No. 6308, Napoleon to Sebastiani, 5 September 1802, 25–26.

50. Ibid., VIII, No. 6599, Napoleon to Decrès, 21 February 1803, 223–224; Coquelle, "L'ambassade du Maréchal Brune," 61–62;

51. Ibid., III, No. 2106, Napoleon to the Minister of Foreign Relations, 16 August 1797, 236–237.

52. Ilari, et al., *Storia militare del Regno Italico*, I, 43–45; Frederick C. Schneid, *Soldiers of Napoleon's Kingdom of Italy: Army, State and Society 1800–1815* (Boulder: 1995), 17–18, 22, 26–27; Frederick C. Schneid, *Napoleon's Italian Campaigns, 1805–1815* (Westport: 2002), 3–4.

53. Paget, *Paget Papers*, II, Paget to Hawkesbury, 23 July 1804, 136–139.

54. Martens, *Recueil des Traités*, II, 405.

55. Paget, *Paget Papers*, II, Paget to Hawkesbury, 23 May 1804, 132–133.

56. Regele, "Mack und Cobenzl," 153; Eysturlid, *Formative Influences of Archduke Carl*, 33–34.

57. Rothenberg, *Napoleon's Great Adversary*, 76–77, Rauchensteiner, *Kaiser Franz und Erzherzog Karl*, 67–69.

58. Martens, *Recueil des Traités*, II, 406.

59. Ibid., 406–421.

60. Rothenberg, *Napoleon's Great Adversary*, 78–79; Rauchensteiner, *Kaiser Franz und Erzherzog Karl*, 71–72.

Chapter 7: The Third Coalition

1. John Holland Rose, ed., *Selected Dispatches from the British Foreign Office Archives Relating to the Formation of the Third Coalition against France, 1804–1805* (London: 1904), Harrowby to Voronstov 26 June 1804, 17.

2. Oscar Browning, "Hugh Elliot at Naples, 1803–1806," *English Historical Review* XIV (April 1889): 216.

3. Michael Bordo and Eugene White, "British and French Finance during the Napoleonic Wars," in Bordo and Capie, ed., *Monetary Regimes in Transition* (Cambridge: 1994), 254–255; John Sherwig, *Guineas and Gunpowder* (Cambridge: 1969), 365–366, provides figures for subsidies during wars of the Revolution and thereafter.

4. Ibid., 165.

5. Napoleon, *Correspondance de Napoleon Ier* (Paris: 1858–1862), VIII, No. 6814, Napoleon to Berthier, 14 June 1803, 352–353.

6. M. De Clerq, M., *Recueil des Traités de la France*, 23 vols. (Paris: 1880), II, 69–71; Simon Schama, *Patriots and Liberators: Revolution in the Netherlands, 1780–1813* (New York: 1992), 442.

7. Simon Schama, "The Politics of Taxation in the Netherlands," in J.M. Winter, *War and Economic Development* (Cambridge: 1975), 117.

8. Ibid., 118, 129.

9. Schama, *Patriots and Liberators,* 451; cf. François Crouzet, "War, Blockades and Economic Change in Europe," 916; Ana Maria Schop, *Las relaciones entre España y Rusia* (Barcelona: 1971), 121–123, 178–179.

10. Jean Gabillard, "Le financement des guerres napoleoniennes et al conjuncture de Premier Empire," *Revue economique* (1953): 549–550.

11. Georges Weill, "Le financier Ouvrard," *Revue historique* CXXVII (1918): 38–41.

12. Ibid.; Philip Walters and Raymond Walters, "The Amercian Career of David Parish," *Journal of Economic History* (1944): 151; G. Labouchère, "Pierre-Cesár Labouchère," *Revue d'histoire diplomatique* XXVII (1913): 430.

13. André Corvisier, ed., *Histoire militaire de la France* (Paris: 1992) II, 371–381.

14. Napoleon, *Correspondance,* X, No. 8206, Napoleon to Villeneuve, 12 December 1804, 63–67; No. 8231, Napoleon to Missiessy, 23 December 1804, 78–81.

15. Ibid., IX, No. 8060, Napoleon to Decrès, 29 September 1804, 551–555.

16. Schop, *España y Rusia,* 121–123.

17. See Paget, *Paget Papers,* and Rose, *Selected Dispatches,* passim.

18. F. Martens, *Recueil des Traités et Conventions conclus par La Russie avec les puissances étrangères,* 14 vols. (St. Petersburg: 1875), II, 418–421; Sherwig, *Guineas and Gunpowder,* 150–161.

19. Gunther E. Rothenberg, *Napoleon's Great Adversary: The Archduke Charles and the Austrian Army, 1792-1814* (Bloomington, IN: 1982), 54–56.

20. Adolf Beer, *Die Finanzen Oesterreichs im XIX. Jahrhundert* (Prague: 1877), 391; Sherwig, *Guineas and Gunpowder,* 110, 366. The exchange rate for gulden (florins):pounds was roughly 10:1.

21. Oscar Criste, *Erzherzog Carl von Österreich,* 3 vols. (Vienna: 1912), II, 310.

22. August Fourier, *Gentz und Cobenzl: Geschichte de österreichischen Diplomatie in den Jahren 1801–1805* (Vienna, 1880), 115–116 fn.; Beer, *Die Finanzen Oesterreichs,* 391–392. In 1793 state debt was 390,130,000 gulden. A decade later in 1803 it was 641,846,000.

23. Sten Carlsson, *Den Svenska Utrikes politikens Historia, III: 1792–1844* (Stockholm: 1954), 91, 93; Gustaf Björlin, *Sveriges Krig I Tyksland åren 1805–1807* (Stockholm: 1882), 20; Sherwig, *Guineas and Gunpowder,* 162–165; Raymond Carr, "Gustavus IV and the British Government, 1804–1809," *English Historical Review* LX, 236 (January 1945): 41–46.

24. Carr, "Gustavus IV," 43; Carlsson, *Svenska Utrikes politikens,* 93; Björlin, *Krig I Tyksland,* 20.

25. Ibid., 20; Carlsson, *Svenska Utrikes politikens,* 94; Carr, "Gustav IV," 44–46.

26. Carlsson, *Svenska Utrikes politikens,* 93; Carr, "Gustav IV," 44–48.

27. Alfred T. Mahan, *The Influence of Sea Power on the French Revolution and Empire, 1793–1812,* 2 vols. (London: reprint n.d.), II, 142.

28. DeClerq, *Recueil des Traités,* II, 117–119.

29. On the divisions among the Second Coalition and reasons for its failure, see Paul Schroeder, "The Collapse of the Second Coalition," *Journal of Modern History* 59 (1987): 244–290.

30. Martens, *Recueil des Traités,* XI, 72.

31. Rose, *Selected Dispatches,* Mulgrave to Gover, 21 January 1805, 88–92.

32. Fourier, *Gentz und Cobenzl,* Colloredo to Cobenzl, 26 January 1805, 151.

33. Ibid., Cobenzl to Emperor Francis, 22 March 1805, 303–304.

34. Rose, *Selected Dispatches*, Anglo-Russian Treaty of April 11, 1805, 266.

35. Rothenberg, *Napoleon's Great Adversary*, 81.

36. Napoleon, *Correspondance*, X, No. 8282, Napoleon to Pino, 22 January 1805, 120–121; cf. no. 8283, Napoleon to Berthier, 121–122.

37. Ibid., X, No. 8379, Napoleon to Ganteaume, 2 March 1805, 182–184; No. 8381, Napoleon to Villeneuve, 2 March 1805, 185–186.

38. Piers Mackesy, *The War in the Mediterranean, 1803–1810* (reprint Westport: 1981). 43. There is often conflicting figures on the number of Spanish ships with Villeneuve. The difference is rather negligible for a general discussion, but is of importance if trying to clearly establish overall Spanish naval strength. Marcus, *Royal Navy*, 251, claims six Spanish sail at Cadiz joined Villeneuve.

39. Mahan, *Influence of Sea Power*, II, 151–154; William Flayhart, *Counterpoint to Trafalgar* (Columbia: 1992), 69–73.

40. G.J. Marcus, *The Age of Nelson* (New York: 1971), 250.

41. Rose, *Selected Dispatches*, Gower to Mulgrave, 7 April 1805, 130.

42. Ibid., Mulgrave to Voronstov, 7 May 1805, 146; Flayhart, 49–51.

43. Flayhart, *Counterpoint to Trafalgar*, 63.

44. Napoleon, *Correspondance*, X, No. 8255, Napoleon to Queen of Naples, 2 January 1805, 103.

45. Rose, *Selected Dispatches*, Mulgrave to Voronstov, 5 June 1805, 155–156

46. Rothenberg, *Napoleon's Great Adversary*, 81–82; Fourier, *Gentz und Cobenzl*, 169–170; Martens, *Recueil des Traités*, II, 426.

47. Paget, *Paget Papers*, II, Paget to Mulgrave, 8 June 1805, 181–182.

48. Mahan, *Influence of Sea Power*, II, 166–171.

49. Ibid., 174–175.

50. Martens, *Recueil des Traités*, II, 430.

51. Ibid., II, 435.

52. Rothenberg, *Napoleon's Great Adversary*, 82, Wilhelm Rustow, *Der Krieg von 1805 in Deutschland und Italien* (Frauenfeld: 1853), 54; Criste, *Erzherzog Carl*, II, 317; Adolf Beer, *Zehn Jahre österreichischer Politik, 1801-1810* (Leipzig: 1877), 139.

53. Ibid., 139, Criste, *Erzherog Carl*, II, 317; Rothenberg, *Napoleon's Great Adversary*, 82.

54. Criste, *Erzherog Carl*, II, 318.

55. Ibid., 139 ; Martens, *Recueil des Traités*, VI, 362. Criste designates Buxhowden as commander of the third army. It was initially General Michaelson who was later replaced by Buxhowden.

56. Rothenberg, *Napoleon's Great Adversary*, 83; Criste, *Erzherzog Carl*, II, 318.

57. Rustow, *Der Krieg von 1805*, 55.

58. Ibid., 55; Rothenberg, *Napoleon's Great Adversary*, 82–83.

59. Ibid., 83; Rustow, *Der Krieg von 1805*, 56.

60. Fournier, *Gentz und Cobenzl*, 184.

61. Marcus Junkelman, *Napoleon und Bayern: von den Anfängen des Königreiches* (Regensberg: 1985), 62, 89.

62. Beer, *Zehn Jahre*, 140–141.

Chapter 8: August–September 1805

1. Napoleon, *Correspondance de Napoleon I*, 32 vols. (Paris: 1858–1862), XI, Napoleon to Eugene, 13 August 1805, 88.

2. John Elting, *Swords Around a Throne: Napoleon's Grande Armée* (New York: 1988), 60. Colonel Elting states one-third of the soldiers and virtually all of the officers and non-commisioned officers served for at least six years. Half the cavalry and 43 percent of the infantry had been in combat. One in thirty entered the army before 1789. For a more detailed examination, see P.C. Alombert and J. Colin, *La campagne de 1805 en Allemagne,* 5 vols. (Paris: 1902), I, 170–172. Alombert and Colin cite 50,338 of 115,582 men had served in at least one campaign.

3. Gunther E. Rothenberg, *The Art of Warfare in the Age of Napoleon* (Bloomington, IN: 1980), 127.

4. Napoleon, *Correspondance,* XI, No. 9070, Napoleon to Talleyrand, 13 August 1805, 80.

5. Ibid., 80.

6. Auguste Fourier, *Gentz und Cobenzl Geschichte der österreichischen Diplomatie in den Jahren 1801–1805* (Vienna: 1880), Cobenzl to Colloredo, 13 August 1805, 175.

7. Arthur Paget, *The Paget Papers, 1794–1807,* 2 vols. (New York: 1896), II, Paget to Mulgrave, 10 August 1805, 204; Paget to Mulgrave, 29 August 1805, 205–206.

8. Alombert and Colin, *Campagne en 1805,* I, 128–134. These pages contain a number of letters sent by Otto and La Rochfocauld to Napoleon concerning Austria's machinations and military buildup.

9. Napoleon, *Correspondance,* XI, No. 9114, Napoleon to Decrès, 22 August 1805, 114.

10. Ibid., No. 9114, Napoleon to Ganteaume, 22 August 1805; No. 9115, Napoleon to Villeneuve, 22 August 1805, 115.

11. Alfred T. Mahan, *The Influence of Sea Power on the French Revolution and Empire* (reprint London: n.d.), II, 179–181.

12. Napoleon, *Correspondance,* XI, No. 9117, Napoleon to Talleyrand, 23 August 1805, 117.

13. Alombert and Colin, *Campagne de 1805,* I, *Note pour le Bureau de l'organisation,* 26 August 1805, 330.

14. Ibid., 331–332.

15. Ibid., 331–332; Wilhelm Rustow, *Der Krieg von 1805 in Deutschland und Italien* (Frauenfeld: 1853), 64–65.

16. Napoleon, *Correspondance,* XI, No. 9137, Napoleon to Berthier, 26 August 1805, 141–144. 95,000 only applies to the corps around Boulogne. It does not include Marmont, Bernadotte, Augereau, the Guard, or cavalry reserve.

17. Frederick C. Schneid, *Napoleon's Italian Campaigns, 1805–1815* (Westport: 2002), 4, 6, 8–10.

18. Ibid., No. 9070, Napoleon to Talleyrand, 13 August 1805, 83–84.

19. Ibid., 83–84.

20. Marcus Junkelmann, *Napoleon und Bayern: von den Anfängen des Königreiches.* (Regensberg: 1985), 90–91; Eberhard Weis, "Bayern und Frankreich in der Zeit des Konsulats und des ersten Empire (1799–1815)," *Historische Zeitschrift* 237 (1983): 582–583.

21. Junkelmann, *Napoleon und Bayern,* 91; M. DeClerq, *Recueil des Traités de la France,* 23 vols. (Paris: 1880), II, 120–123.

22. B. Erdmansdörfer and K. Obler, eds., *Politische Correspondenz Karl Friedrichs von Baden 1783–1806,* 2 vols. (Heidelberg: 1901), II, 278, Maltiz (Russian ambassador to Württemberg) to Edelsheim (first minister of Baden), 30 August 1805; 283, M. Thiard (Napoleon's Chamberlain on special mission to Baden) to Talleyrand, 2 September 1805; Paul Sauer, *Adler über Württemberg, Baden und Hohenzollern* (Stuttgart: 1987),

78–81; Rudolfine von Oer, *Der Friede von Pressburg: Ein Beitrag zur Diplomaticgeschichte des Napoleonischen Zeitalters* (Munster: 1965), 36–37.

23. Sauer, *Adler über Wurttember, Baden und Hohenzollern*, 78–82.

24. Obler, *Correspondenz Karl Friedrichs*, V, Thiard to Talleyrand, 2 September 1805, 283; Lady Jackson, ed., *Jackson Diaries*, 2 vols. (London: 1872), I, 28 August 1805, 315.

25. Obler, *Politische Correspondenz*, 279, *Precis de l'ouverture faite à Carlsrouhe le 31 août par le ministre de France M. Didelot*, and 284–285, Didelot to Talleyrand, 2 September 1805. The Austrian province of Vorarlberg bordered Württemberg to the southeast.

26. De Clerq, *Receuil des Traités*, II, 123–124, *Traité d'alliance, conclu à Baden le 5 septembre 1805 entre France et l'Electeur de Bade pour la garantie de l'indépendence et l'integrité de l'Electorate*.

27. Ibid., II, 126–128, *Traité d'alliance conclu à Louisbourg entre la France et l'Electeur de Wurtemberg*.

28. Napoleon, *Correspondence*, X, No. 8329, Napoleon to Frederick William III, 148–150; Napoleon to Frederick William III, No. 8502, 276–277.

29. Brendan Simms, *The Impact of Napoleon: Prussian High Politics, Foreign Policy and the Crisis of the Executive, 1797–1806* (Cambridge: 1997), 176–178; Philip Dwyer, "Duroc Diplomate: Un militaire au service de la diplomatie napoléonniene," *Souvenir Napoleonién* 58 (1995): 32.

30. Simms, *Impact of Napoleon*, 181–182; Dwyer, "Duroc," 34.

31. Harold Deutsch, *The Genesis of Napoleonic Imperialism* (Cambridge, MA: 1938), 239. Pays particular attention to Hesse-Cassel.

32. Napoleon, *Correspondence*, XI, No. 9184, Napoleon to Bernadotte, 5 September 1805, 180–181.

33. Paul Bailleu, ed., *Preußen und Frankreich von 1795–1807: Diplomatische Correspondenzen*, 2 vols. (Leipzig: 1887), II, Duroc to Napoleon, 377.

34. Ibid., II, Duroc to Talleyrand, 3 September 1805, 373; and Duroc to Napoleon, 8 September 1805, 377, which establishes Bernadotte's route to Wurzburg via Hesse-Cassel and the principality of Fulda; Napoleon, *Correspondance*, XI, No. 9180, Napoleon to Talleyrand, 5 September 1805, 178, and No. 9184, *Pièce annexée au Maréchal Bernadotte*, 180–181.

35. Rainer von Hessen, *Wir Wilhelm von Gottes Gnaden: Die Lebenserinnerungen Kürfürst Wilhelms I von Hessen 1743–1821* (Frankfurt: 1996), 344–345; Phillip Losch, *Kürfürst Wilhelm I, Landgraf von Hessen: Ein Fürstenbild aus Zopfzeit* (Marburg: 1923), 252.

36. Jackson, *Jackson Diaries*, I, 317.

37. von Hessen, *Gottes Gnaden*, 344–345; Jackson, *Jackson Diaries*, 323.

38. Ibid., 345.

39. J.R. Dietrich, "Die Politik Landgraf Ludwigs X. von Hessen-Darmstadt von 1790–1806," *Archiv für hessische Geschichte und Alterrumskunde* 7 (1910): 434–435.

40. Ibid., 435–436.

41. Ibid., 436; On the Bavarian and Württemberg note, see, Obler, *Politische Correspondenz*, V, Maltiz to Edelsheim, 30 August 1805, 278; Simms, *Impact of Napoleon*, 187–188.

42. Obler, *Politische Correspondenz*, II, 326, Collini (Baden representative at Regensberg) to Edelsheim, 20 September 1805; Napoleon, *Correspondance*, XI, No. 9157, Napoleon to Talleyrand, 29 August, 1805, 158.

43. Alombert and Colin, *La Campagne de 1805*, II, 116–151. Alombert and Colin cover each day of I Corps's march to Wurzburg.

44. Ibid., II, elector of Hesse-Cassel to Bernadotte, 25 September 1805, 138–139.

45. von Hessen, *Gottes Gnaden*, 345.

46. F. Martens, *Recueil des Traités et Conventions conclus par la Russie avec les puissances étrangères*, 14 vols. (St. Petersburg: 1875), VI, Alexander to Alopeus, 7 August 1805, 362.

47. Ibid., 362. Frederick William's sister was the princess of Orange.

48. *Großen Generalsstabe, "Die Preußischen Kriegsvorbereitungen und Operationspläne von 1805," in Kriegsgeschichtliche Einzelschriften*, heft 1 (Berlin: 1898), 2, 61.

49. Ibid., 62–63.

50. Martens, *Recueil des Traités*, VI, 365; Dwyer, "Duroc", 34.

51. Curt Jany, *Geschichte der Preußischen Armee vom 15 Jahrhundert bis 1914*, (Osnabrück: 1967), III 511; Generalsstabe, "Preußischen Operationspläne," 5–6.

52. Ibid., 64–67.

53. Martens, *Recueil des Traitès*, VI, 365. Letter to Alexander sent 21 September.

54. Bailleu, *Preußen und Frankreich*, II, Duroc to Talleyrand, 18 September 1805, 387.

55. Oskar Criste, *Erzherzog Car von Österreich*, 3 vols. (Vienna: 1912), II, 320; Adolf Beer, *Zehn Jahre österreichischer Politik, 1801–1810* (Leipzig: 1877), 141; Gunther Rothenberg, *Napoleon's Great Adversaries: The Archduke Charles and the Austrian Army* (Bloomington, IN: 1982), 83–84. The numbers concerning the Austrian army of Italy vary.

56. Oscar Regele, "Karl Frieherr von Mack und Johann Ludwig von Cobenzl. Ihre Rolle im Kriegsjahr 1805," *Mitteilungen des österreichischen Staatsarchivs* XX, 1 (1969): 148–145; Manfred Rauchensteiner, *Kaiser Franz und Erzherzog Karl* (Munich: 1972), 74. The logistical assessment was drawn from Charles' staff officer upon his arrival in Italy at the end of September shortly after the war began. This was the state of the main Austrian army. One can imagine the condition of Mack's army in Germany.

57. Rauchensteiner, *Franz und Karl*, 75; Rustow, *Der Krieg von 1805*, 77; Rothenberg, *Napoleon's Great Adversaries*, 84;

58. Criste, *Erzherzog Carl*, II, 317.

59. Ibid., 321, 328–329; Beer, *Zehn Jahre*, 141. On 9 September 1805 Francis declared Mack the general commander of all forces in Vorarlberg, north Tyrol, and on the Bavarian border.

60. Rustow, *Der Krieg von 1805*, 75; Paget, *Paget Papers*, II, Paget to Mulgrave 5 September 1805, 211

61. Rothenberg, *Napoleon's Great Adversaries*, 84.

62. Rustow, *Krieg von 1805*, 75; Junkelmann, *Napoleon und Bayern*, 92–95. 6,000 Bavarian troops remained throughout southern Bavaria, while 16,000 withdrew to the Upper Palitinate.

63. Obler, Politische Correspondenz, V, Edelsheim to von Maltiz, 18 September 1805, 317–319.

64. Ibid., Collini to Edelsheim, 20 September 1805, 326.

65. Ibid., Murat to Karl Friedrich, 24 September 1805, 339.

66. *Archives de la guerre. Service historique de l'armée du terre*, Chateau de Vincennes, Paris. [hereafter AG] C² 3, Max Joseph to Bernadotte 24 September 1805; C² 3, Bernadotte to Berthier, 28 September 1805.

67. Rustow, *Der Krieg von 1805*, 81.

68. Ibid., 81.

69. Beer, *Zehn Jahren*, 483; *Allerhöchtes Handschreiben an Erzherzog Ferdinand*, 5 October 1805.

Chapter 9: From the Rhine to the Inn

1. Napoleon, *Correspondance de Napoleon I*, 32 vols. (Paris: 1858–1862), XI, No. 9227, *Ordre*, 17 September 1805, 211–214; orders revised, 29 September 1805, in Napoleon, *Unpublished Correspondence of Napoleon I*, 3 vols. (New York: 1913), I, Special Dispositions, 122–127.

2. Ibid., I, 29 September 1805, 122–127.

3. Nicolas Mollien, *Mémoires d'un Ministre du Trésor Public*, 1780–1815, 4 vols. (Paris: 1845), I, 409.

4. Ibid., I, 408.

5. Napoleon, *Correspondence*, XI, No. 8178, *Décision*, 11 November 1804, 52.

6. Gabriele B. Clemens, "Napoleonische Armeelieferanten und die Entstehung des Rheinischen Wirtscahftsbürgertums," *Francia* 24, 2 (1997): 161–166.

7. Napoleon, *Correspondance*, XI, No. 9150, Napoleon to General Dejean, 28 August 1805, 153; Napoleon, *Unpublished Correspondence*, I, No. 187, Napoleon to Andreossy, 26 September, 1805, 116.

8. Napoleon, *Correspondance*, XI, No. 9134, Napoleon to the elector of Bavaria, 25 August 1805, 139. A good discussion of logistical concerns in 1805 can be found in Martin van Crevald, *Logistics from Wallenstein to Patton* (Cambridge: 1977), 40–61. In his chapter, "An Army Marches on Its Stomach," van Crevald provides a clear examination of Napoleon's logistical difficulties. He fails, however, to take into account the agreements made between Napoleon and the German electors of Baden and Württemberg, which enabled his army to acquire great quantities of food and supplies in an extremely short time.

9. Napoleon Correspondance, XI, No. 9150, Napoleon to General Dejean, 28 August 1805, 153; No. 9231, Napoleon to Murat, 18 September 1805, 218; M. de Clerq, *Recueil des Traités de la France*, 23 vols. (Paris: 1880), II, 122.

10. Napoleon, *Unpublished Correspondence, I*, Napoleon to Ney, 20 September 1805; Napoleon to Lannes, 20 September 1805; Napoleon to Davout, 20 September 1805, 108–111.

11. Van Crevald, *Logistics*, 52.

12. P. Alombert and J. Colin, *La campagne en Allemagne: 1805*, 5 vols. (Paris: 1902), II, 62–65; cf. volume I, 583, reprint of archival document listing quantity of biscuits and bread available and the amount each city was able to produce each day, 26 September 1805.

13. Napoleon, *Correspondance*, XI, No. 9218, Napoleon to Berthier, 15 September 1805, 204.

14. Bernadotte to Berthier, 2 letters, 28 September 1805, AG C²3; Max Joseph to Bernadotte, 24 September 1805, AG C²3.

15. B. Erdmansdorfer and K. Obler, *Politische Correspondenz Karl Friedrichs von Baden 1783–1806*, 2 vols. (Heidelberg: 1901), II, Thiard to Edelsheim, 19 September 1805, 322. Refer to articles 9 and 10; Karl Friedrich informed his privy council of the French army's logistical needs; and *Kürfürstliches Reskript an der Geheimen Rath.*, 25 September 1805, 341.

16. Ibid., II, *Vollmacht für den Geh. Referandar Oehl*, 26 September 1805, 342.

17. Ibid, II, Oehl to Karl Friedrich, 28 September 1805, 342 and Oehl to Karl Friedrich, 29 September 1805, 343.

18. Ibid.,II, Oehl to Karl Friedrich, 29 September 1805, 343; Napoleon, *Correspondance*, XI, No. 9320, 3 October 1805, 280;

19. Obler, *Karl Friedrichs*, II, 349fn. Payment of vouchers did not occur until the spring of 1806, and French paper had little value in the Electorate through the remainder of 1805 and into 1806.

20. Paul Sauer, *Adler über Württemberg, Baden und Hohenzollern: Südwestdeutschland in der Rheinbundzeit (Stuttgart: 1987)*, 82–89.

21. Napoleon, *Unpublished Correspondence,* Special Dispositions, 29 September 1805, 124.

22. Napoleon, *Correspondance*, XI, No. 9301, Napoleon to Joseph, 1 October 1805, 269; No. 9306, Napoleon to Josephine, 2 October 1805, 272.

23. Sauer, *Adler über Württemberg, Baden und Hohenzollern*, 87.

24. Napoleon, *Correspondance*, XI, No. 9330, Napoleon to Cambaceres, 4 October 1805, 285–286.

25. M. DeClerq, *Recueil des Traités des France*, 23 vols. (Paris: 1880) , II, *Traité d'alliance*, 5 October 1805, 126–127.

26. Sauer, *Adler uber Württemberg, Baden und Hohenzollern*, 86. Negotiations for supply contracts began three days prior to Napoleon's arrival at Ludwigsberg; van Crevald, *Logistics*, 54–55, provides figures for the quantities gathered by French corps at Heilbronn and later Hall.

27. Berthier to Bernadotte, 28 September 1805, AG C^{2}3.

28. Napoleon, *Correspondance*, XI, No. 9314, Napoleon to Max Joseph, 2 October 1805, 277.

29. Bernadotte to Berthier, 1 October 1805, AG C^{2}4.

30. Three letters from Bernadotte to Berthier, 3 October 1805, AG C^{2}4 3; three letters from Bernadotte to Berthier, 4 October 1805; one letter from Bernadotte to Berthier, 5 October 1805, AG C^{2}4 3.

31. Clemens von Metternich, *Memoirs of Prince Metternich: 1773–1815*, II (New York: 1970), Metternich to Colloredo, 7 October 1805, 63–64.

32. Paul Bailleu, *Preußen und Frankreich von 1795–1807, Diplomatische Correspondenzen*, 2 vols. (Leipzig: 1887), II, Frederick William to Hardenberg, October 1805, #298, 400. He called it "the Bavarian insolence."

33. Brendan Simms, *The Impact of Napoleon: Prussian High Politics, Foreign Policy and the Crisis of the Executive, 1797–1806* (Cambridge: 1997), 191–192.

34. Jany, *Geschichte der Preußischen Armee*, 511–512.

35. Dennis Showalter, "Hubertusberg to Auerstädt: The Prussian Army in Decline?" *German History* 12, 3 (1994): 308.

36. For further discussion of the Prussian canton and reserve system, see William O. Shanahan, *Prussian Military Reforms, 1786–1813* (New York: 1966), 35–60.

37. Philip Dwyer, "Duroc Diplomate: Un militaire au service de la diplomatie napoléonniene," *Souvenir Napoleonién* 58 (1995): 34.

38. Bailleu, *Preußen und Frankreich*, Lombard to Hardenberg, n.d. October 1805, 400–401n.

39. Ibid., Hardenberg to Laforest, 17 October 1805, #299, 401.

40. Jany, *Geschichte der Preußischen Armee*, 513. Potsdam conference 9 October 1805, Brunswick, Möllendorf, Kalkreuth, Kökritz, Kleist, Hardenberg, and Haugwitz were present.

41. Shanahan, *Prussian Military Reforms*, 82.

42. Jany, *Geschichte der Preußischen Armee*, 514.

43. Rustow, 116–117, 122–123; cf. Napoleon, *Correspondance*, XI, note date and location of headquarters on correspondence *passim*.

44. Adolf Beer, *Zehn Jahre österreichischer Politik, 1801–1810* (Leipzig: 1877), 147.

45. Ibid., Ferdinand to Francis, 6 October 1805, 484; *Allerhöchtes Handschreiben an der Erzherzog Ferdinand*, 7 October 1805, 485.

46. Wilhelm Rustow, *Der Krieg von 1805 in Deutschland und Italien* (Frauenfeld: 1853), 120–122.

47. Ibid., 127–135.

48. Ibid., 123–150; two letters from Bernadotte to Berthier, 11 October 1805 provides first report of Russian troops in Bavaria, AG C^{2}5; Bernadotte to Berthier, 12 October 1805, AG C^{2}5, places 20,000 Russians at Braunau.

49. Rustow, *Krieg von 1805*, 132–135; Gunther Rothenberg, *Napoleon's Great Adversaries, the Archduke Charles and the Austrian Army, 1792–1814* (Bloomington, IN: 1982), 92.

50. Rustow, *Krieg von 1805*, 156–163; Napoleon, *Correspondance*, XI, No. 9403, Napoleon to Murat, 20 October 1805, 341.

51. Rothenberg, *Napoleon's Great Adversaries*, 92.

52. Ibid., 93.

53. Arthur Paget, *The Paget Papers, 1794–1807*, 2 vols. (New York: 1896), Paget to Mulgrave, 24 October 1805, 231–234.

54. Richard Metternich, ed., *Memoirs of Prince Metternich, 1773–1815*, 3 vols. (New York: 1970), II, Metternich to Colloredo 29 October 1805, 81–82.

55. Bailleu, *Preußen und Frankreich*, Duroc to Napoleon, 27 October 1805; Duroc to Napoleon, 30 October 1805, 401–402.

56. Napoleon, *Correspondance*, XI, No. 9434, Napoleon to Frederick William III, 27 October 1805, 360–362. In the note at the bottom of the letter, the editors of the *Correspondance* indicate that they were unable to discover whether this letter was actually sent to Berlin. Nonetheless, its content provides the reader with a wonderful illustration of Napoleon's logic of argument. Whether he was sincere is another question.

57. Joseph Wirth, *Le Maréchal Lefebvre: Duc de Danzig (1755–1820)* (Paris: 1904), 139.

58. Napoleon, *Correspondance*, XI, 9137, Napoleon to Berthier, 26 August 1805, 142–144. The following regiments and battalions remained on the Channel coast: 72nd Line from IV Corps, 21st Light from VI Corps, from III Corps "the regiment which was weakest and possessed the most conscripts." Furthermore, the 3/23, 2/17, 3/17, 3/36, 3/45, 3/55, 3/46, 3/28, and 3/65 Lines were ordered to Ambleteuse and Boulogne. On Holland, see *Correspondance*, XI, 9252, *Instructions pour la défense de Boulogne*, 22 September 1805, 234–237. The state of Brune's divisions can be found in *Situations des Troupes Composant les Premier Corps de Reserve*, August–December 1805, AG C^{2}486.

59. Ibid., XI, 9248, Napoleon to Berthier, 21 September 1805, 230. Estimate of 40,000 derived from calculating 1,200 men per battalion times 34 battalions on the Rhine. The state of Lefebvre's corps can be found in *Situations des Troupes Composant les II Corps des Reserve*, September–December 1805, AG C^{2}489; the state of Kellerman's corps can be found in *Situations des Troupes Composant les III Corps des Reserve*, September–December 1805, AG C^{2}489.

60. Corvisier, *Histoire Militaire*, II, 306.

61. As the standard age for conscription was 20, the range was determined by adding the number of years prior to 1805 from which the conscripts of the reserve were called.

62. Refer to Lefebvre and Kellerman's respective reports in *Situations des Troupes Composant les Corps des Reserve*, 6 December 1805, AG C^{2}489.

63. Ibid., 9248, Napoleon to Berthier, 21 September 1805, 230–231; the corps was composed of the 5th Light, 7th, 66th, 82nd, and 86th Line regiments.

64. Napoleon, *Correspondance*, XI, 9256, Napoleon to Berthier, 22 September 1805, 238–239 and 9285, Napoleon to Menou, 29 September 1805, 258–259. The reserve

division included the 13th and 67th Lines, 3rd Light, a Swiss battalion, and the Hanoverian Legion.

65. Desmond Gregory, *Napoleon's Italy* (Madison, WI: 2001), 114.

66. Napoleon, *Correspondance*, XI, 9226, Napoleon to Lacèpéde, 17 September 1805, 211; André Fugier, *Napoléon et l'Espagne (1799–1808)*, 2 vols. (Paris: 1930), II, 30–31. The Spanish contingent consisted of three infantry regiments, two cavalry regiments, and an artillery detachment.

67. Napoleon, *Correspondance*, XI, 9214, *Note sur l'organization des Gardes Nationales*, 15 September 1805, 197–199; on Italian departments, see 9223, Napoleon to Lebrun, 16 September 1805, 206; Alain Pigeard, *L'armée Napoléonnienne* (Currandra, France: 1993), 431; L. Levy-Schneider, "Napoléon et la Garde Nationale," *La Revolution Française* 56 (January 1909):19–23.

68. Alfred Rambaud, *L'Allemagne sous Napoleon Ier (1804–1811)* (Paris:1897), 3.

Chapter 10: November 1805

1. Napoleon, *Correspondance de Napoleon I*, 32 vols. (Paris: 1858–1862), XI, No. 9210, Instructions to Villeneuve, 14 September 1805, 195–196; No. 9220, Napoleon to Decrès , 15 September 1805, 204–205; Alfred T. Mahan, *The Influence of Sea Power on the French Revolution and Empire, 1793–1812,* 2 vols. (London: reprint n.d.), II, 185; Piers Mackesey, *The War for America 1775–1783* (Lincoln, NE: reprint 1993), 74–76.

2. Napoleon, *Correspondance*, XI, No. 9230, Instructions for Rosily, 17 September 1805, 216–217.

3. Mahan, *Influence of Sea Power*, II, 186–187.

4. Ibid., II, 188–195; Alan Schom, *Trafalgar: Countdown to Battle, 1803–1805* (Oxford: 1990), 307–356.

5. Napoleon, *Correspondance*, XI, No. 9507, Napoleon to Decrès, 18 November 1805, 424.

6. M. de Clerq, *Recueil des Traités de la France*, 23 vols. (Paris: 1880), II, *Traité de neutralité*, 124–125.

7. O'Farrill's division did not leave Spain until late November, and it arrived in Tuscany by February 1806.

8. Frederick C. Schneid, *Napoleon's Italian Campaigns* (Westport: 2002), 20; William Flayhart, *Counterpoint to Trafalgar: The Anglo-Russian Invasion of Naples, 1805–1806* (Columbia, SC: 1992), 110.

9. Schneid, *Italian Campaigns*, 4.

10. Napoleon, *Correspondance*, XI, No. 9262, 23 September 1805, 246.

11. Ibid., XI, No. 9258, Napoleon to Eugene, 22 September 1805, 242.

12. Archduke Charles to Bellegarde, 8 September 1805, *Kriegsarchiv*, Vienna, *Feldakten* [hereafter KAFA] KAFA-II Reg 90/1805 Fasz. 9, NF 1363.

13. O. Criste, *Erzherzog Carl von Österreich*, 3 vols. (Vienna: 1912), II, 335–337 and Charles to Duke Albrecht, 21 September 1805, 572; Archduke Ferdinand complained that Charles's army had not taken the field and the French were bearing down on him. This was not a criticism of Charles, but an indictment of Mack. Adolf Beer, *Zehn Jahre Österreichischer Politik, 1801–1810* (Leipzig: 1877), Erzherzog Ferdinand, 5 October 1805, 483.

14. Schneid, *Italian Campaigns,* 22–23; Edouard Gachot, *Histoire militaire de Massena* (Paris: 1911), 36.

15. Criste, *Erzherzog Carl,* II, Charles to Albrecht, 1 October 1805, 577.

16. Napoleon, *Correspondance*, XI, No. 9281, Napoleon to Glutz, 29 September 1805, 256.

17. Napoleon to Massena 7/8 October 1805, KAFA-II Reg. 90/1805 Fasz. 10/b, NF 1364. There is no indication of when the dispatch was taken en route to Italy. Nonetheless, it is safe to assume that Charles had it by 14 October; Charles to Francis I, 17 October 1805, KAFA-II Reg. 90/1805 Fasz. 10/152 NF 1364; Criste, *Erzherzog Carl*, II, Charles to Albrecht, 20 October 1805, 584.

18. Schneid, *Italian Campaigns*, 18–19; Criste, *Erzherzog Carl*, II, 345–347.

19. Schneid, *Italian Campaigns*, 28–29.

20. Criste, *Erzherzog Carl*, II, 345.

21. Charles to generals of the army in Italy, ten letters, 25 October 1805, KAFA-II, Reg. 90/1805 Fasz.10/231, NF 1364.

22. Criste, *Erzherzog Carl*, II, 345.

23. Schneid, *Italian Campaigns*, 29–32.22.

24. Ibid., 33.

25. Ibid., 36–39; Gachot, *Histoire militaire*, 59–81; Wilhelm Rustow, *Der Krieg von 1805 in Deutschland und Italien* (Frauenfeld: 1853), 105–109; Criste, *Erzherzog Carl*, 349–354.

26. Schneid, *Italian Campaigns*, 40.

27. Charles to Francis, 3 November 1805, KAFA-II, Fasz. 25 Reg. ¼ NF 1364.

28. Schneid, *Italian Campaigns*, 41.

29. Bernadotte to Napoleon, 12 October 1805, AG C^{2}5; Bernadotte to Napoleon 14 October 1805, AG C^{2}5.

30. Bernadotte to Napoleon, 17 October 1805, AG C^{2}5. Frederick William approved the Tsar's request to move Buxhowden's army through Prussian Silesia after Bernadotte's corps violated the neutrality of Anspach.

31. Moritz von Angeli, "Ulm und Austerlitz," *Österreichischer militär Zeitschrift*, III (1878): 285–286.

32. Gustaf Björlin, *Sveriges Krig I Tyksland åren 1805–1807* (Stockholm: 1882), 24, 28–29.

33. Ibid., 75; F. Martens, *Recueil des traités et conventions conclus par La Russie avec les puissances étrangères*, 14 vols. (St. Petersburg: 1875), VI, 346–350.

34. Paul Bailleu, *Preußen und Frankreich von 1795–1807, Diplomatische Correspondenzen*, 2 vols. (Leipzig: 1887), II, Hardenberg to Laforest, 17 October 1805, 401.

35. Richard Metternich, ed., *Memoirs of Prince Metternich: 1773–1815*, 3 vols. (New York: 1970), II, Metternich to Colloredo, 4 November 1805, 86.

36. Leopoled von Ranke, ed., *Einhändige Memoiren des Saatskanzlers Fürsten von Hardenberg*, 5 vols. (Leipzig: 1877), II, Brunswick's military plans in full, 317–324, dated 1 November 1805. Estimates of army strengths are Brunswick's own, 317.

37. Ibid., 320.

38. Karl Linnebach, ed., *Scharnhorsts Briefe, I: Privatbriefe* (Munich: 1914), Scharnhorst to Knesbeck, No. 168, November 1805, 257.

39. Ranke, ed., *Hardenberg*, II, 323, Brunswick's Second Memorandum; Curt Jany *Geschichte der Preußischen Armee vom 15 Jahrhundert bis 1914*, 4 vols. (Osnabrück: 1967), III, 514; Linnebache *Briefe*, Scharnhorst to Ompteda, 29 October 1805, No. 167, 256; *Großen Generalsstabe*, "Die Preusischen Kriegsvorbeitungen und Operationspläne von 1805," in *Kriegsgeschicteliche Einzelschriften*, heft 1 (Berlin: 1898), 26–27.

40. Martens, *Recueil des Traités*, II, 491–493.

41. Angeli, "Ulm und Austerlitz," 310.

42. Manfred Rauchensteiner, *Kaiser Franz und Erzherzog Karl* (Munich: 1972), Charles to Josef, 30 November 1805, 78.

43. Napoleon, *Correspondance*, XI, No. 9425 and No. 9426, Napoleon to Petit, 24 October 1805, 355–356; No. 9441, 14th Bulletin of the Grande Armée, 30 October 1805, 367.

44. Angeli, "Ulm und Austerlitz," 286–287; Rainer Egger, *Das Gefecht bei Dürnstein-Loiben 1805* (Vienna: 1986), 10.

45. Napoleon, *Correspondance*, XI, No. 9451, Napoleon to Francis, 3 November 1805, 376; Rudophine von Oer, *Der Friede von Pressburg* (Munster: 1965), 245–247.

46. Napoleon, *Correspondance*, XI, No. 9464, Napoleon to Francis, 8 November 1805, 386.

47. Ranke, ed., *Hardenberg*, II (Leipzig: 1877), 324–332, articles of Treaty of Potsdam; Martens, *Recueil des Traités*, II, 480–489.

48. Metternich, *Memoirs,* II, 85–88.

49. 49. Lady Jackson, ed., *The Diaries and Letters of Sir George Jackson,* 2 vols. (London: 1872), I, J. Jackson to G. Jackson, 9 November 1805, 365.

50. Martens, *Recueil des traités*, II, 487. Article IX , Treaty of Potsdam.

51. J. Holland Rose, *Selected Dispatches* (London: 1904), three letters, Mulgrave to Harrowby, 27 October 1805, 207–220.

52. Ibid., Harrowby to Mulgrave, 17 November 1805, 221–226.

53. Arthur Paget, *The Paget Papers, 1794-1807*, 2 vols. (New York: 1896), Paget to Mulgrave, 8 November 1805, 241.

54. Angeli, "Ulm und Austerlitz," 314; Egger, *Dürnstein-Loiben*, 9, 11; Criste, *Erzherzog Carl*, II, 360.

55. Egger, *Dürnstein-Loiben*, 14–21.

56. Angeli, "Ulm und Austerlitz," 329–331; Gunther Rothenberg, *Napoleon's Great Adversaries, the Archduke Charles and the Austrian Army* (Bloomington, IN: 1982), 96–98.

57. Ibid., 98; Rainer Egger, *Das Gefecht bei Hollabrunn und Schöngrabern 1805* (Vienna: 1982), 12–18; Angeli, "Ulm und Austerlitz," 332–333.

58. Napoleon, *Correspondance*, XI, No. 9495, Napoleon to Marmont, 15 November 1805, 412–413.

59. Criste, *Erzherzog Carl*, II, 364–366.

60. Schneid, *Italian Campaigns,* 42.

61. Ibid., 47; William Flayhart, *Counterpoint to Trafalgar, the Anglo-Russian Invasion of Naples, 1805–1806* (Columbia, SC: 1992), 121–132.

Chapter 11: Austerlitz, Pressburg, and Prussia.

1. André Bonnefons, *Un allié de Napoleon, Frédéric-Auguste Premier roi de Saxe et Grand-Duc de Varsovie, 1763–1827* (Paris: 1902), 128–133.

2. Ibid., 132–135; *Großen Generalsstabe, "Die Preusischen Kriegsvorbeitungen und Operationspläne von 1805,"* in *Kriegsgeschichteliche Einzelschriften*, heft 1 (Berlin: 1898), 26, 27, 35.

3. Ibid., 34–36.

4. Phillip Losch, *Kürfurst Wilhelm I, Landgraf von Hessen* (Marburg: 1923), 253–254.

5. J.R. Dietrich, "Die Politik Ludwigs X. von Hessen-Darmstadt von 1790–1806," *Archiv für hessische Geschichte und Altertumskunde* 7 (1910): 437–440.

6. *Generalsstabe, "Kriegsvorbeitungen und Operationspläne,"* 33–35, 37.

7. Ibid., 29; Gustaf Björlin, *Sveriges Krig i Tyksland åren 1805–1807* (Stockholm: 1882), 76, 82, 87.

8. Leopold von Ranke ed., *Einhändige Memoiren des Saatskanzlers Fürsten von Hardenberg*, 5 vols. (Leipzig: 1877), V, 185–186, *Mémoire du Comte Haugwitz pour lui servir d'instructions lors de son voyage à Vienne en novembre 1805*; Brendan Simms, *The Impact of Napoleon: Prussian High Politics, Foreign Policy and the Crisis of the Executive, 1797–1806* (Cambridge: 1997), 207; *Generalsstabe, "Kriegsvorbeitungen und Operationspläne,"* 27–28.

9. Paul Bailleu, *Preußen und Frankreich von 1795–1807, Diplomatische Correspondenzen*, 2 vols. (Leipzig: 1887), II, Haugwitz to Hardenberg, 20 November 1805, 408n.

10. Ibid., II, Laforest to Talleyrand, 14 November 1805, 405–406.

11. Napoleon, *Correspondance de Napoleon I*, 32 vols. (Paris: 1858–1862), XI, No. 9516, Napoleon to Talleyrand, 22 November 1805, 430–431.

12. Ibid., XI, No. 9466, *Décret*, 8 November 1805; No. 9488, Napoleon to Lefebvre, 15 November 1805, 409.

13. *Situation des Troupes composant le 2e corps d'armée de Reserve*, 29 November 1805, AG C^{2}489; *Situation des Troupes composant le 3e corps d'armée de Reserve*, 21 November 1805, AG C^{2}489; *Situation des Troupes composant le Premier Corps d'armée de Reserve*, 21 November 1805, AG C^{2}486.

14. Moritz von Angeli, "Ulm und Austerlitz," *Mitteilungen des k.k Kriegs Archivs*, III (1878): 357.

15. Napoleon, *Correspondance*, XI, No. 9532, 30 November 1805, 440.

16. For the battle of Austerlitz consult, Christopher Duffy, *Austerlitz* (London: 1973); David Chandler, *The Campaigns of Napoleon* (New York: 1966); Rustow, *Der Krieg von Italien* and Angeli, "*Ulm und Austerlitz.*"

17. Napoleon, *Correspondance*, XI, No. 9535, *Dispositions Générales pour le journée du 11 frimaire* (2 December), 442–443.

18. Ibid., XI, No. 9539, Napoleon to the Bishops, 3 December 1805, 445–446; No. 9540, Napoleon to Talleyrand, 3 December 1805, 446; No. 9542, Napoleon to Talleyrand, 4 December 1805, 453–454.

19. M. De Clerq, *Recueil des Traités de la France*, 23 vols. (Paris: 1880), II, Armistice, 6 December 1805, 134–135.

20. Oskar Criste, *Erzherzog Carl von Österreich*, 3 vols. (Vienna: 1912), II, 366–369;cf. Charles to Duke Albrecht, 6 December and 7 December 1805, 597–599.

21. De Clerq, *Recueil des Traités*, II, Treaty with Bavaria, 10 December 1805, 135–137; Treaty with Württemberg, 11 December 1805, 138–140; Treaty with Baden, 12 December 1805, 140–143.

22. *Generalsstabe, "Kriegsvorbeitungen und Operationspläne,"* 39–40, 43–46.

23. Bailleu, *Preußen und Frankreich*, II, Hardenberg to Frederick William, 9 December 1805, 415–419; Hardenberg to Frederick William, 11 December 1805, 419.

24. *Generalsstabe, "Kriegsvorbeitungen und Operationspläne,"* 46–47.

25. De Clerq, *Recueil des Traités*, II, Treaty of alliance, 15 December 1805, Article 2, 144.

26. Ibid., 143–145.

27. Napoleon, *Correspondance*, XI, No. 9582, 16 December 1805, 484–485.

28. Bailleu, *Preußen und Frankreich*, II, Frederick William to Friedrich August, 20 December 1805, 427–428.

29. Ibid., II, Hardenberg to Lucchesini, 22 December 1805, 428.

30. Napoleon, *Correspondance*, XI, No. 9571, Napoleon to Massena, 13 December 1805, 476–477; No. 9587, Napoleon to Berthier, 18 December 1805, 487–488.

31. Gunther Rothenberg, *Napoleon's Great Adversaries: The Archduke Charles and the Austrian Army* (Bloomington, IN: 1982), 101; Criste, *Erzherzog Carl*, 372.

32. De Clerq, *Recueil des Traités*, II, Treaty of Pressburg, 26 December 1805, 145–151.

33. William Flayhart, *Counterpoint to Trafalgar* (Columbia: 1992), 141–142.

34. Frederick Schneid, *Napoleon's Italian Campaigns* (Westport: 2003), 48–50.

35. Gustaf Björlin, *Sveriges Krig I Tyksland* (Stockholm: 1882), 100–102.

36. De Clerq, *Recueil des Traités,* II, 154–155.

37. Björlin, *Krig I Tyksland*, 100–115; Sten Carlsson, *Den Svenska Utrikes Politikens Historia*, 3 vols. (Stockholm: 1954), III, 100–105.

38. See Brendan Simms, "An Odd Question Enough." Charles James Fox, "The Crown and British Policy during the Hanoverian Crisis of 1806," *Historical Journal* 38 3 (1995): 567–596.

39. Napoleon, *Correspondance*, XI, No. 9671, 16 January 1806, 539–540.

40. Jacques Barbier and Herbert Klein, "Revolutionary Wars and Public Finance: The Madrid Treasury, 1784–1807," *Journal of Economic History* XLI, 2 (June 1981): 329. Figure refers to revenue in the treasury of Cadiz, which was the primary port for Indies trade.

41. Marcel Marion, *Histoire Financière de la France depuis 1715*, 4 vols. (Paris: 1927), 283–285.

42. Victor de Grimouard,"Les origins du domatine extraordinaire: Le Receveur Général des Contributions de la Grande Armée, 1805–1810," *Revue des questiones historique* 39 (1908): 162–166. These figures do not include contributions collected from Venice.

BIBLIOGRAPHY

Alombert, P.C., and J. Colin. *La Campagne de 1805 en Allemagne*. 5 vols. Paris: 1902.

Angeli, Moritz von. "Ulm und Austerlitz." *Österreichischer militär Zeitschrift*. Vol. III. (1878): 283–394.

Arentin, Karl Ottmar Freiherr von. *Heiliges Römisches Reich, 1776–1806*. 2 vols. Weisbaden: 1967.

Bailleu, Paul, ed. *Preußen und Frankreich von 1795–1807, Diplomatische Correspondenzen*. 2 vols. Leipzig: 1887.

Barbier, Jacques A. "Peninsular Finance and Colonial Trade: The Dilemma of Charles IV's Spain." *Journal of Latin American Studies* 12, 1 (1980): 21–37.

———. "Indies Revenues and Naval Spending: The Cost of Colonialism for the Spanish Bourbons, 1763–1805." *Jahrbuch fur Geschichte von Staat, Wirtschaft und Gesellschaft Lateinamerikas* 21 (1984): 171–184.

Barbier, Jacques A., and Herbert S. Klein. "Revolutionary Wars and Public Finances: The Madrid Treasury, 1784–1807." *Journal of Economic History* XLI, 2 (June 1981): 315–339.

Beccera de Beccera, Emilio. "El Ejercito Español desde 1788 hasta 1802." *Rivista de historia militar* 28, 56 (1984): 91–134.

Beer, Adolf. *Die Finanzen Oesterreichs im XIX. Jahrhundert*. Prague: 1877.

———. *Zehn Jahre österreichischer Politik, 1801–1810*. Leipzig: 1877.

Bernath, Mathias. "Die Auswärtige Politik Nassaus 1805–1812: Ein Beitrag zur Geschichte des Rheinbundes der politischen Ideen am Mittelrhein zur Zeit Napoleons." *Nassauische Annalen* (1952).

Beumer, Karl, ed. *Quellensammlung zur Geschichte der deutschen Reichsverfassung im Mittelalter und Neuzeit*. 2 vols. Tübingen: 1913.

Bien, David. "La réaction aristocratique avant 1789: l'example de l'armée." *Annales* 29, 1 (1974): 23–48; 29, 2 (1974): 505–534.

———. "The Army in the French Enlightenment: Reform, Reaction and Revolution." *Past and Present* 85 (1979): 68–98.

Billinger, Robert. "Good and True Germans: The Nationalism of the Rheinbund Princes, 1806–1814." In *Reich Oder Nation? Mitteleuropa 1780–1815*, edited by Heinz Durchhardt and Andreas Kunz. Mainz: 1998.

Biro, Sydney. *The German Policy of Revolutionary France: A Study in French Diplomacy during the War of the First Coalition.* 2 vols. Cambridge, MA: 1957.

Björlin, Gustaf. *Sveriges Krig I Tyksland ären 1805–1807.* Stockholm: 1882.

Black, Jeremy. *France From Louis XIV to Napoleon: The Fate of a Great Power.* London: 1999.

Blanning, T.C.W. *The French Revolutionary Wars, 1787–1802.* London: 1986.

Bonnefons, André. *Un Allié de Napoléon, Frédéric-Auguste, Premier Roi de Saxe et Grand-Duc de Varsovie, 1763–1827.* Paris: 1902.

Bordo, Michael, and Eugene White. "A Tale of Two Currencies: British and French Finance During the Napoleonic Wars." *Journal of Economic History* 51, 2 (June 1991): 303–316.

———. "British and French Finance during the Napoleonic Wars." In *Monetary Regimes in Transition,* edited by Michael Bardo and Forrest Capie. Cambridge, MA: 1994.

Bottineau, Yves. *Les Bourbons d'Espagne: 1700–1808.* Paris: 1993.

Brandes, Karl Friedrich. "Hannover in der Politik der Grossmachte. 1801–1807." *Forschungen zur brandenburgischen und preußischen Geschichte* LI. (1939): 239–274.

Browning, Oscar. "Hugh Elliot at Naples, 1803–1806." *English Historical Review* XIV (April 1889): 209–228.

Camon, Hubert. *La Guerre Napoléonienne: Précis des campagnes.* Paris: 1911.

Carlsson, Sten. *Den Svenska Utrikes politikens Historia.* Vol. III, *1792–1844.* Stockholm: 1954.

Carr, Raymond. "Gustavus IV and the British Government, 1804–1809." *English Historical Review* LX, 236 (1945): 36–44.

Carrington, Dorothy. "The Achievement of Pasquale Paoli (1755–1799) Its Consequences." *Proceedings of the Consortium on Revolutionary Europe* (1986): 56–69.

———. *Napoleon and His Parents.* New York: 1990.

Chandler, David. *The Campaigns of Napoleon.* New York: 1966.

———, ed., *Napoleon's Marshals.* New York: 1987.

Chastenet, Jacques. *Godoy: Master of Spain. 1792–1808.* London: 1953.

Chuquet, Arthur. *La Jeunesse de Napoleon.* Paris: 1897.

Clemens, Gabriele. "Napoleonische Armeeleiferanten und die entstehung des Rheinischen wirtschaftsbürgertums." *Francia* 24, 2 (1997): 159–180.

Colin, Jean. *L'education militaire de Napoléon.* Paris: 1900.

Connelly, Owen. *Napoleon's Satellite Kingdoms.* New York: 1965.

Coquelle, P. "L'ambassade du Maréchal Brune á Constantinople (1803–1805)." *Revue d'histoire diplomatique* 8 (1904): 53–73.

Corvisier, André, ed. *Histoire militaire de la France.* 2 vols. Paris: 1992.

Crevald, Martin van. *Logistics from Wallenstein to Patton.* Cambridge: 1977.

Criste, Oscar. *Erzherzog Carl von Österreich.* 3 vols. Vienna: 1912.

Crouzet, François. "War, Blockades and Economic Change in Europe, 1792–1815." *Journal of Economic History* 24 (1964): 70–79.

De Clerq, M. *Recueil des Traités de la France.* 23 vols. Paris: 1880.

Defanceschi, John. "Le Corse et la Revolution française: La Rêve brisé." *Proceedings of the Consortium on Revolutionary Europe* (1986): 70–79.

Deutsch, Harold. *The Genesis of Napoleonic Imperialism.* Cambridge, MA: 1938.

Dietrich, J. R. "Die Politik Landgraf Ludwigs X. von Hessen-Darmstadt von 1790–1806." *Archiv für hessische Geschichte und Alterrumskunde* 7 (1910): 417–453.

Driault, Edouard. *Napoléon en Italie, 1800–1802.* Paris: 1906.

———. "Bonaparte et les Recès Germanique de 1803." *Revue historique* 100 (1909): 269–310.

———. *La Politique extérieure du premier Consul 1800–1803.* Paris: 1910.

Duffy, Christopher. *Austerlitz.* London: 1977.

Dwyer, Philip. "The Politics of Prussian Neutrality, 1795–1805." *German History* 12, 3 (1994): 351–374.

———. "Duroc Diplomate: Un militaire au service de la diplomatie napoléonniene." *Souvenir Napoleonien* 58 (1995): 21–40.

———. "Two Definitions of Neutrality: Prussia, the European State-System and the French Invasion of Hanover in 1803." *International History Review* 19, 3 (August 1997): 522–540.

Elting, John. *Swords Around a Throne: Napoleon's Grande Armée.* New York: 1988.

Egger, Rainer. *Das Gefecht bei Hollabrunn und Schöngrabern 1805.* Vienna: 1982.

———. *Das Gefecht bei Dürnstein-Loiben 1805.* Vienna: 1986.

Erdmansdörfer, B., and K. Obler, eds. *Politische Correspondenz Karl Friedrichs von Baden 1783–1806.* 2 vols. Heidelberg: 1901.

Esteban, Javier Cuenca. "Statistics of Spain's Colonial Trade, 1792–1820: Consular Duties, Cargo Inventories and Balances of Trade." *Hispanic American Historical Review* 61, 3 (1981): 381–428.

Eysturlid, Lee. *The Formative Influences, Theories, and Campaigns of the Archduke Carl of Austria.* Westport, CT: 2000.

Feldbæk, Ole. *Denmark and Armed Neutrality 1800–1801.* Copenhagen: 1980.

———. "Denmark in the Napoleonic Wars: A Foreign Policy Survey." *Scandinavian Journal of History* 26, 2 (June 2001): 89–101.

Fisher, Hal. *Studies in Napoleonic Statesmanship: Germany.* Oxford: 1903.

Fisher, John. "Imperial Response to 'Free Trade': Spanish Imports from Spanish America, 1778–1796." *Journal of Latin American Studies* 17 (1985): 35–78.

————. "Commerce and Imperial Decline: Spanish Trade with Spanish America, 1797–1820." *Journal of Latin American Studies* 30 (1998): 459–479.

Flayhart, William. *Counterpoint to Trafalgar, The Anglo-Russian Invasion of Naples, 1805–1806.* Columbia: 1992.

Ford, Guy Stanton. *Hanover and Prussia, 1795–1803: A Study in Neutrality.* New York: reprint 1967.

Fourier, August. *Gentz und Cobenzl: Geschichte de österreichischen Diplomatie in den Jahren 1801–1805.* Vienna, 1880.

Frey, Linda, and Marsha Frey. "The Reign of Charlatans Is Over: The French Revolutionary Attack on Diplomatic Practices." *Journal of Modern History* 65 (December 1993): 706–744.

Fugier, André. *Napoleon et l'Espagne: 1799–1808.* 2 vols. Paris: 1930.

Gabaillard, Jean. "Le Financement des guerres napoleonniennes et la conjoncture du Premier Empire." *Revue Economique* 4 (1953): 548–572.

Gachot, Edouard. *Histoire Militaire de Massena.* Paris: 1911.

Gagliardo, John. *Reich and Nation: The Holy Roman Empire as Idea and Reality, 1763–1806.* Bloomington, IN: 1980.

Godoy, Manuel de. *Principe de la Paz Memorias.* Madrid: 1956.

Grandmaison, Geoffrey de. *L'Espagne et Napoleon.* Vol. I, *1804–1809.* Paris: 1908.

Grimouard, Henri de. "Les origines du Domaine Extraordinaire: Le Receveur Général des contributions de la Grande Armée ses Attributions, ses comptes, 1805–1810." *Revue des questions historiques* 39 (1908): 160–192.

Grimstead, Patricia Kennedy. *The Foreign Ministers of Alexander I: Political Attitudes and the Conduct of Russian Diplomacy, 1801–1825.* Berkeley, CA: 1969.

Großen Generalsstabe, "Die Preusischen Kriegsvorbeitungen und Operationspläne von 1805." In *Kriegsgeschichte Einzelschriftenliche, heft* 1. Berlin: 1898.

Hall, C.D. "Addington at War: Unspectacular but Not Unsuccessful." *Historical Research* LXI (1998): 306-315.

Hall, Thadd. "The Development of Enlightened Interest in Eighteenth Century Corsica." *Studies on Voltaire and the Eighteenth Century* 64 (1968): 165–185.

————. "Thought and Practice of Enlightened Government in French Corsica." *American Historical Review* 74, 3 (February 1969): 880–905.

————. "Corsica and Its World." *Proceedings of the Consortium on Revolutionary Europe* (1987): 49–55.

————. "Jean-Jacques Rousseau and the Corsican Connection." *Studies on Voltaire and the Eighteenth Century* 267 (1989): 199–215.

Hammett, Brian R. "The Appropriation of Mexican Church Wealth by the Spanish Bourbon Government—The 'Consolidación de Vales Reales.' 1805–1809." *Journal of Latin American Studies* 1, 2 (November 1969): 85–113.

Hansard, T.C. *The Parliamentary Debates from the Year 1803 to the Present Time,* III. London: 1812.

Harbon, John D. *Trafalgar and the Spanish Navy.* Annapolis, MO: 1988.

Hertenberger, Helmut, and Franz Wiltschek. *Erzherzog Karl: Die Sieger von Aspern.* Graz: 1983.

Hessen, Rainer von. *Wir Wilhelm von Gottes Gnaden: Die Lebenserinnerungen Kürfürst Wilhelms I von Hessen 1743–1821.* Frankfurt: 1996.

Hilt, Douglas. *The Troubled Trinity: Godoy and the Spanish Monarchs.* Tuscaloosa, AL: 1987.

Ilari, Virgilio, Piero Crociani, and Ciro Paoletti. *Bella Italia Militar: Escerciti e Marine nell'Italia pre-napoleonica (1748–1792).* Rome: 2000.

———. *La Guerra della Alpi (1792–1796).* Rome: 2000.

———. *Storia Militare dell'Italian Giacobina: dall'armistizo di Cherasco alla pace di Amiens, (1796–1802).* 2 vols. Rome: 2001.

———. *Storia militare del Regno Italico, 1802–1814.* 2 vols. Rome: 2002.

Lady Jackson, ed., *Jackson Diaries.* 2 vols. London: 1872.

Jahns, Max. "Zur Geschischte der Kriegsverfassung des Deutschen Reiches." *Prußische Jahrbücher* 39 (1877): 1–28.

Jany, Curt. *Geschichte der Preußischen Armee vom 15 Jahrhundert bis 1914.* 4 vols. Osnabrück, Germany: 1967.

Junkelman, Marcus. *Napoleon und Bayern: von den Anfängen des Königreiches.* Regensberg: 1985.

Klüpfel, Karl, "Die Friedensunterhandlungen Würtembergs mit der französischen Republik: 1796–1802." *Historische Zeitschrift* 46 (1881).

Krebs, Lèonce, and Henri Moris. *Campagnes dans les Alpes pendant la Révolution.* 2 vols. Paris: 1891.

La Parra López, Emilio. "Les changements politiques en Espagne après Brumaire." *Annales historiques de la Révolution française* 4 (1999): 695–696.

Labouchère, G. "Pierre-César Labouchère." *Revue d'histoire diplomatique* XXVII, (1913): 425–455.

Levy-Schneider, L. "Napoléon et la Garde Nationale." *La Revolution Française* 56 (January 1909): 18–45.

Linnebach, Karl, ed. *Scharnhorsts Briefe, I: Privatbriefe.* Munich: 1914.

Losch, Phillip. *Kürfürst Wilhelm I, Landgraf von Hessen: Ein Fürstenbild aus Zopfzeit.* Marburg, Germany: 1923.

Lundh, Herbert. *Gustaf IV Adolf och Sveriges Utrikespolitik 1801–1804.* Uppsala: 1926.

Lynch, John. "British Policy and Spanish America, 1763–1808." *Journal of Latin American Studies* 1, 1 (1968): 1–30.

———. *Bourbon Spain, 1700–1808.* London: 1994.

Mackesy, Piers. *The War in the Mediterranean, 1803–1810.* Westport, CT: reprint 1981.

———. *The War for America 1775–1783.* Lincoln, NE: reprint 1993.

Mahan, Alfred T., *The Influence of Sea Power on the French Revolution and Empire, 1793–1812.* 2 vols. London: reprint n.d.

Marcus, G.J. *The Age of Nelson* New York: 1971.

Marichal, Carlos, and Matilde Souto Mantecón. "Silver and Situados: New Spain and the Financing of the Spanish Empire in the Caribbean in the Eighteenth Century." *Hispanic American Historical Review* 74, 4 (1994): 587–613.

Marion, Marcel. *Histoire Financière de la France depuis 1715.* 4 vols. Paris: 1927.

Martens, F. *Recueil des Traités et Conventions conclus par La Russie avec les puissances étrangères.* 14 vols. St. Petersburg: 1875.

Masson, Frederick, and Guido Biagi. *Napoleon innconu: papiers inedit.* 2 vols. Paris: 1895.

McErlean, John. "Between Paoli and Bonaparte: Philippe Masseria, An Anglomaniac in Corsica, 1789–1793." *Proceedings of the Consortium on Revolutionary Europe* (1986): 80–90.

McGrew, Roederick E. *Paul I of Russia: 1754–1801.* Oxford: 1992.

Metternich, Richard, ed. *Memoirs of Prince Metternich, 1773–1815.* 3 vols. New York: 1970.

Mollien, Nicolas. *Mémoires d'un Ministre du Trésor Public, 1780–1815.* 4 vols. Paris: 1845.

Mowat, R.B. *The Diplomacy of Napoleon.* London: 1924.

Muriel, Andreas. *Carlos IV.* Madrid: 1959.

Napoleon I. *The Confidential Correspondence of Napoleon Bonaparte with His Brother Joseph.* 2 vols. New York: 1856.

———. *Correspondance de Napoleon Ier.* 32 vols. Paris: 1858–1862.

———. *Unpublished Correspondence of Napoleon I.* 3 vols. New York: 1913.

Oer, Rudolfine von. *Der Friede von Pressburg: Ein Beitrag zur Diplomaticgeschichte des Napoleonischen Zeitalters.* Munster, Germany: 1965.

Paget, Arthur. *The Paget Papers, 1794–1807.* 2 vols. New York: 1896.

Parker, Harold. "The Formation of Napoleon's Personality: An Exploratory Essay." *French Historical Studies* 7 (1971): 6–26.

———. "Napoleon's Changing Self-Image to 1812: A Sketch." *Proceedings of the Consortium on Revolutionary Europe* (1983): 449–450

———. "The Broken Dream." *Proceedings of the Consortium on Revolutionary Europe* (1986): 91–95.

———. "Napoleon Reconsidered: An Invitation to Inquiry and Reflection." *French Historical Studies* 15 (spring 1987): 142–156.

———. "Napoleon and French Army Values: The Early Phases." *Proceedings of the Annual Meeting of the Western Society for French History* 18 (1991): 233–242.

Phipps, Ramsey Weston. *The Armies of the First French Republic and the Rise of the Marshals of Napoleon I.* 5 vols. London, 1926–1935.

Pigeard, Alain. *L'armée Napoléonnienne.* Currandra, France: 1993.

Ragsdale, Hugh. "Russian Influence at Lunéville." *French Historical Studies* 5 (1968): 274–284.

———. *Russian and the Mediterranean, 1797–1807*. Chicago: 1970.

———. "A Continental System in 1801: Paul I and Bonaparte." *Journal of Modern History* 42, 1 (March 1970): 70–89.

Rambaud, Alfred. *L'Allemagne sous Napoleon Ier (1804–1811)*. Paris:1897.

Ranke, Leopold von, ed. *Einhändige Memoiren des Saatskanzlers Fürsten von Hardenberg*. 5 vols. Leipzig, Germany: 1877.

Rauchensteiner, Manfred. *Kaiser Franz und Erzherzog Karl*. Munich: 1972.

Regele, Oskar. "Karl Frieherr von Mack und Johann Ludwig von Cobenzl. Ihre Rolle im Kriegsjahr 1805." *Mitteilungen des Österreichischen Staatsarchivs* XX, 1 (1969): 142–164.

Roider, Karl. *Baron Thugut and Austria's Response to the French Revolution*. Princeton, MJ: 1987.

Rose, John Holland. "Gustavus IV and the Formation of the Third Coalition." *Revue Napoléonienne* 2 (1901–1902): 88–93.

———, ed. *Selected Dispatches from the British Foreign Office Archives Relating to the Formation of the Third Coalition against France, 1804–1805*. London: 1904.

Ross, Steven T., *Quest for Victory: French Military Strategy, 1792–1799*. New York: 1973.

Rothenberg, Gunther. *Napoleon's Great Adversaries, the Archduke Charles and the Austrian Army, 1792–1814*. Bloomington, IN: 1982.

Rustow, Wilhelm. *Der Krieg von 1805 in Deutschland und Italien*. Frauenfeld, Switzerland: 1853.

Sauer, Paul. *Adler über Württemberg, Baden und Hohenzollern: Südwestdeutschland in der Rheinbundzeit*. Stuttgart, Germany: 1987.

Schama, Simon. "The Politics of Taxation in the Netherlands." In *War and Economic Development*, J.M. Winter. Cambridge, MA: 1975.

———. *Patriots and Liberators: Revolution in the Netherlands, 1780–1813*. New York: 1992.

Schneid, Frederick C. *Soldiers of Napoleon's Kingdom of Italy: Army, State and Society 1800–1815*. Boulder, CO: 1995.

———. *Napoleon's Italian Campaigns, 1805–1815*. Westport, CT: 2002.

Schop Soler, Ana Maria. *La relaciones entre España y Rusia en la época de Carlos IV*. Barcelona: 1971.

Schroeder, Paul. "The Collapse of the Second Coalition." *Journal of Modern History* 59 (1987): 244–290.

———. *The Transformation of European Politics*. Oxford: 1994.

Scott, Sam. *The Response of the Royal Army to the French Revolution*. Oxford: 1978.

Secco Serrano, Carlos. *Godoy: El hombre y el politico*. Madrid: 1978.

Shanahan, William O. *Prussian Military Reforms, 1786–1813*. New York: 1966.

Sherwig, John. *Guineas and Gunpowder: British Foreign Aid in the War with France, 1793–1815.* Cambridge, MA: 1969.

Showalter, Dennis. "Hubertusberg to Auerstädt: The Prussian Army in Decline?" *German History* 12, 3 (1994): 308–333.

Simms, Brendan. "The Road to Jena: Prussian High Politics 1804–1806." *German History* 12, 3 (1994): 374–394.

———. "'An Odd Question Enough.' Charles James Fox, the Crown and British Policy during the Hanoverian Crisis, 1806." *Historical Journal* 38, 3 (1995): 567–596.

———. *The Impact of Napoleon: Prussian High Politics, Foreign Policy and the Crisis of the Executive, 1797–1806.* Cambridge, MA: 1997.

Stamm-Kuhlmann, Thomas. *König in Preußens großer Zeit: Freidrich Wilhelm III der Melancholiker auf dem Thron.* Berlin: 1992.

Tulard, Jean. *Napoleon: The Myth of A Savior.* New York: 1977.

Walters, Philip, and Raymond Walters. "The American Career of David Parish." *Journal of Economic History* (1944): 149–166.

Weill, Georges. "Le financier Ouvrard." *Revue historique* CXXVII, (1918): 31–61.

Weis, Eberhard. "Bayern und Frankreich in der Zeit des Konsulats und des Ersten Empire (1799–1815)." *Historische Zeitschrift* 237 (1983).

White, Edward. "The French Revolution and the Politics of Government Finance, 1770–1815." *Journal of Economic History* 55, 2 (June 1995).

Wilkenson, Spencer. *The Rise of General Bonaparte.* Oxford: 1930.

Wilson, Peter. *War, State and Society in Württemberg, 1677–1793.* Cambridge, MA: 1995.

———. *German Armies: War and German Politics, 1648–1806.* London: 1998.

Wirth, Joseph. *Le Maréchal Lefebvre: Duc de Danzig (1755–1820).* Paris: 1904.

Zawadzki, W.H. "Prince Adam Czartoryski and Napoleonic France, 1801–1805: A Study in Political Attitudes." *Historical Journal* XVIII, 2 (1975): 245–277.

INDEX

ABOUT THE AUTHOR

FREDERICK C. SCHNEID is a Professor of History at High Point University. He is the author of *Napoleon's Italian Campaigns, 1805–1815* (Praeger, 2002) and *Soldiers of Napoleon's Kingdom of Italy: Army, State and Society, 1800–1815* (1995). He serves on the board of directors of the Consortium on Revolutionary Europe and is southern regional director for the Society for Military History.